The Road to
WATERLOO

The British Army and the Struggle Against Revolutionary and Napoleonic France, 1793-1815

Edited by Alan J Guy

ALAN SUTTON

NATIONAL ARMY MUSEUM

ALAN SUTTON PUBLISHING LIMITED
PHOENIX MILL · FAR THRUPP · STROUD · GLOUCESTERSHIRE

ALAN SUTTON PUBLISHING INC.
WOLFEBORO FALLS · NH 03896–0848

THE NATIONAL ARMY MUSEUM · ROYAL HOSPITAL ROAD · CHELSEA
LONDON SW3 4HT

First published 1990

ISBN 0 86299 919 7

Cover Picture: Attack on the British Squares by French Cavalry (detail)
Watercolour by Denis Dighton, 1815
National Army Museum 7505-7-2

Designed by Alastair Pether and Amy Bridgman
Photography by Ian Jones
Colour origination by
Yeo Valley Graphic Reproductions, Wells
Printed in Great Britain by
The Bath Press, Avon

CONTENTS

Foreword, **Ian G Robertson** MA FMA, Director, National Army Museum 2

Glenn A Steppler, The British Army on the Eve of War 4

G J Evelyn, 'I learned what one ought not to do': The British Army in

Flanders and Holland, 1793-95 16

Michael Duffy, The Caribbean Campaigns of the British Army, 1793-1801 . . . 23

Ian F W Beckett, The Militia and the King's Enemies, 1793-1815 32

Clive Emsley, The Volunteer Movement 40

De Witt Bailey and **David Harding**, From India to Waterloo: The 'India Pattern' Musket 48

Brian Robson, 'Warranted Never to Fail': The Cavalry Sword Patterns of 1796 . . 58

A S Bennell, Arthur Wellesley: The Sepoy General as Politician and Diplomat, 1797-1805 . 69

Randolf G S Cooper, New Light on Arthur Wellesley's Command-Apprenticeship in India:

The Dhoondiah Waugh Campaign of 1800 Reconsidered 81

Kenneth Ferguson, The Army and the Irish Rebellion of 1798 88

Piers Mackesy, Abercromby in Egypt: The Regeneration of the Army 101

Alan J Guy, A Good Man at Falmouth: Captain Philip Melvill, Defender of

Pendennis Castle, 1796-1811 111

Peter B Boyden, 'A System of Communication Throughout Each County': Fire-Beacons

and their Role in the Defence of the Realm, 1803-11 126

Charles Esdaile, The British Army and the Guerrilla War in Spain 132

Michael Ball, An Artist's Road to Waterloo: The Sketch-Book of

Ensign Robert Batty, 1813-14 142

Peter B Boyden, The Postal Service of Wellington's Army in the Peninsula and

France, 1809-1818 149

Rory Muir, From Soldier to Statesman: Wellington in Paris and Vienna, 1814-15 . . 155

Lesley Smurthwaite, Glory is Priceless!: Awards to the British Army during

the French Revolutionary and Napoleonic Wars 164

David G Chandler, Captain William Siborne and his Waterloo Models 184

Hew Strachan, The British Army's Legacy from the Revolutionary and Napoleonic Wars . 197

Alan J Guy, Guide to Further Reading 206

List of Contributors 213

Index 216

IAN G ROBERTSON

It would have been inconceivable for the National Army Museum to have failed to have marked the 175th Anniversary of the Battle of Waterloo, fought, of course, on 18 June 1815 and unquestionably on everyone's list of the most decisive engagements ever contested by the British Army. It was decided that the Museum's tribute to those who participated would be the opening of a new Permanent Gallery entitled *The Road to Waterloo: The British Army and the Struggle against Revolutionary and Napoleonic France, 1793-1815*, which would be the first complete refurbishment of any part of the Museum's permanent displays since the opening in Chelsea in 1971. This Gallery includes not only our most important items relating to the Wars with Revolutionary and Napoleonic France, but also sets before the public once again the famous 1838 Siborne Model of the Battlefield, properly cleaned and conserved.

The Road to Waterloo Permanent Gallery was opened by The Duke of Wellington, descendant of The Iron Duke and President of The Waterloo Committee, on 6 December 1990. The choice of the end of the 175th Anniversary Year was deliberate, as it presages the continuing public interest in the anniversaries of these wars which will certainly be underway in 1993 and culminate in the 200th Anniversary of the Battle of Waterloo itself in 2015. It is earnestly hoped that our visitors will find in this new Gallery the inspiration, through seeing the original objects, reading the captions, reflecting on the reconstructed model figures wearing uniforms now lost to us, sufficient to help them make up their own minds about key issues during those troubled decades.

This Volume, published to coincide with the opening of the new Permanent Gallery, is not, and was never intended to be, either a comprehensive treatment of the Wars with France between 1793 and 1815, or indeed a bland re-statement of received knowledge, which is why in particular it does not contain yet another narrative description of the Battle of Waterloo. Instead, a team made up of some of the most distinguished historians working in this field today, joined by representatives of a new generation of scholars, have supported the National Army Museum in marking this particular Anniversary by writing a series of essays which focuses attention on work in progress on a limited number of themes. It would be invidious to pick out any one or two of these scholars for especial mention in this Foreword, but it is right that all should be thanked for their kind, willing and prompt co-operation in the production of this Book.

In addition to the Collections of the National Army Museum itself, information has been gathered from many quarters by the contributors, and grateful acknowledgements are offered to the governing bodies and staff of the following institutions: the *Archivo Histórico Nacional*, Madrid; the Bodleian Library; the British Library; the Buckinghamshire Record Office; the Cornwall Record

Office; the Essex Record Office; the India Office Library and Records; the National Archives, Dublin Castle; the Ministry of Defence Whitehall Library; the National Library of Scotland; the National Register of Archives (Scotland); Northumberland Record Office; the University of Nottingham; the Post Office Archives; the Public Record Office; the Royal Armouries, HM Tower of London; the Royal Commission on Historic Manuscripts; the Scottish Record Office; the Scottish United Services Museum, and the University of Southampton.

It is a particular pleasure that papers by members of the staff of the National Army Museum are included, as well as illustrations drawn from items in the Collections here. Dr Alan Guy, Assistant Director (Collections), the Editor of the Volume, has also contributed a survey of recent secondary literature dealing with this period, which it is intended will guide the general reader and indeed indicate areas in which research still clearly needs to be done. Above all, as a guide to further reading, it provides a good frame of reference for the conflicts of the period 1793-1815, which were known, of course, as 'The Great War' to the pre-1914 generation.

As with the Permanent Gallery, so this Volume demands that credit be given to the Production Team and especially its designer, Alastair Pether of the Museum's Department of Design, assisted by Amy Bridgman. Additional research was carried out by Dr Peter Boyden and Michael Ball, and the index was compiled by Miss Elizabeth Talbot Rice. Special acknowledgement for assistance rendered to the Editor is due to Randolf G S Cooper (who is also one of the contributors), Dr Stephen Roberts of the Royal Commission on Historic Manuscripts and David Smurthwaite, Assistant Director (Museum Services), also to Miss June Hicks who typed the manuscript.

Ian G Robertson MA FMA   November 1990
Director, National Army Museum

G A STEPPLER

1. Lt-Gen Sir Henry Bunbury, *Narratives of Some Passages in the Great War with France, from 1799 to 1810*, London (1854) pp vii-xviii.

2. Sir John Fortescue, *A History of the British Army*, Vol III, London (1911) *passim*; *The British Army, 1783-1802*, London (1905) *passim*.

Officers who remembered the Army of 1793 did not necessarily recall it with any pride. Sir Henry Bunbury's unflattering reflection is perhaps the best known. 'Our army', he recalled, 'was lax in its discipline, entirely without system, and very weak in numbers. Each Colonel of a regiment managed it according to his own notions, or neglected it altogether. There was no uniformity of drill or movement; professional pride was rare; professional knowledge still more so'. Nor were the regiments well supported, for 'Every department of the Staff was more or less deficient, particularly the commissariat and Medical branches'. It seemed there 'Never was a kingdom less prepared for a stern and arduous conflict...'.[1]

Such opinions have long condemned the late-eighteenth century Army to ridicule and the Government of the day to scorn. Sir John Fortescue was unsparing in his criticism of the younger Pitt,[2] whose first Administration spanned most of the decade before the outbreak of war with Revolutionary France in 1793. The years before the war have come down to us as a period of shameful neglect, and what is worse, of corruption too. But, has such a judgement been fair? What *are* we to make of Bunbury's remarks? What was the state of the British Army on the eve of war with France? What sort of army was it?

Pitt's Administration, the Army and the Tribulations of Peace and War

As Bunbury said, the Army was 'very weak in numbers'. With a population in Great Britain and Ireland of about fourteen-and-a-half million, a Regular Army of only 50,000 men (divided between separate British and Irish Establishments) was small indeed, especially so when set beside those of other major European powers. It was certainly not for lack of financial means that the British Army was so small. Quite the contrary, Britain was the wealthiest of nations. Rather it was a conscious reluctance by Government to spend any more than seemed absolutely necessary on an institution whose power Parliament had long feared. Many of the Army's troubles stemmed from this simple fact. Parliament's wary eye kept it low in numbers, held its pay down, and denied it the benefits of being regularly housed in barracks. For a century and more, Parliamentarians had indulged in anti-Army rhetoric, and if by the 1790s the Army's very existence was no longer seriously questioned, the embers of hostility could still be made to glow, and nothing fanned them faster than the suggestion of new military expenses.[3]

The administration of the Army reflected further the age-old fear that permanent armies were a threat to liberty. This, as well as the financial constraints imposed by Parliament, must be given due weight in any assessment of Pitt's Ministry and of the state of the Army.

Responsibility for the Army's affairs was kept in civilian hands and diffused through various departments and officials - the result, as Bunbury saw it, being that 'Every department of the Staff was more or less deficient...'. To further reconcile military with civilian power, two distinct patterns of control had evolved, one suitable for peace, another required for war.[4] In peacetime, the Army was often without a military Commander-in-Chief (as was the case before 1793), relying instead on the King himself to act in this role. At the centre of the peacetime administration was the Secretary at War, a relatively minor official without ministerial rank. Although a strong central authority was lacking, this worked well enough, on a day to day basis, but in wartime, both to spread the work-load and to provide the executive authority which the Secretary at War lacked, the active intervention of a Secretary of State and the appointment of a professional Commander-in-Chief became imperative. The amount of work increased dramatically, and inevitably there was some administrative dysfunction as new men took office and responsibilities were re-apportioned.

The embarrassment, indeed the danger, of the Army's 'very weak' numbers was felt most acutely at those moments when the nation lurched from peace to war, and back again. Sudden expansion to several times its former size caused untold problems for the Army:

3. In 1786 and 1787 proposals to re-fortify the naval dockyards and to raise a corps of Royal Military Artificers aroused much opposition.

4. J L Pimlott, 'The Administration of the British Army, 1783-1793', unpublished doctoral thesis, University of Leicester (1975) pp365-69.

immense strain on its peacetime administrators, chicanery of every sort in recruiting and serious disciplinary problems in old and new regiments alike. Almost as stressful was the rapid contraction of the Army upon the return of peace, a process never without pain but, at the end of the American Revolution, an especially traumatic experience, the effects of which were felt for some time afterwards. In 1783, against a background of mutinies and mass desertion, the ministers of two different Administrations had moved in haste to disband the wartime Army. Plans for the orderly re-assignment of a much-reduced peacetime force then fell into disarray and, in December 1783, when Pitt formed his Ministry, he found an Army which was dangerously under strength, low in morale and poorly deployed, its battalions packed into Ireland and Great Britain at the expense of colonial commitments.

Historians have always assumed that Pitt did nothing to change this situation. The Army's weak state in 1783, and its apparently dismal performances during 1793-95, have been taken as proof that the decade of peace had been a time of '…political interference, of neglect of training, discipline, and the proper selection of officers [which] had gone far toward rotting the British Army's capacity for war'.[5] Yet the troubles of 1783 and 1793-95 do not afford such proof. A more sympathetic scrutiny of the 'missing years' reveals a very different picture.[6] The damage done in 1783 was eventually reversed, but the Army's re-construction and re-deployment, so as to create a better balance between colonial and domestic needs, not only took time of itself, but had also to be reconciled with financial constraints and the further complication of two crisis augmentations, in 1787 and 1790, in response to deteriorating foreign relations. The crisis of 1787 in the United Provinces proved a decisive turning point which prompted significant improvements in both the organizational and administrative detail of the Army. Despite fiscal retrenchment, six new battalions were raised for service abroad (five regiments had already been saved from disbandment in 1783-85), all infantry battalions were restored to ten companies (ending the 1783 experiment of only eight),

5. Richard Glover, *Peninsular Preparation: The Reform of the British Army, 1795-1809*, Cambridge (1963) p2.

6. See Pimlott, *op cit*. *This* much-needed re-evaluation of the period deserves to be more widely known. The present article owes a great deal to Dr Pimlott's work.

archaic units such as the regiments of Irish Horse were reformed and important steps were taken to assimilate the British and Irish Establishments. Some central control was established over recruiting, especially for regiments serving overseas. Most important of all however, was the development of a definite military policy reconciling the defence of British interests both at home and abroad.[7] The benefits of these changes were seen during the Nookta Sound Crisis of 1790.

7. *Ibid, pp358-59.*

Nor were other military matters ignored. As Sir John Fortescue noted (with approval), Pitt turned his attention to improving fortifications at home (to defend the naval dockyards), and in the West Indies. In 1787, the Corps of Engineers was reorganized as the Royal Engineers and a corps of Royal Military Artificers was formed. The long festering problem of the soldier's pay, seen to be at the root of many troubles affecting the Army's rank and file, was also brought to Pitt's attention, and after investigation, significantly improved in 1792. Desertion-rates fell quickly, and in May of that year, Sir George Yonge, the Secretary at War, initiated a scheme to rehabilitate apprehended deserters.[8] In June the publication of the *Rules and Regulations for the formations, field exercise and movements of his Majesty's forces* officially ended the tactical uncertainty which had followed the end of the American Revolution, though its complete implementation took time. In January 1793, the Royal Artillery incorporated a new species of gunner with the formation of the Royal Horse Artillery.

8. Fortescue, in criticising what he saw as Pitt's negligent delay in dealing with the soldier's pay, seems to have been unaware of the fact that losses from desertion diminished in 1785, and only became serious again following the very bad harvest of 1789.

Contrary to popular impression, the years of peace had witnessed steady improvement, but the outbreak of war immediately changed everything. Although Bunbury condemned the Army of 1793, his personal experience as an officer only began in 1795, by which time the very real achievements of the Army's peacetime administrators had been lost from view in the rush to expand it. Troubles abounded. What good works there had been were already forgotten. The chaos experienced upon the outbreak of war was not due to unusually incompetent individuals, nor to an extraordinarily inept peacetime

Administration. Its real cause lay in the distrust of military power which left the Army very weak in numbers in times of peace, while it created a pattern of peacetime administration completely unsuitable for the prosecution of war.

The King's Regiments

Bunbury had drawn attention to the individuality of the Army's regiments. 'Each Colonel of a regiment managed it according to his own notions, or neglected it altogether. There was no uniformity of drill or movement...'. His criticism followed closely that made in 1788 by a future Commander-in-Chief, Colonel David Dundas, who was soon to play an important role in reforming the Army's tactical training. Nor were 'drill or movement' the only matters that lacked uniformity. As Dundas observed, the '...irregularities...equally take place in the internal composition and management of our battalions; each has its singular mode of discipline unknown to the other, and often as opposite as those of two distinct services'. What was needed was 'the promulgation of a general *military code*', applicable to the whole Army.[9]

Unlike the Prussians, whose infantry and cavalry regiments had benefited from such codes for over 60 years, British regiments were brought into discipline and order partly through the provisions of Parliament's annual Mutiny Act and the King's *Articles of War*, partly through occasional royal warrants, general orders and regulations, but most importantly through their own daily orders, and, should they possess them, their own 'standing orders'. Additionally, many things were carried on simply by 'the custom of the British service'. There were, David Dundas noted, '...many proper and excellent regulations and customs, existing in the Biritsh service', but the difficulty was '...to know which are obsolete, and which in force'.[10]

Such orders as governed the daily affairs of the regiment were by custom left to the field officer commanding. This officer's zeal and ability were decisive in moulding the regiment's character, but the final authority in all matters regimental rested with its colonel. Each

9. Col David Dundas, *Principles of Military Movements, Chiefly Applied to Infantry...*, London (1788) pp12, 16.

10. *Ibid*, p16.

8

of the Army's colonels, though seldom present with his own corps, undertook to maintain for the King a regiment which was 'fit for service'. In return, he expected a free hand in directing the regiment's internal affairs, and his wishes were largely respected. Nor was this surprising, for, as Bunbury knew, the colonels were very important men; over half had direct peerage connections. Moreover, they were almost invariably general officers. By attendance at the Board of General Officers they assisted in certain matters of routine administration and, when called upon, acted as military advisers to the King and his ministers. As 'Reviewing Generals' they conducted the annual regimental inspections which informed the King of the general state of his Army. Should reforms be contemplated, they would be vital participants, offering advice, implementing change - and reporting on the results.

The distinctive identity stamped upon each regiment by its colonel and his field officers was further accentuated by frequent colonial service, a distinguishing characteristic of the Army's infantry in particular and quite unlike the experience of the stay-at-home soldiers of other European powers. Remaining abroad often for lengthy periods of time, regiments quite naturally turned in upon themselves. It was difficult to sustain a flow of replacements from Britain, and the regiments were often further dispersed in small detachments. None of this was conducive to creating or sustaining one uniform system in the Army, be it in the minutiae of regimental finance or in the details of tactical training. Nor was this all, for regiments regularly returned from their foreign postings in such a weakened state as to require a complete re-building.

If broadening for the individual, the lessons of colonial service did not necessarily seem of relevance to the Army in general, indeed, they might even appear detrimental. Much of the tactical inconsistency of which Bunbury complained had grown out of the Army's experience in North America. The American Revolution generated a decided preference for a looser style of tactics, which, taken together with the absence of any universally agreed system, had resulted in a chaos that

11. Piers Mackesy, 'What the British Army Learned', in Ronald Hoffman, Peter J Albert, eds., *Arms and Independence: The Military Character of the American Revolution*, Charlottesville (1984) pp191-215.
12. For training problems, see J A Houlding, *Fit for Service: The Training of the British Army 1715-1795*, Oxford (1981) *passim*.

seemed likely to prove disastrous. This at least was what Colonel Dundas thought, and when one system of tactical manoeuvre was finally adopted officially, in 1792, it was based on a Prussian model, and not one derived from recent colonial experience.[11]

Even when stationed in the British Isles, the regiments struggled with difficulties which impaired both their tactical training and discipline.[12] In the absence of any alternative force, the cavalry and infantry regiments of the line were routinely broken down into smaller detachments and deployed on policing duties which required their wide dispersal. Riot-control, the suppression of smuggling and escort duties took up much time and, as barrack accommodation on any scale was not yet available in Britain, detachments were scattered in alehouse billets, hardly an atmosphere likely to foster the best 'soldier-like' discipline. In Ireland there was a greater number of barracks but, when troops were obliged to quarter on the local population, conditions were even worse than in Britain. Nonetheless, despite all these disadvantages, many units were well managed, and those 'pattern regiments,' held to be exemplars, were disciplined according to principles, and to a standard, which would do them credit in any age.

One 'universal regulation' was needed to counteract the worst effects of the Army's foreign and domestic regimen, and in June 1792 the tactical debate of the preceding decade was brought officially to a close by the issue of a comprehensive set of instructions. Such a regulation had been 'long demanded', but it was only a first stop. Dundas, its originator, saw his reform of the Army's tactical training as but 'one great division' of the much larger task of creating a 'general system' or 'general military code' governing all aspects of the British soldier's life. In February 1793, when the war with Revolutionary France began, that great task as yet remained undone.

'Brothers of the Blade'

Not surprisingly, the interests of most officers strayed little beyond the boundaries of their own regiment. Bunbury was scathing; '...professional pride was rare; professional knowledge still more so'. If by 'professional knowledge' he meant a detailed technical understanding of military matters, Bunbury would certainly have found many supporters among other observers of the eighteenth century Army. If by 'professional pride' he envisaged a close attention to duty and a strict obedience to orders, he would also have found many who would have agreed with him. Why should this have been so? What sort of man held the King's commission?

The Army's officers, although more diverse in their social origins than is popularly supposed, were nonetheless drawn disproportionately from the landed classes in general and the aristocracy in particular.[13] The aristocracy and the landed gentry, especially younger sons, would seem to have accounted for at least a quarter of regimental officers, and more than half of the colonels and general officers. Birth, wealth and superior social connections favoured their advancement, but the majority of officers were men of more modest means and background. While conforming to the social requirement of being 'a gentleman', they might come from good families involved in commerce or the professions. They might be the sons of clergymen, or from families originally foreign in origin, notably the descendants of the Huguenot refugees. There were also some men who had been promoted from the ranks, but save in exceptional cases, their lack of means and humble social background confined them to the most junior positions. Officers of Scottish origin formed a significant part of the Army, quite out of proportion to the size of the Scottish population. In 1792 they accounted for more than a quarter of the infantry officers, their English colleagues little more than two-fifths (approximately 42%).[14]

A proper social background for the Army's officers was deemed necessary for political stability, and was believed to be ensured through the institution of purchase for the majority of peacetime commissions and many subsequent promotions.[15] Although a considerable number of commissions were obtained through a variety of non-purchase means, generally speaking all commissions in the infan-

13. Much research remains to be done on the social origins and career patterns of eighteenth and nineteenth century British officers. For further discussion and references, see J Hayes, 'The Social and Professional Background of the Officers of the British Army, 1714-63', unpublished MA thesis, University of London, (1956); Alan J Guy, *Oeconomy and Discipline: Officership and Administration in the British Army 1714-63*, Manchester (1985); Anthony Bruce, *The Purchase System in the British Army 1660-1871*, London (1980) and Houlding's *Fit for Service*.

14. Public Record Office, War Office Papers, WO27 series, Inspection Returns 1789-92.

15. For the workings of purchase system, see Bruce and Pimlott, op cit pp82-92.

try and cavalry below the rank of colonel could be bought and sold. As the negotiations and manoeuvres for advancement could be tortuous, the system favoured those who could seize an opportunity with ready cash. Despite this, King George III tried, wherever possible, to give preference to men of experience and merit. Strict regulations were laid down to govern promotion, though exceptional circumstances, like the crisis augmentation of 1787, might allow an officer to bypass the rules. Commissions in the Royal Artillery and the Engineers were supposedly exempt from purchase and advancement was regulated instead by strict seniority which, if free from other influences, led unfortunately to promotion stagnation.

In peacetime, advancement for the majority of officers could be painfully slow, and from 1783 to 1787 was made worse by the trial retention in each regiment of a number of supernumerary officers, 'en second' who were supposed to accede to any vacancies. New blood was thus denied an easy entry and there was much grumbling, but Pitt's Secretary at War, Sir George Yonge, seems to have administered the complexities of the system as diligently as he could.[16] Though the years of peace before 1793 were not free of problems, the Army had been permitted, despite financial retrenchment, to retain a higher number of officers on full pay than in any period of peace during the century. The unforeseen intensity and duration of the ensuing war, however, soon demanded more young officers than ever before, not just for the regular forces, but for an unprecedented number of auxiliaries as well. The new men brought with them much enthusiasm, but also a condition of ignorance which only time could correct.

Length of service is, of course, no guarantee of professional competence, and Bunbury's reproof was an echo of a criticism which had been made by others before 1793 and would continue to resound long after. Although an aspiring young gentleman might himself seek private tuition at home or abroad, officers in the infantry and cavalry were not required to undergo any formal training. Instead, the rudiments of their profession were acquired in the course of their regimental duties. The situation in the Artillery and Engineers was

16. *Ibid*, pp15-16, 85-87; Glover, *op cit*, pp147-53, levels the traditional charge of corruption, but without hard proof. The regulations governing promotion which he attributes to the Duke of York were in fact those operated by Sir George Yonge as Secretary at War in the 1780s.

very different. These officers began their careers as cadets at the Royal Military Academy, Woolwich. The quality of their training in the 1780s was high, but the exacting standards required by the Duke of Richmond, then the Master General of the Ordnance, resulted in many vacancies being unfilled. When war came, standards had to be lowered and the number of cadets greatly increased.[17]

Young gentlemen who became members of 'the epaulette gentry' did not expect their personal affairs, interests and pastimes to be unduly cramped by their new military duties, let alone by a laborious study of 'military science'. Officer absenteeism in peacetime was a constant of regimental life - absences of a year were common, but furloughs of two or even three years were not unknown. Although difficulties experienced during the United Provinces Crisis of 1787 resulted in new attendance regulations, there was no strong central authority to enforce them and determined truants continued to be troublesome, as leave was still easily obtained and extended.

As for those officers present with their battalions, more important than a complete 'professional knowledge' was their strength of character: the stoic fortitude necessary to risk danger and endure pain - what contemporaries referred to as 'bottom' - and the confidence to lead others in adversity. Bunbury says nothing on this, but gentlemanly ideals were at this point well matched to the military requirements of the period. Though regularity of performance might be wanting, a commanding officer could expect, not unreasonably, that most of his officers would possess courage, physical toughness and a certain habit of command. As Bunbury declared, there was 'no lack of gallantry' in evidence during the first campaign of 1793.[18]

The Private Soldier

The common soldier was left out of Bunbury's terse analysis of events, but must receive mention here. While not a few officers came from near the pinnacle of the social pyramid, the great mass of their soldiery came from its broad base, with every stratum in between given at least some representation. The American Revolution had

17. *Ibid*, pp187-91.

18. Bunbury, op cit p xiii.

19. For the common soldier, see G A Steppler, 'The Common Soldier in the Reign of George III, 1760-1793', unpublished doctoral thesis, University of Oxford (1984).

20. PRO.WO30/8/242, 'Memorandum', 10 Aug 1787.

21. G A Steppler, 'British Military Law, Discipline, and the Conduct of Regimental Courts Martial in the later Eighteenth Century', *English Historical Review*, Vol CII (1987) pp859-86.

brought many Irish recruits into the lowest ranks of the Army, but the Scots remained the nationality whose numbers were disproportionately high, about one-fifth of the infantry.

Soldiering in the 1780s had been extremely hard.[19] The relentless pressure of rising prices left the soldier's fixed pay of eight pence per day (from which all 'stoppages' and maintenance costs had to be taken), looking very slender indeed. In such 'Commercial Manufacturing and Enlightened times' recruits had been difficult to attract - '...either grown up Vagabonds or young Boys', according to the Adjutant-General[20] - and just as difficult to hold on to. Desertion was an option which was closely linked to times of economic distress. It had been heavy at the close of the American Revolution, and rose sharply again following a very bad harvest in 1789. Long complained of, the soldier's 'necessitous situation' was finally improved in 1792 by the removal of a number of stoppages and by the fixing of a definitive list of his 'necessaries', and their regulation cost. For the moment, losses from desertion fell dramatically, a great improvement which the outbreak of war and further economic distress was all too quickly to reverse.

The military life was a peripatetic one, with the prospect of much service abroad and of constant marching, even within Great Britain and Ireland. Discipline was anchored in a paternal relationship between the soldier and his captain. It could be strict, but its grasp was hardly continuous or unrelenting. The restrictions of garrison life regularly gave way to the latitude enjoyed by the small detachment billeted in scattered quarters. Time on duty or at 'the Drill', was followed by hours spent in pursuit of amusement or gainful employment in the community. Obedience was customarily enforced through admonition and minor punishments, graded according to regimental practice, the more serious step of assembling a regimental court martial (with the prospect of a flogging), normally being the last resort.[21] The ordinary soldier lived for the moment. His outlook was extremely conservative, and though his officers might expect him to obey, they were well advised to treat him with strict fairness, and in particular to respect what the soldier referred to as 'his rights'. The British soldier had a good reputation as a fighting man and would willingly follow an officer of proven courage, but how well his discipline would be maintained off the battlefield was more problematic, being ultimately dependent upon that same gentleman.

'Never was a kingdom less prepared...'?

Historians, influenced by the statements of contemporaries like Bunbury, have dismissed the hapless Army of 1783-93 as an exceptionally '...useless body of men',[22] a view which has certainly been sharpened by the temptation to use the years before 1793 as a foil for the later reforms of the Duke of York and the successes of Wellington's Peninsular army. Indeed, Sir Henry himself made this very contrast. Though hardly unique to this period of the Army's history, much of what he said was justified, but much of it was also beyond its control, being the result of deep-seated political attitudes. Nonetheless, the Army had ample potential. Collectively, its officers were men of considerable experience, with a greater number on full and half-pay than at any other time of peace. There were more battalions of foot, and regiments of horse available for service than before. Moreover, in its recent colonial campaigns the Army had demonstrated great flexibility. Contrary to popular belief, its peacetime administrators had been neither idle nor neglectful. Although uniformity of practice was lacking, improvement had begun. Many regiments were well drilled and their discipline was now based on sound and agreed principles. This is hardly to suggest perfection, for there was much still to be done (especially to the supporting services), as the subsequent reforms of the Duke of York were to demonstrate. Nevertheless, the Army on the eve of war in 1793 was in many ways better prepared than most of its predecessors were for earlier (and, arguably, less demanding) conflicts. Indeed, it is hard to imagine what level of preparedness would have been sufficient for a struggle unsurpassed until the next 'Great War' of 1914-18.

22. Glover op cit, pp1-2, 118.

15

G J EVELYN

1. Philip Henry, 5th Earl Stanhope, *Notes of Conversations with the Duke of Wellington*, London (1889) p182.

2. Lincelles (18 Aug 1793); the Defence of Nieuport (Oct 1793); Villers-en-Couches (24 Apr 1794); Beaumont (26 Apr 1794); Willems (10 May 1794); Tournay (22 May 1794).

3. By the summer of 1794 the *Armée du Nord* had evolved reasonably sophisticated battlefield tactics, making use of column, line and skirmish-order to good effect. The *levée en masse*, proclaimed in the autumn of 1793, generated the numbers which made these mixed formations appear as 'swarms' or 'hordes' to their opponents.

'I learned what one ought not to do'. With this curt dismissal, spoken more than 40 years after the events they described and with a wealth of experience and success behind him, the Duke of Wellington pronounced the British Army's first campaign against the French as an unmitigated failure, condemning it to historical oblivion.[1] Yet, on closer inspection, it proved the efficacy of the Army's newly-digested drill system, produced six battle honours,[2] and provided the tactical bedrock upon which his own roll of victory was founded. Moreover, what he did learn was that individual regiments possessed sound systems of internal management and control, which responded quickly and efficiently to the vaguaries of being in the field again after a lapse of ten or more years; and that basic vitality led, in turn, to their unique ability to withstand the bewildering onslaught of the French 'horde' tactics[3], although overwhelmed at last by sheer numbers.

Wellington (or Lieutenant-Colonel Arthur Wesley as he was at that time) also learned the importance of providing the cutting edge of an army with a well-organised system of support services. The bitter experience of woefully inadequate and, at times, hopelessly misman-aged transport and supply - especially during the winter retreat of 1794-95 - taught him to take immense pains over reducing wastage, and his campaigns in India and the Peninsula testify to this. In those theatres of war the autonomy that he enjoyed in the field enabled him virtually to do as he liked; there was no effective interference with the running of the campaigns from the War Office. Here was another lesson which he had absorbed in Flanders - made all the more painful as a result of command-divisions engendered by a perceived require-ment to conform to the political objectives of the Austrians - senior partners in the anti-French alliance. In future he would try to prevent this from happening when he was in command (a conviction which was to be reinforced in the Talavera campaign of 1809). And, finally, Arthur grasped the importance of uniting an army under senior commanders who would not allow jealousies of rank to take precedence over their duty and who were supported by a well-organized and experienced staff.

Preparation for Battle

By the time of the annual review circuit in the summer of 1792, the Army's new unified system of battalion drill and discipline had been assimilated, and was demonstrated to be working in practice.[4] Colonel David Dundas' *Principles of Military Movements*, published in 1788, had been embodied in an official regulation earlier in 1792,[5] and by February 1793 the regular regiments were being used to instruct Militia units, so proficient had they become.[6] Dundas' primary concern was to unify the Army's tactics by imposing a common system of drill for use in action, and, by so doing, to enable a commander in any situation to handle any unit or combination of units at a time. This essential framework, common to infantry as well as cavalry (who were instructed to comply with '...the general principles of Formation and Movement...on all occasions for the future, as far as circumstances, and the natural and unavoidable difference between Cavalry and Infantry in their respective modes of service will permit'),[7] provided sufficient flexibility to cope with most tactical situations. But necessary as this framework was at the time, it contained a flaw which quickly became apparent under active service conditions. For, in his zeal to codify the Army's tactical arrangements, Dundas had concentrated on the evolutions of the 'heavy' infantry - that is, the close-order line whose firepower won battles. In so doing he virtually ignored the role of 'light' infantry, whom he perceived to be an adjunct of the battalion line and entirely dependent upon it. Although permitted to act in extended order as circumstances demanded, battalion light infantry companies were not to do so in total isolation from the main body. This effectively negated any value they might have as *bona fide* skirmishers, for, as Dundas saw it, their use was merely '...to cover the front, rear, or flanks of the column when in march; to protect the forming of the line, or to cover its retreat'.[8] And, although his 'General Conclusion' conceded that '...where it may be improper rigidly to follow all the

4. See Public Record Office, WO27 series, 1792 Inspection Returns, for example WO27/73, 4 Aug 1792 when the 8th (King's) Regiment of Foot was inspected by David Dundas in person; 'Manual Exercise - performed agreeable to His Majesty's late order. Movements and Evolutions - on the Principles of the New System of Field Exercise as lately ordered by His Majesty...General Remarks - fired well. Marched well in line. Performed their formations and movements with steadiness and attention both in officers and men. An improving Regt. and fit for service...'.
5. Col David Dundas, *Principles of Military Movements Chiefly Applied to Infantry, Illustrated by Manoeuvres of the Prussian Troops, and by An Outline of the British Campaigns in Germany, During the War of 1757...*, London (1788, 2nd rev. edn. 1795). The general tenets of Dundas' book were made regulation in March 1792. The actual drillbook was issued in June that year. Dundas was promoted Major-General on 28 Apr 1790.
6. PRO.WO3/27/129, Col William Fawcett, Adjutant-General, to Lt-Col Christoper Maxwell, 30th Foot, Lt-Col Hay Macdowall, 57th Foot, Col The Hon Henry Fox and the Lieutenant Governors of Portsmouth and Plymouth, 5, 6 Feb 1793. The specific instruction was for the regulars to assist in the teaching of the manual and platoon exercises, but the general implication of the circular was that they should provide overall assistance, which would extend to battalion manoeuvre.
7. PRO.WO3/27/114, Circular from Fawcett to the colonels and commanding officers of all regiments of cavalry, 26 Jun 1792. Dismounted action was to be in strict compliance with the regulation.
8. Dundas, *op cit*, Appendix p67. There are tantalising inconsistencies throughout Dundas's work, particularly in the first part of his book, which is a discussion of why a close-order formation, the ultimate battle-winner, should be insisted upon. See, for example, p13, where foreign light troops 'perform regular and eminent service as advance guards, rear guards and patrols', or p14, where it is argued that British light infantry's 'frequent dispension and peculiarities...should be considered as occasional exceptions', or p64, where it is stated that '...extended order is an occasional exception that may be taken when [light companies] are single, detached, and when necessary'.

9. *Ibid*, Appendix pp85-86. Light companies grouped as a single combat unit were, however, expected to act as 'heavy' infantry.

formal rules of method' a commander might be permitted a degree of latitude in his tactical arrangements,[9] Dundas attached by far the greatest importance to training the infantry in close-order movements.

This shortcoming however, does not lessen Dundas' achievement in providing the British Army with something it badly needed after a decade of uncertainty - tactical uniformity, sustained as it was by a regimental 'interior economy' which enabled recruits to be trained to a level sufficient to enable them to take their place in the line in about two months.

The Army in the Field

Beginning in 1793 with a small detachment from the Guards of about 2,500 men, the Duke of York's army in the Low Countries grew to some 37,500 by the autumn of 1794. This total included troops from Hanover, Hesse-Cassell, and sundry French *emigré* and loyalist units, and a number of privately-raised corps.[10] However, increased numbers on paper never approximated to the effective fighting strength of the Duke's force. Foreign contingents arrived on a haphazard, job-lot basis and York had to beg the War Office for reinforcements and recruits. Sickness bedevilled his army, reaching epidemic proportions - over 60% - by late-December 1794.[11] The practice of taking men out of the line to serve as officers' batmen sapped the battalions' strength even further.[12] The situation became so dire that infantry-men had to be used as gunners; gunners were used as artillery drivers and the Duke even had to plead for drafts of sailors to do the work of artillerymen. It is no small wonder that his army was able to remain in the field for so long. That it did so, and the fact that the French came to respect the British soldier's fighting ability both in attack and defence,[13] pre-figured the Army's battlefield domination of the French in Egypt and the Peninsula.

In the field, Dundas' ideas, supplemented by new *Manual and Platoon Exercises* for the infantry[14] were put into practice under his own eye[15] and the Duke of York's General Orders suggest the degree of flexibility which could be obtained from them if they were astutely

10. PRO.WO1/170/135, 137, Return, 5 Aug 1794; WO1/171/289, Return, 1 Sep 1794.

11. PRO.WO1/171/621, Return, 24 Dec 1794.
12. PRO.WO1/170/555, Return, 1 Sep 1794. In the cavalry, batmen accounted for 236 men out of 3,105 present and fit for duty, and in the infantry, 782 men out of 14,861.
13. This is, it must be said, a very subjective judgment, but see, among correspondence from the front, PRO.WO1/168/211, Col (later Lt-Gen Sir) James Craig, Adjutant-General to the Duke of York to Evan Nepean, Under Secretary of State, 31 Jan 1794, also WO1/170/283, same to same, 31 Aug 1794.
14. This was The M*anual and Platoon Exercises*, London (1792), issued 'By His Majesty's Command' on 20 April. It is interesting to note that the order 'Present' included the words '...the left eye shut...look along the barrel with the right eye from the breech pin to the muzzle...' pp14, 26, 17, which suggests aimed fire of a sort.
15. Dundas commanded a brigade of cavalry from May 1794, and remained on the Continent in command of the entire British Cavalry from April to December 1795.

interpreted. The two-deep line, for example, was to be employed where there was no expectation of an attack by cavalry,[16] and this formation was practised regularly on such occasions as a *feu de joie* or an inspection. In combat, the prescribed third rank (where there were men sufficient to form one) was used as a reserve, and did not contribute to the battalion's firepower.[17]

As the campaign progressed, greater stress was laid on firepower,[18] a development attributable in part to the ever-increasing number of the enemy thrown forward in skirmishing 'clouds'. As these *tirailleurs* blazed away at their lines, the British realised that they were suffering from inadequate protection, lacking as they did any effective light infantry screen. Although a light company was included in the establishment of each battalion, these men were considered to be far too valuable to risk in a genuine skirmishing role,[19] and so this essential task was performed, in the main, by the polyglot foreign units. Some of these fulfilled the role splendidly, but the majority quickly went to pieces and degenerated into marauders. In the last few months of the campaign the British took over the duty themselves, and out of that experience came a realization of the need for a properly-trained and disciplined body of riflemen.[20] In addition, the cry for effective, dependable (and preferably British) light infantrymen had been heeded,[21] and from now on the light companies were liberated from their parent battalions' apron-strings.

The British cavalry, meanwhile, was in its element during 1793 and the first half of 1794. The open countryside around the border towns of France and the Austrian Netherlands favoured the *arme blanche*, and with the French cavalry in a weakened state, vulnerable and isolated parties of the enemy were swept aside with contemptuous ease by both heavy and light formations. April and May 1794 saw the British at their best, their crowning achievement taking place at the Battle of Willems on 10 May where, in a co-ordinated, all-arms attack, 22 squadrons broke three squares of French infantry, having previously routed a covering force of cavalry.[22] Taking part in the charge that day, and largely instrumental in its success, were the 2nd Royal

16. National Army Museum, 8512-15-4, Manuscript General Orders of Maj-Gen Gerard Lake, 1 Jun 1793, 26 Aug 1794; NAM 8512-9-1, Orderly Book of the 28th Foot, 27 Nov 1793. The two-deep line continued to receive official sanction despite Dundas' recommendation of three ranks; PRO.WO3/27/109, General Order, 23 Apr 1792.

17. NAM.8512-15-6, Lake General Orders, 27 Jul 1794.

18. PRO.WO1/168/175 York to Charles, 3rd Duke of Richmond, Master General of the Ordnance, 25 Jan 1794; same to Henry Dundas, Home Secretary, 28 Mar 1794.

19. PRO.WO1/168/199, Craig to Nepean, 31 Jan 1794.

20. The need for riflemen was raised as early as May 1793; PRO.WO1/166/263, Maj-Gen Sir James Murray to Dundas, 17 May 1793. See also same to same, 7 Jun, 12 Jul 1793, 31 Jan 1794.

21. PRO.WO1/168/377, Craig to Nepean, 4 Mar 1794; WO1/168/675, same to same, 11 Apr 1794. It is noteworthy that the 1792 drill-book, *Rules and Regulations for the Formations, Field Exercises, and Movements of His Majesty's Forces* (derived from David Dundas, *op cit*) contained general instructions for light infantry, including firing in extended order; general movement in quick time; taking cover; running, and the defence of wooded terrain; pp332-41.

22. It should be noted that contemporary accounts of the action are neither altogether clear nor entirely in agreement as to whether the French were formed in square.

North British Dragoons (the Scots Greys) who, after their return to England in 1795, were to spend the next 20 years on home service. Not until 18 June 1815 were they given another opportunity to ride over Frenchmen, when, perhaps frustrated by their intervening years of inactivity and recalling their earlier triumph too fondly, they over-reached themselves, lost all order and control, and were cut to pieces. Wellington in the Peninsula was to complain of his cavalry's inability to retain *any* sort of control, but during 1793-95 it was deployed, on the whole, in squadron strength rather than as complete regiments, and this made it that much easier to handle at speed.

Furthermore, throughout the campaign the duties of outposts and patrols were efficiently carried out by both heavy and light cavalry. Until April 1795 for example, the 5th and 6th Dragoon Guards had two light troops each. Unfortunately, it seems that these skills came to be neglected in favour of the charge, especially when in 1796 *Instructions and Regulations for the Formations and Movements of the Cavalry* were published (under Dundas' guidance), wherein it was emphasized that 'the great force of Cavalry is more in the offensive than the defensive: therefore the attack is its principal object'.

The Duke of York's artillery, despite a shortage of trained personnel, was well served in its close-support of the infantry, and was invariably a major factor in both the attack and the defence. Wellington was never to neglect the importance of artillery support, especially after the system of attaching light 6 pounders to the infantry as 'battalion guns' fell into disuse around the turn of the century.

A Grim Reckoning

Although frequently successful at the tactical level, the British Army was fighting a losing battle overall. Once the pressure of the French *lévee en masse* began to be felt and the Austrians (senior partners in the alliance) lost heart,[23] the Duke of York was left to fend for himself, an impossible task in purely numerical terms. After the defeat of the Allied army at the Battle of Tourcoing (17-18 May 1794),[24] the French established themselves firmly in control of the

23. This tendency became evident from the end of May 1794.
24. The British attack-column was left unsupported by the Austrians, and despite being surrounded and almost cut off by the enemy, blasted its way to safety in a brilliantly executed fighting withdrawal.

strategic initiative, and by making almost casual threats to the Duke's flanks whilst demonstrating in his front they pushed him back into unfriendly Dutch territory. A gruelling winter campaign developed along the river lines - indefensible when frozen solid - and although the British could still show a sting in their tail, fighting at least half-a-dozen minor actions, their strength began to wither away, largely on account of defective logistics. There was a dearth of wagon-drivers, which resulted in painfully accumulated stores of ammunition being abandoned and destroyed for want of transport. Biscuit had to be issued instead of bread. New clothing, sent out in pieces to be made up in the field (as was normal), could not be tailored, and as a result the troops froze. There was an equally desperate lack of shoes. Above all, the chronic mismanagement of the medical service, in particular the army's General Hospital, sent many a potential convalescent to the mortuary.

Throughout this time of misery the men of York's battered regiments continued to march, fight and march again, generating amongst themselves an immense pride in their achievements; '...the enemy were formidable only in their numbers', declared Captain Lewis Jones of the 14th Foot, 'and to their numbers also were they indebted for their conquests'.[25] Discipline held firm - only 27 men had been flogged by order of a General Court Martial during the campaign and a mere seven condemned to death.[26] In spite of the horrors of the winter retreat into northern Holland which left many a man, woman and child frozen to death, the army held together, but although many stragglers eventually found their way back to their regiments some battalions had suffered losses of 45%.[27] Recruiting parties scoured Britain for replacements, sweeping up a class of man they would have spurned in better times,[28] and providing a market for the notorious 'crimps' - civilian contractors who kidnapped men for military service.[29] In addition to the human cost of the campaign and its aftermath, a mass of equipment was also lost, captured or destroyed. The 7th Light Dragoons, for example, had to replace (amongst many other items), 87 saddles, 203 saddle-pads, 93 holsters, 136 carbine-

25. Capt L T Jones, *An Historical Journal of the British Campaign on the Continent in the Year 1794; with the Retreat through Holland in the Year 1795*, Birmingham (1797) p183.
26. NAM.8512-15-4, Lake General Orders, 1793-95. One of the condemned men was eventually pardoned. Additionally, 27 men were acquitted for insufficiency of evidence, six were suspended or reduced in rank, two were reprimanded and one officer was cashiered. (A total of 9 officers was tried during the campaign). Thirteen men were awarded 1,000 lashes each; the mildest sentence, 300 lashes, was imposed on a gunner who had stolen an officer's horse. Three NCOs and 16 men of the 8th Light Dragoons were acquitted after an affray on 16 August 1795 during which two men were killed as no witnesses could be found.
27. See PRO.WO17 series, Monthly Returns, for 1795. A number of regiments had as many as 50% of their men on the sick-list on their return to Britain, some of whom would have been incapable of further service.
28. Fifteen cavalry regiments and 34 battalions had participated in the campaign to varying degrees. As an example of the poor quality of recruit being enlisted, see PRO.WO27/77, 'Return of Men of the 107th Reg'. who by Age and Disease are unfit for Actual Service', which records 182 men unfit out of 539; the defectives include 14 suffering from ruptures, 70 with damaged limbs and 53 rheumatics. The eldest was 80 years of age and the youngest sixteen.
29. For the notorious crimping houses and mob attacks on them, see Clive Emsley, *British Society and the French Wars, 1793-1815*, London (1979) pp27, 37-38, and J Stevenson, 'The London "Crimp" Riots of 1794', *International Review of Social History*, Vol XVI (1971).

straps, 119 swords and scabbards, 150 sets of reins and 300 pairs of boots.[30]

The veterans of the British Army, however, had absorbed a great deal from their campaigning in Flanders and Holland. They understood that man for man they could beat anything that the French could throw against them, and that individual regiments, unfamiliar with each other, could operate harmoniously together in the performance of any task. Men who had fought in the Low Countries would carry the struggle to the enemy in India, Egypt, the West Indies and the Far East, Portugal, Spain, North and South America and, finally, back once more to Flanders fields. Their confidence in their ability to conquer is perhaps the lesson which, above all, was taken to heart, and the one which was ultimately to raise Lieutenant-Colonel Arthur Wesley of the 33rd Regiment of Foot to a dukedom and the final overthrow of Napoleon Bonaparte two decades later.

Between 1793 and 1801, 69 line infantry regiments of the British **MICHAEL DUFFY**
Army saw service in the Caribbean (15 wholly or in part serving there
twice). This was greater than the 65 which served in the Peninsular
War or the 28 (and three Guards Regiments) in the Waterloo campaign. In addition to those 69 were eight British light dragoon
regiments, four of foreign hussars, eight foreign infantry regiments,
three captured Dutch garrisons and twelve negro West India Regiments, making a total of over 95,000 officers and men. Why were so
many soldiers sent to an area now more famous for its tourist industry
and a superlative cricket team?

The Caribbean in British Strategy

Two hundred years ago the Caribbean contained the most important overseas colonies of Britain and France, their largest overseas
capital investments by far, tied up in sugar, cotton and coffee planta-
tions and the largest concentration of slaves in the world - 465,000 in
the British colonies and 594,000 in the French (1787-88). These
investments generated about one-fifth of all British foreign trade,
serviced by over one-eighth of all British merchant shipping tonnage
and seamen. Their value to France was even higher, generating two-
fifths of her foreign trade, a quarter of her merchant tonnage (including two-thirds of its ocean-going shipping) and over a third of her
seamen.

It was felt that whichever of the rival powers could deprive the other
of these highly exposed assets would secure a decisive margin of
superiority in the century-old Anglo-French contest for maritime and
commercial supremacy. France made a major attempt in a recent war
(1778-83), which Britain survived only at the expense of losing Tobago
to the French and granting her American mainland colonies their
independence. The French Revolution however weakened France's
navy and disrupted her colonies through conflict between republicans
and royalists, slaves and masters. It was inevitable when war broke
out between Britain and France in 1793 that William Pitt's Adminis-

tration would seek to take advantage of this situation to strike at the Caribbean foundations of French seapower.

The Course of the Caribbean Campaigns

The very first offensive British strike of the War was the recapture of Tobago by units of the Caribbean garrisons (April 1793). Although a subsequent landing on Martinique failed (June), a lodgement was successfully made in Saint-Domingue (September), before a 6,000 strong expedition under Lieutenant-General Sir Charles Grey arrived in January 1794 and in a vigorous and well-executed campaign captured Martinique, whose main strongpoint, Fort Bourbon, was reputedly the strongest fortress in the Caribbean (March), followed by St Lucia and Guadeloupe (April). Grey sent part of his force on to capture Port-au-Prince, capital and main port of Saint-Domingue in June. But with the latter (modern-day Haiti, then the richest colony in the world), at its mercy, Grey's small expedition was struck by disease and ran out of numbers to complete the conquest. When, unexpectedly, a small French expedition got back into Guadeloupe in June, Grey lacked the resources to turn it out. His gamble for victory by a night attack on Point-à-Pitre on 1 July turned into a disaster when his élite grenadier and light infantry battalions were caught in the streets of the town and shot to pieces.

Not until a similar disaster at Buenos Aires in 1807 was Britain to suffer such a crucial set-back in the overseas war, upsetting hopes of building a vast new American empire. The French expedition to Guadeloupe brought with it the whole panoply of the now rampant French Revolution. All slaves were declared emancipated and males of military age were promptly conscripted by *levée en masse* to provide the energetic and ruthless republican *commissaire* Victor Hugues with a large strike-force of coloured troops, with which he expelled the remnant of the British from Guadeloupe in December, recaptured St Lucia (May 1795), and stirred up revolt in the British islands of Grenada and St Vincent (March) and Dominica (June). This last uprising was quickly suppressed, but the others became serious and devastated two productive colonies. Further west, republican commissioners on Saint-Domingue used the same methods and pushed the British invaders back to the water's edge. When revolt broke out among the native Maroon population of Britain's richest colony, Jamaica, in August the position of her Caribbean empire began to look desperate.

To lose the Caribbean threatened losing the war - the Secretary for War, Henry Dundas, warned a year later that the loss of Jamaica would paralyze Britain's finances by ruining her credit. It was imperative to recover the lost ground quickly and expel the French republicans completely before they stirred up further revolt. The result was the biggest single military expedition ever yet sent overseas from Britain. Thirty-three thousand soldiers were despatched to the Caribbean in the autumn of 1795 - a concentration of over half of the line regiments of the British Army.

Composed of the survivors of the Flanders campaign and the best of the new army recruited in 1794-95, and commanded by Major-General Sir Ralph Abercromby, this massive effort was disrupted by its sheer size. It proved impossible to assemble it all by the planned departure date of mid-September 1795, and when the main body finally set off in November in a vast armada of 155 ships, it was twice driven back by storms, finally arriving piecemeal over the first four months of 1796. In view of the fate of most of those who finally reached their destination, it was perhaps fortunate for this present publication that Lieutenant-Colonel Arthur Wellesley was amongst those safely driven back when a storm in Lyme Bay wrecked the first sailing, after which his 33rd Regiment was diverted to India.

The late and fragmented arrival of Abercromby's expedition prevented him from achieving total victory. Nevertheless his achievement was impressive and important. The Guiana colonies of France's Dutch ally were captured in April 1796 and St Lucia regained in May. The Maroon uprising in Jamaica collapsed in January and the Grenada and St Vincent revolts were suppressed in June. Abercromby resumed the offensive in the following year by capturing Trinidad (where Lieutenant-Colonel Thomas Picton of the 56th was installed as Governor) in February 1797, and although repulsed from San Juan, Puerto Rico, in April, he had stabilized the position and restored British credit. Victor Hugues was intimidated into looking to his own defences and turned to the more financially rewarding field of privateering instead of trying to stir up revolt in the British islands.

The human price however was enormous. Nineteen thousand British troops died in the Caribbean in the 1795-96 and 1796-97 campaigns, while the costs in particular of sustaining the British forces and their French royalist allies on Saint-Domingue escalated fast as armies of ex-slaves and free coloureds strengthened their position in that populous colony. By 1797 it was clear to the Government that it could not continue its extensive Caribbean offensives. It was fast running out of troops to send and money with which to sustain them. A new policy of retrenchment was inaugurated. No more big expeditions were sent from Britain; negro regiments were recruited (by purchase of slaves) to conserve white manpower; operations on Saint-Domingue were wound down and in 1798, Brigadier-General Thomas Maitland skillfully extracted British forces without letting the French back in again by negotiating an unmolested withdrawal and a non-agression pact directly with the rebel leader, Toussaint l'Ouverture. There were still windfall gains to be made by garrison forces - Surinam (1799) and Curaçao (1800) from the Dutch - and in early 1801 a small expedition was sent from Britain which helped capture the Danish West Indian islands and the French and Dutch colonies on St Martins.

West Indian Warfare

Comparing military operations in the Caribbean with those in Europe, Sir Ralph Abercromby wrote that;

'There is little amusing in talking of Windward and Leeward situations, of Tides, Currents and Winds and yet these are circumstances to us of the utmost importance. In short this is a most uninteresting warfare, you see perhaps one or two days in the Campaign the Troops you command, the moment that you begin to act you are obliged to parcel out your little army in small detachments, and the instant the Service is over they go on shipboard to return to their respective garrisons. The real service of a campaign here might be comprised in the operation of a fortnight in Europe. Everything depends on a good understanding between the sea and land services. Seldom can a family quarrel be justified, on no occasion can the disagreement of an Admiral and a General be excused.[1]

1. Scottish Record Office, Hope of Luffness Papers, TD 73/25, Bundle 1081, Sir Ralph Abercromby to Col Alexander Hope, 21 Mar 1797.

Amphibious operations faced hazards unknown on the mainland and required specialist skills. The prevalent trade winds necessitated fighting from east to west (windward to leeward) and placed a premium on mastery of the Windward Islands chain which commanded the rest. Hence, although Saint-Domingue to leeward was the richest prize, over two-thirds of British troops were employed in fighting to control the strategically dominant Windward Islands.

A typical attack on an enemy colony set up multiple landings, threatened or actual, under cover of naval bombardment, in order to distract the enemy from concentrating his forces against the point of landing where the invaders would be at their most vulnerable. This was followed by the march of the various divisions to concentrate against the one major strongpoint each colony usually possessed. Set-piece battles on open ground were rare because of the lack of open ground and the dispersed nature of operations. Instead there were attacks on minor defences barring the way, culminating in the assault or siege of the major strongpoint, depending on its strength. The main obstacle was often less the subsidiary defences than the mountainous and wooded terrain - Major-General Perryn compared the topography of St Lucia to the Alps - and the climate. The latter restricted campaigning to the healthier winter months, but even then Brigadier-General John Hope thought the heat 'too intense';

'...it requires an uncommon degree of exertion in this climate where a man naturally is apt to feel himself languid and enfeebled, and where, when under the pressure of disease, every ache every pain is doubled by that lassitude which is the universal attachment of loss of health here, and in a degree unfortunately greater than is experienced at home.[2]

2. SRO.TD 73/25/1082, Brig-Gen John Hope to Col Alexander Hope, 17 Mar 1796.

Ensign Ross-Lewin recalled of one march on Saint-Domingue;

'The troops only moved off at 9 a.m., and before that time the greater number of the men had emptied their canteens, for a considerable distance we had to pass through a deep and close ravine, and were half suffocated by clouds of red dust; we had not advanced above two miles when the serjeant-major and thirteen privates of the 67th expired. Those who had improvidently drunk their grog before moving off were soon seen sucking the sleeves of their jackets for the perspiration that oozed through them; the tongues of several were hanging out of their mouths, amazingly swollen and black with flies; and in many instances, *horresco referens*, the men had recourse to the last extremity to allay their thirst...[3]

3. J Wardell ed., H Ross-Lewin, *With 'The Thirty Second' in the Peninsular and Other Campaigns* , Dublin (1904) pp22-23.

Thoughtful generals like Sir Charles Grey preferred to march in the cool of the night and attack in the early dawn to avoid such distress, but what could be done often depended on the quality of the troops. Grey's army included many veterans of the American War and the élite flank companies of all the regiments in Ireland, out of which he formed three grenadier and three light infantry battalions. It was probably the finest British strike-force assembled in the whole war and Grey used it in brilliantly successful shock-tactics, storming with the bayonet wherever possible and demoralizing opponents into submission. Abercromby's army was newer, brave certainly, but much less disciplined and poorly led at company level by inexperienced officers. It needed all the nursing and coaxing that Abercromby and his able subordinates, John Moore and John Hope, could bestow on it. Abercromby often relied on the skilled mercenary German rifle regiments he took with him and which helped inspire the subsequent development of British rifle corps.

The French Revolution added a new guerrilla-warfare element to Caribbean operations which had usually hitherto ended when the major strongpoints surrendered. Now the insurgent slaves frequently took to the woods and mountains and continued a bush war, tying down and exposing to the ravages of disease large numbers of troops who might otherwise have been removed to healthier climes before the onset of the deadly 'sickly season'.

The Human Cost

The Caribbean was the most deadly theatre in which the British Army served during the French Revolutionary and Napoleonic Wars. Of 89,000 white officers and men who served there between 1793 and 1801 some 45,000 died. Over 95% of these were killed by disease rather than the enemy. The 31st Foot, for example, lost 55 killed and 664 dead from disease in less than two years on St Lucia in 1796-97; the 13th Light Dragoons lost one killed and 305 from disease in two-and-a-half-years on Saint-Domingue.

Losses had indeed been anticipated, but casualties on such a scale were unprecedented. The vast influx of Europeans, lacking immunity to the killer tropical diseases of yellow fever and malaria, seems to have cruelly coincided with the arrival of a more virulent yellow fever strain from Africa and successive hotter, wetter summer seasons which greatly multiplied the mosquito vectors of these diseases.

The strategic needs were such that these losses had to be risked, but Pitt's war minister, Henry Dundas, did not wantonly send men to their deaths. He did all he could to keep them alive by sending as many as possible to Gibraltar to be 'seasoned' in a warmer clime before transfer to the Caribbean. He ordered a major medical enquiry in 1795 and implemented its recommendations (unfortunately contemporary medicine was ignorant of the real causes of these diseases). And he forced reluctant colonial governments to accept the creation of twelve negro regiments which were eventually built up to a third of the garrison strength in order to avoid sending out so many British troops. Dundas's successors were even more careful. When the conquered islands, restored by the Peace of Amiens, had to be re-won in the Napoleonic Wars, ministers avoided sending large expeditions from Britain, relying largely on 'seasoned' garrison forces supplemented by the West India Regiments, and for larger operations, such as the capture of Martinique (1809) and Guadeloupe (1810), reinforced these with troops closer at hand in Bermuda and Nova Scotia, removing them quickly as soon as the operation was successful. In these ways annual casualty-rates among British troops in the Windward and Leeward Islands fell from 41% in 1796 to 13.8% in 1803-16.

Nevertheless, much psychological as well as physical damage had by then been done to the Army. George Pinckard, physician to Abercromby's 1795-96 expedition, recorded that '...a sense of terror attaches to the very name of the West Indies'.[4] There were incentives to go for those willing to run the risks. Prize money was greater for the capture of those rich colonies than on any other service, while almost certain promotion beckoned those officers who survived. 'Terror' however predominated. It affected recruiting, and Dundas only managed to raise an army to invade Holland in 1799 by promising recruits from the Militia that they would not be obliged to serve outside Europe. Six regiments mutinied in 1795 when their men were drafted into others going with Abercromby. Some troops inflicted disabling sores on themselves to avoid Caribbean service. Others deserted - indeed desertion was so rife that an embarkation officer was ordered in 1797 to tell the 87th Regiment it was going to the Cape of Good Hope rather than the Caribbean in order to get it on board ship whole.

Most soldiers, like Dr Pinckard, resignedly hoped that it would be their lot to escape the dreaded 'black vomit' (yellow fever). When it struck however its suddenness and extent were overwhelming. Lieutenant Howard's York Hussars lost eight officers and 186 men in ten days in 1796. 'Some regiments', he wrote, 'seeing the Mortality around them gave themselves totally up for lost, and instead of attempting to stop the progress of the Disease did everything in their Power to promote it in order to be the sooner out of their Misery'.[5]

4. G Pinckard, *Notes on the West Indies*, London (1806) Vol 1 p15.

5. R N Buckley ed., *The Haitian Journal of Lieutenant Howard, York Hussars, 1796-1798*, Knoxville (1985), p50.

Many seized on the lethal new island rum as the solution to their troubles one way or another. Yet when there was a prospect of fighting human enemies, Pinckard noted that;

'The spirit of attack seemed to operate as a specific remedy. Many actually recovered, and were allowed to join their comrades. Others stole off, without reporting themselves, fearful the doctors should not allow that they were well enough to be reported efficient...[6]

6. Pinckard; *op cit*, Vol II p169.

Military action raised morale above the general demoralization of service in the Caribbean in the 1790s.

Results

Demoralizing though they might have been for the men involved, the Caribbean campaigns and their conquests were vital to Britain's ability to keep fighting until a sufficiently strong European coalition emerged to defeat Napoleon. They ensured the security of one of Britian's principal wealth-producing areas in what became a war of financial endurance, and their part in destroying France's maritime empire helped to establish the clear maritime superiority that was the basis of the 'Pax Britannica' of the nineteenth century. French trade did not regain its 1788 level until 1825; French merchant tonnage failed to regain its 1788 level until mid-century, by which time Britain's was three times greater. The Battle of Waterloo extinguished the immediate menace of Napoleon, but it was the many British overseas campaigns during these wars which ensured the undermining of the longer-term French maritime threat to Britain.

Ian F W Beckett

The English and Welsh Militias enshrined the ancient principle that the citizen owed a military obligation in defence of the state. Indeed, since a standing army might pose a threat to the state, the 'old constitutional force' had been regarded traditionally as preferable as a means of defence. The increasing professionalism of warfare in the late-seventeenth and eighteenth centuries clearly demonstrated the need for a regular military establishment but, given the reluctance of politicians in a predominantly maritime nation to maintain a large army, it was unavoidable that the Militia would play a major wartime role. Such was the case between 1793 and 1815 but, in the process, the Militia not only became increasingly unpopular but also lost its distinctiveness as an independent military force.

Ballot and Subversion

It was hardly the case that Militia obligations enjoyed universal support even before the mid-eighteenth century, but popular resentment had been greatly increased by the reform of the Militia system between 1757 and 1769. Whereas liability had been previously assessed on property, the 'new Militia' decisively shifted the burden of service to the lower end of the social scale by compelling each county to ballot compulsorily to find a proportional quota of its able-bodied males between the ages of 18 and 50 to serve for three years. Since the Militia was liable to be called out for 20 days (28 from 1762), continuous training each summer, the system promised a more efficient military instrument and most of the new county regiments were also embodied for permanent wartime service during the latter stages of the Seven Years' War. They performed the same role in the more severe test of the country's defences when both France and Spain allied themselves to the American rebels in 1778. But, popular opposition to the ballot - there were widespread anti-Militia disturbances in 1757 - was to endure well beyond its final abandonment in 1831, despite the various exemptions granted and the ability to avoid personal service by paying a £10 fine or providing a substitute.

Changing the Guard at St James's Palace
Coloured line engraving, artist unknown, published 1792.
The three Regiments of Foot Guards were a long-established part of London life, an ornament to royal occasions and a force to police the city's turbulent populace.
National Army Museum   6307-32

'Foot Soldier'
Coloured stipple engraving by François Soiron after Henry William Bunbury, published by Thomas Macklin, London, 20 July 1791.
Henry Bunbury the caricaturist (who was at one time Colonel of the West Suffolk Militia must not be confused with his son, Lieutenant-General Sir Henry Edward Bunbury, the military memoirist often quoted in this book.
National Army Museum 8211-169-1

'A Field Day in Hyde Park'
Coloured aquatint by Thomas
Malton after Thomas Rowlandson,
published by S W Fores, London,
15 May 1789.
Satirical views of military 'behaviour' or individuals were common
fare throughout the Revolutionary
and Napoleonic War period.
National Army Museum   7907-144

'Light Infantry Man'
Watercolour, probably the original
by Henry Bunbury for the coloured
stipple engraving by François
Soiron, published by Thomas
Macklin, London, 20 July 1791.
National Army Museum 6007-178-2

His Royal Highness
FREDERICK DUKE of YORK.

'His Royal Highness Frederick Duke of York'
Stipple engraving by and after William Hincks, published by John Fairburn, London, 1 December 1794.
Frederick Augustus, Duke of York and Albany, seen here as a young man, was the second and favourite son of King George III. He commanded the British contingent in Flanders, 1793-95 and was a brave but inexperienced general. Appointed Field Marshal in 1795 and Commander-in-Chief from April 1798, he presided over a number of significant Army reforms. He was obliged to quit his post in March 1809 after it was revealed that his mistress, Mary Anne Clarke, had made money from traffic in commissions, but was reinstated in May 1811 to almost unanimous satisfaction.
National Army Museum   7801-15

Sʳ DAVID DUNDAS, KB, COMMANDER in CHIEF.

'Sr. David Dundas, KB, Commander in Chief'
Coloured etching by and after Robert Dighton Snr., published by Robert Dighton Snr., London, April 1810.
A veteran of the German campaigns of the Seven Years' War, who did not serve in America, he published the book that made his reputation, *The Principles of Military Movements*, in 1788. Following a succession of staff and field-command appointments he became Commander-in-Chief in March 1809 in succession to the Duke of York, then under a cloud on account of the Mary Anne Clarke scandal. He willingly resigned the post of C-in-C to York in May 1811.
National Army Museum 6412-139-14

'The New Manual and Platoon Exercises, as Practised by His Majesty's Army'
Coloured engraving by and after Robert Dighton Snr., published by Bowles and Carver, London, 2 January 1795.
National Army Museum   8407-69

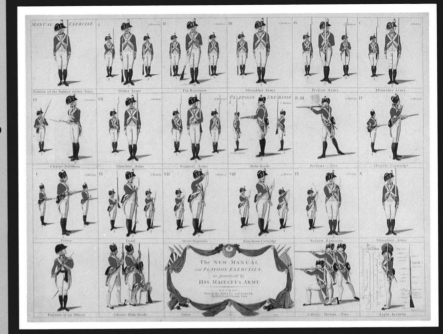

'Flannel Coats of Mail…'
Coloured etching after Isaac Cruikshank, published by S W Fores, London, 25 November 1793. The misadventures of the Duke of York's army in Flanders were the subject of much coarse humour, of which this is an early and typical example.
National Army Museum   7507-24

'Sir Charles Grey, KB'
Stipple engraving by Joseph Collyer
after Thomas Lawrence, published
by William Austin, London, 29 May
1797.
A distinguished veteran of the Seven
Years' War and the War of American Independence, Lieutenant-
General Sir Charles Grey was
appointed to command the land
forces sent to the West Indies in
1793. This campaign, though costly
in manpower, was attended by
considerable success - later marred
by the French recapture of
Guadeloupe and accusations that
Grey was too interested in seeking
after prize money and places of
profit in the captured islands.
National Army Museum   8208-103

**A Private of the 5th West India
Regiment**
Coloured aquatint by Joseph
Stadler after Charles Hamilton
Smith, from the series 'Costume of
the British Army', published by
Colnaghi and Co, London, 1815.
The West India Regiments were
recruited from 1795 among Creole
slaves and newly imported Africans.
The British Army's reliance on the
slave trade to recruit these forces
was a factor in prolonging that
trade to 1807.
National Army Museum 8204-203-44

'S.W. View of Forts Bourbon & Louis, in the Island of Martinique', 1794
Coloured aquatint by Samuel Alken after the Revd C Willyams, published by the Revd C Willyams, 1 August 1796.
National Army Museum 7102-33-250

'N.E. View of Fort Louis in the Island of Martinique', 1794
Coloured aquatint by Samuel Alken after the Revd C Willyams, published by the Revd C Willyams, 1 August 1796.
Sir Charles Grey's army took Fort Louis by storm on 20 March 1794.
National Army Museum 7102-33-249

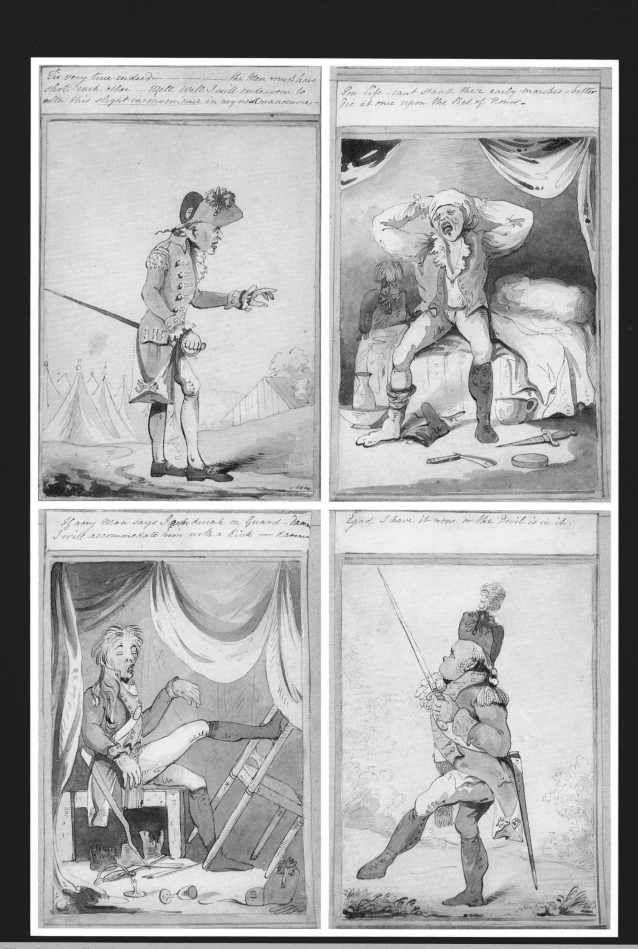

The Cornwall Militia, c1796

From a set of ten watercolours, based on regimental 'characters', artist unknown, the originals for the coloured aquatint 'A Peep into Camp', published by S W Fores, London, 8 May 1797.
National Army Museum   7210-3

Do not believe them Mem — we military Gemmin
are the Protectors not the Violators of the Fair

Soudafais equipp'd for Conquest 'fore Ged —

O La! La! Dear Sweet Wind spare me but tile
I pass the General! —

Go the Rounds d'ye say? — d — y what d'ye mean
by that? can't you hedid it rain you Scoundrel?

Coupled with popular resentment against compulsion was the fact that a Militiaman was not differentiated from the population in the same way as a regular soldier and he retained his civilian interests and opinions at least in the initial period of any embodied service before habits of discipline prevailed. Consequently, there was a possibility of subversion in a force which - upon wartime mobilisation - would become not only the main defence against enemy raids but also the principal force for the maintenance of domestic order. The perceived revolutionary potential in Britain following the French Convention's decree in November 1792 promising assistance to all those seeking to overthrow their monarchies was sufficiently feared for the Militia to be embodied on 1 December as a precautionary and preventative measure against insurrection. It was not therefore surprising that signs of unrest should soon be detected amid a force composed predominantly of manual workers.

In November 1792 it had already been reported that 'little books' were circulating among Militiamen from northern and industrial areas and six regiments - those of Cumberland, Derbyshire, Nottinghamshire, Warwickshire, Westminster and Yorkshire - were suspected of disaffection. One result was a barrack building programme, while another was the practice of stationing Militia regiments as far away as possible from their own counties - in 1793 the authorities in County Durham and Northumberland actually requested that their own Militias be sent away. But such measures did not necessarily isolate the Militia and Militiamen figured in at least 16 of the food and grain riots during the course of 1795.

Much of the difficulty was due to poor discipline and officer absenteeism but, more importantly, the Militia was as vulnerable to price rises as any consumer. The food allowance was just five pence a day and flour was needed for dressing regulation pigtails, while there was also often a determination to identify with local grievances. Men of the Gloucestershire Militia forced butchers to lower prices in Portsmouth; South Hampshire Militiamen were involved in disturbances at Canterbury; Northamptonshire Militiamen at Plymouth and Herefordshire Militiamen at Chichester. The most serious outbreak took place at Seaford in April 1795, involving as many as 400 Oxfordshire Militiamen, of whom five were subsequently executed.

Concessions forthcoming included bread at fixed prices, increased pay and the abolition of the pigtail and, thereafter, there was an understandable tendency to distrust the Militia, at least in its own areas. In 1802 it was alleged that leading shearmen opposed to the introduction of mill machinery in Yorkshire included discharged Militiamen, while the Luddite disturbances in the north in 1811 and 1812, when the bulk of the 12,000 troops deployed was drawn from the Militia, also brought renewed warnings in the West Riding and Cheshire that it was unwise to employ northern Militia. However, such fears appear to have been unfounded after 1795. In 1797 seditious handbills distributed in barracks invariably invoked strong protestations of loyalty from Militia regiments. The widespread food riots of 1800 saw no repetition of Militia indiscipline and in 1812 there was but one occasion - in the Cumberland Militia - when a Militiaman declined to fire upon rioters.

Of course, over ten years had passed since the height of the initial food riots and, for many Militiamen, this had meant ten years of steady assimilation into the military life. In this regard, the unique autobiography of the farm servant, Joseph Mayett, who served in the Royal Bucks King's Own Militia from 1803 to 1815, provides a glimpse of the mentality of the ordinary Militiaman, regularly shunted around from one garrison to another and restricted to mundane military tasks such as guarding prisoners of war or escorting deserters. The Royal Bucks had 25 stations in 12 years during Mayett's service, excluding a period in Ireland and the service of some elements in France in 1814. Mayett was distanced from many of his peers both by his literacy and also by his intermittently strong Baptist faith but even he '...carried a very small political universe in his baggage'[1], its parameters closely defined by his reactions to arbitrary military authority and injustice, frequent illnesses and immoral temptations. For Mayett and his fellows, being ordered to 'fire ball' in Stockport on three occasions

1. Ann Kussmaul ed., *The Autobiography of Joseph Mayett of Quainton, 1783-1839*, Bucks Record Society, No 23 (1986) p21.

had little significance compared with the arduous marching and countermarching in wet weather that accompanied the deployment to the north.

Notwithstanding the unpopularity of compulsion and the fact that the Militia's loyalty was not immediately apparent in the 1790s, the Government could not forego the ballot as a means of raising the additional forces it believed necessary for home defence. Hasty legislation in March 1794 allowed the augmentation of the Militia by voluntary means but in November 1796 it was proposed effectively to treble county quotas by raising a 60,000 strong Supplementary Militia. As it was not intended to embody it at once, it was hoped to avoid undue opposition. However, there was another wave of anti-Militia riots in 1797 which brought forth a far more vigorous response than 40 years previously. The legislation was not thereafter disputed, but some regiments did not complete their quotas until the autumn of 1798 and there were familiar problems in finding men prepared to serve in person ('principals'), despite the fine for exemption being raised to £15. Similar opposition was generated by the extension of the Militia to Scotland between July and September 1797 with over 40 riots, the restriction of the ballot to those aged between 18 and 23 not recognising the economic importance of this age-group north of the border. The disturbances were more violent than those in England and at Tranent in East Lothian, Fencibles fired on a crowd of over 5,000 on 29 August, killing at least 12 people - a higher death toll than at 'Peterloo' in 1819.

The threat of the ballot greatly stimulated the Volunteer Movement after 1794 but the 105,000-strong Militia and Supplementary Militia still represented 46% of all forces available in Britain in 1798. However, this numerically impressive array was rapidly dissipated after the signing of the preliminaries of the Peace of Amiens in October 1801. Both Militia and Supplementaries were disembodied, and legislation in April 1802 reduced the establishment to 70,000 men, of which only 49,000 would actually be trained. It was also anticipated that any future conflict would require the embodiment of only the youngest and fittest of five classes into which the Militia was to be divided according to age, marital status and health. Peacetime training was also curtailed to 21 days per annum. However, peace lasted but fourteen months and it was as early as 11 March 1803 that the Militia was re-embodied with an immediate extension of annual training to the customary 28 days. On 28 May the Supplementary Militia was also re-embodied.

Militia and Regulars

The renewal of the War marked a growing debate over the precise relationship between the Militia and the Army, which had become apparent even during the earlier conflict. The raising of the Supplementary Militia had made it more difficult to find recruits for the Army, while prices of substitutes had soared. Consequently, in January 1798, the Government had tried to obtain up to 10,000 Supplementary Militiamen for the Army, but Lords Lieutenant opposed any part of the Militia becoming merely a draft-finding body. Similarly, they opposed any extraction of grenadier or light companies from ordinary Militia regiments in April 1798, although the Marquess of Buckingham did suggest enabling the Militia to serve in Ireland, where rebellion had erupted, and his own regiment was the first to be despatched there. (Offers to serve in Ireland declined noticeably once the difficulties pertaining to military life there became apparent). Nevertheless, in June 1799, the Militia was reduced to 66,000 men to allow Militiamen to enlist up to a quarter of the new county quotas. In July, regular Army commissions were also opened to Militia officers where at least 60 men transferred, and in October the establishment was again reduced to enable the surplus to enlist. By such means, over 26,000 Militiamen had enlisted in the Army by the end of 1799 and, despite their inexperience and occasional indiscipline, they proved good military material in the expedition to North Holland that year. Sir Ralph Abercromby proclaimed them '...a superior race of men, and a great acquisition to the army',[2] and it has been argued that their arrival helped to regenerate the army he was soon to lead to victory in Egypt.

2. Piers Mackesy, *War Without Victory, The Downfall of Pitt 1799-1805*, Oxford (1984) p78.

However, due to the opposition among Lords Lieutenant and Militia commanding officers, the 1802 legislation firmly prohibited Militiamen from entering the Army. As a result, successive administrations turned to expedients such as the 'Army of Reserve' in June 1803 and the 'Permanent Additional Force' in June 1804 - the latter incorporating both Army of Reserve and Supplementary Militia forces - as a means of reinforcing the regular Army. As Secretary of State for War in the 'Talents' administration, William Windham substituted a Training Act for the Permanent Additional Force Act as a basis for national military training, although without conspicuous success. At the same time, he launched an assault on the Volunteers, whose exemption from the ballot had also contributed to the high price of substitutes and the concommitant uncompetitiveness of Army recruiting bounties. Another part of Windham's scheme was to suspend the ballot for two years from July 1806 in the expectation of improving Militia recruitment but his measures merely deprived the Volunteers of any real enducement to efficiency, without materially assisting the Militia's cause and it was left to his successor in the Perceval and Liverpool Administrations, Lord Castlereagh, to structure national military organisation in a way that clearly defined the relationship of Army and Militia.

In fact, Castlereagh had briefly occupied the War Office at the close of Pitt's final Administration and, in order to create a 'disposable force', he had revived the 1799 precedent in April 1805 by permitting the enlistment of the equivalent of four-fifths of those added as Supplementary Militia. Some safeguards were offered to commanding officers to forbid the enlistment of selected men and 10,696 Militiamen had transferred to the regulars. Castlereagh clearly appreciated the ready reinforcement that had thus been obtained from the Militia and, following the decision to mount the Copenhagen Expedition (1807), he announced the intention to seek a further 28,000 Militiamen for the Army. He also revived the ballot to fill vacancies, although this would be suspended until January 1810 where sufficient volunteers came forward towards quotas. The

3. Sir John Fortescue, *The County Lieutenancies and the Army, 1803-1814*, London (1909) p195.

revival of the ballot inevitably brought what Sir John Fortescue aptly described as a 'wild traffic in substitutes',[3] but Castlereagh succeeded admirably in augmenting the Army with some 27,505 Militiamen.

The precedent thus re-established, the experiment was repeated in March 1809 to bring in 16,429 Militiamen to compensate for casualties suffered during the retreat to Corunna and in time for the Walcheren Expedition. Thereafter, the Militia increasingly fed the Army in the Peninsula, with legislation in April 1811 allowing a fixed annual draft into the Army with vacancies filled primarily by voluntary means, the ballot being suspended successively to January 1812 and then to July 1813. Some 11,453 Militiamen entered the Army in 1811, 9,927 in 1812 and 9,095 in 1813. Further service was also obtained by allowing for the interchange of Irish and British Militia regiments on a voluntary and rotating basis for periods of up to two years from 1811 onwards; seeking offers to form provisional battalions for service overseas in November 1813 and, in the following month, removing all restrictions to universal Militia service throughout the United Kingdom.

Unfortunately, the call for provisional battalions coincided with a further request for 30,000 men to transfer to the Army. Amid the resulting confusion, only 3,243 men were enlisted into the Army by June 1814 while only 2,700 came forward for the provisional battalions. Three provisional battalions were formed in February 1814 from 16 separate county contingents. Embarking at Portsmouth in March they only landed at Pauillac in the Gironde on 23 April to be attached to the British 7th Division. The French had already withdrawn and, without seeing action, the battalions re-embarked on 29 May 1814. According to one somewhat prejudiced account they 'were constantly tipsy', while the local inhabitants clustered to view the frequent parades solely 'to gaze on the commanding officers, whom they denominated *Les boeufs-gras anglais*'.[4]

4. *The Reminiscences and Recollections of Captain Gronow*, London (1900) Vol II pp217-19.

Undoubtedly, there was greater willingness on the part of the Militia and, especially, their commanding officers, to serve overseas as an entity. Nine regiments had already volunteered for the Peninsula by January 1809 and such offers were repeated regularly thereafter. However, it was clearly more beneficial to the Army to direct Militia recruits where they were needed without having to accommodate the susceptibilities of independently-minded Militia colonels. The latter continued to resent the indiscipline and drunkenness that often resulted as those enlisting in the regulars expended their bounty money in the shortest possible time, and they also resented the loss of trained men, since those longest in the Militia were usually the most likely to enlist. That such men were of high quality can be illustrated by noting just how many of the most celebrated accounts of the Peninsular War emanating from the Army's rank-and-file were penned by those who had first served in the Militia, including Private Wheeler, William Surtees, Edward Costello, William Green and Thomas Jackson.

Thus, not only did the Militia invariably supply approximately half the trained men available for home defence in Britain, but it also produced the manpower necessary to maintain the Army at strength, even if the flurry of additional measures in 1814 suggested that the system was under strain. Militiamen were certainly hastily enlisted again during the Hundred Days and some of those who fought at Waterloo reputedly did so still wearing their Militia uniforms. Naturally enough, there were then considerable problems of adjustment after the end of almost 20 years of continuous warfare, with the Militia swelling the number of demobilised servicemen on the labour market, even if parishes were immediately relieved of the not inconsiderable wartime burden of maintaining the families of those on Militia service.

In the latter aspect alone, the Militia would have had a great impact on the lives of ordinary citizens during the Revolutionary and Napoleonic Wars but, of course, there had also been the almost universal distaste for the Militia ballot. Of all the auxiliary forces to survive through or emerge from, this period, it was the Militia whose very basis had been most threatened. But there was also the challenge from the increasing assumption among soldiers and politicians that the Militia served only as an adjunct to the Army. In contributing so distinctly to the defeat of the King's enemies, the Militia had undermined both its independence and its acceptability.

CLIVE EMSLEY

Until 1914 Britons generally referred to the wars against Revolutionary and Napoleonic France as 'the Great War'. These wars were the climax of a century of conflict fought between Britain and France across the world, but they were fought on a much larger scale than their predecessors; the armies and navies were bigger, the expense was colossal, and the threat of invasion was greater, especially while the *Grande Armée* was encamped on the French Channel coast between 1803 and 1805. The Revolutionary Wars also had a pronounced ideological element and this led to fears of a 'fifth column' within Britain, fomenting and encouraging disorder; when riots occurred over food shortages in 1795-96 and again in 1799-1801, British Jacobins were suspected of involvement. To fight the French overseas, armies and navies of unprecedented size were raised, enormous loans were negotiated, and taxes of unprecedented levels and types were voted. To protect the country from invasion the Militia was embodied and periodically augmented; a further line of internal defence against Jacobinism, both foreign and British, was provided by the Volunteer Movement.

For King, Constitution and Country

Volunteer companies had been organised for home defence during the American War of Independence when the rebel colonists' French allies threatened a descent on British coasts. In December 1792, before the declaration of war on Britain by France's new republican government but when fears of subversion were acute, at least one gentleman, Sir Thomas Gooch of Benacre Hall near Saxmundham, was contemplating organising a corps of cavalry from men of property to maintain internal order.[1] The Declaration of War on 1 February 1793 led rapidly to gentlemen on the south coast organising mounted patrols, and offering to embody themselves as volunteer companies if the Government felt their services were necessary and was prepared to issue them with weapons. Pitt's Administration was sympathetic to these proposals, yet it was over a year before legislation was passed for encouraging and disciplining corps of Volunteers. The Act of April 1794 (34 Geo. III cap. 31) was the first of several passed at different

1. British Library, Add. MSS. 16922/ 133-34, Gooch to John Reeves, 16 Dec 1792.

stages of the war to encourage volunteering and to organise the country in case of French invasion. In April 1798, a second round of volunteering was engendered by the Defence of the Realm Act (38 Geo.III cap.27) which authorised the raising of 'Armed Associations' and required local authorities to make returns of all males aged between 15 and 60 in each county, together with the numbers of livestock, carts, boats, barges and corn mills. Similar legislation, the 'Levy en Masse Act' (43 Geo.III cap.96), was passed in July 1803 after the rupture of the short-lived Peace of Amiens, but the enormous number of independent Volunteer corps which came forward at the re-commencement of hostilities rendered many of its clauses for training the nation's manpower superfluous. A key problem in 1803 was that the Volunteer corps were established under such a variety of acts and regulations: the Volunteer Consolidation Act of 1804 (44 Geo.III cap.54) went some way towards clarifying the situation. The Local Militia Acts of 1808 (48 Geo.III caps.111 and 150), which enabled Volunteer infantry companies to transfer into a new Local Militia for a bounty was an attempt to impose a greater degree of uniformity in the system which had developed over the preceding years. The Volunteers appear to have reached their numerical peak towards the end of 1803 when there were estimated to be some 368,000 in England, Scotland and Wales, with another 72,000 in Ireland; by the summer of 1807 these numbers had fallen to 228,000 and 66,000 respectively.[2]

There were artillery, cavalry and infantry among the Volunteers. Most of the artillery were to be found in seaports and harbours manning gun-batteries against a French invasion. The cavalry was generally drawn from men of property who brought their own horses and who, in many instances, paid for all, or much, of their accoutrements and uniforms. The Light Horse Volunteers of London and Westminster had originated in the American War and were reorganised in May 1794 on the basis of six troops of 50 men; in that year, and again in 1795, they refused generous offers of financial assistance from gentlemen who were not members of the corps, insisting that they could not depart from their original principle of each man supplying his own equipment. Charles Herries, the prosperous London merchant who became colonel of the corps, published an in-

2. This essay is not concerned with the Irish Volunteers in any detail; before 1801, when the Act of Union was passed, Ireland had its own Parliament in Dublin. Irish Volunteer units were similar to those elsewhere in Britain, but the Yeomanry were almost exclusively Protestant and were deployed as a sectarian force. Moreover, the Rebellion of 1798 and the landing of General Humbert with 1,000 veterans from the Italian campaign, also gave them a very different military experience.

3. James N Collyer, John Innes Pocock, *An Historical Record of the Light Horse Volunteers of London and Westminster*, London (1843) *passim*; NAM.7704-82-73-77, Documents relating to the London and Westminster Light Horse Volunteers, 1779-1818, accumulated by Col-Commndt Charles Herries.

4. NAM.6012/266/4, Papers of Brig H Bullock; cutting from the *Wilts and Gloucestershire Standard*, 8 June 1957.

5. Northumberland Country Record Office, Sir Paul Butler [Ewart MSS] B8/1-17, Papers relating to Royal Cheviot Legion and North Northumberland Militia.

struction book on cavalry movements, drill and the use of arms which became a text book for Yeomanry and Volunteer cavalry.[3] The Yeomanry cavalry regiments of the counties were generally recruited from the well-to-do farmers and gentry; they adopted flamboyant uniforms and were officered by the cream of county society. The Volunteer infantry units, especially during the first stage of the wars, were largely urban. They were a cross-section of society, drawn from local notables, shopkeepers and tradesmen, artisans and the occasional labourer; the 95 officers and men of the Cirencester Volunteers in October 1799, for example, contained, among others, five lawyers, nine grocers and victuallers, eight carpenters and chairmakers, three barbers, three tailors, two woolcombers, and a gardener.[4] A few corps combined both infantry and cavalry. The Royal Cheviot Legion was raised by Horace St Paul around Wooler in 1798; originally it consisted of four infantry companies and two cavalry troops all of 50 men each; when it was reformed in May 1803 there were ten infantry companies and four troops of cavalry.[5]

Volunteering - A Mixture of Motives

Men joined the Volunteers for a variety of reasons. Patriotism was obviously a key motive; the eighteenth century Englishman was xenophobic and fiercely proud of the liberties which he claimed to enjoy as a result of the Glorious Revolution of 1688. The French had become the traditional enemy during the century and, in Government and loyalist propaganda, their Revolution had transformed them from the ignorant slaves of an absolutist, Catholic monarch into atheistical monsters; the situation was little different when Jacobin revolutionaries were replaced by 'the Corsican ogre', General Bonaparte. For the staunch British loyalist, those who espoused even the most liberal and moderate of the principles associated with the French Revolution were seditious and designing traitors. Some of the early Volunteer corps evolved out of the Association Movement, launched towards the end of 1792 by the respected lawyer John Reeves to demonstrate loyalty to King and Constitution and to counteract the propaganda of political radicals with French sympathies. The parades of such corps became a further focus for loyal speeches and sermons, and presented opportunities for the intimidation of the radicals.

But patriotism was only one motive for volunteering. Men who volunteered for corps organised by their employer or their landlord may have been patriotic, but they may also have been wary of their job prospects or their tenancies. Some of the poorer Volunteers, especially, enrolled because this gave them immunity from the ballots for the county Militia regiments. As a Volunteer a man only had to train for, perhaps, one day a week and he would only be called out for actual service in case of emergency; if he was ballotted for the Militia he would either have to serve in person, (and in wartime the Militia was embodied on a permanent footing), or else pay a fine or find the money to hire a substitute to serve in his place. The pay allowed to a poor man when he turned out as a Volunteer for training could be a valuable source of additional income in times of unemployment or underemployment. The Volunteers also provided opportunities for conviviality, for patronage, and even in the case of some local clothiers, boot and shoemakers, for profit. As an anonymous (and cynical) Sussex poetaster asked, with reference to Lord Egremont's troop of Yeomanry;

'Why does the baker on the saddle rise

Who'd better stay at home and make mince pies?

Is it to war with gnats and butterflies?

Why does the grocer draw the ruthless sword?

In hope to gain the custom of my lord.

Why is the ploughshare to the cutlass bent?

To bribe the steward to curtail the rent.[6]

The urban infantry reflected the growing self-confidence and civic-mindedness of the middle class, something which led members of the traditional élite to look askance at such corps, particularly those which insisted on electing officers who were not drawn from the gentry.[7] There was concern towards the end of the 1790s that some political extremists were joining the Volunteers to obtain weapons and to learn their use;[8] and the Gloucestershire magistrate, Sir George Onesiphorus Paul, while conceding that if the workers in the local clothing industry were armed

6. Quoted by Ann Hudson, 'Volunteer Soldiers in Sussex during the Revolutionary and Napoleonic Wars, 1793-1815', *Sussex Archaeological Collections*, Vol 122 (1984) p176.

7. Linda Colley, 'Whose Nation? Class and National Consciousness in Britain 1750-1830', *Past and Present*, No.113 (1986) pp114-15; J E Cookson, 'The English Volunteer Movement of the French Wars, 1793-1815: Some Contexts', *Historical Journal*, Vol XXXII (1989) pp867-91.
8. Clive Emsley, 'The Military and Popular Disorder in England 1790-1801', *Journal of the Society for Army Historical Research*, Vol. LXI (1983) pp99-100.

9. J R Western, 'The Volunteer Movement as an Anti-Revolutionary Force, 1793-1801', *English Historical Review*, Vol. LXXI (1956) p610.

10. For the Brixham riot, see John Bohstedt, *Riots and Community Politics in England and Wales 1790-1810*, Cambridge, Mass. (1983) p53. For the Volunteers in general during the food riots, see Roger Wells, *Wretched Faces: Famine in Wartime England 1793-1803*, Gloucester (1988), especially pp260-73.
11. Public Record Office, Home Office Papers, HO42/74/30, John Bennett to Charles Yorke, Home Secretary, 29 Dec 1803; HO/42/78 John Wright to Yorke, 4, 15 Feb 1804.

12. Cecil Sebag-Montefiore, *A History of the Volunteer Forces*, London (1908) pp170-71.

13. PRO.HO42/37/113-14, Townshend to Portland, 22-23 Dec 1795.

then they could be relied on to fight the French, also feared that when the danger of invasion was passed, then the same weapons might be used to prevent the introduction of new machinery.[9]

As the names of many of the units imply, the Volunteer corps were very much local bodies; some of the original corps specified in their articles of agreement that they would not be deployed more than a few miles from their home. Their local nature made them vulnerable to pressure in certain kinds of police action that they were called upon to perform. During the food shortages, and the consequent riots, of 1795-96 and especially 1799-1801, the poorer urban Volunteers were increasingly regarded as unreliable by the authorities. These men and their families were themselves suffering from high prices and shortages; on some occasions when Volunteer infantry were called out to face hungry rioters, many men did not appear, and those who did were sometimes subjected to verbal abuse and physical ill-treatment afterwards. In Brixham, Devon, disorder over high prices in March 1801 was actually orchestrated by the officers of the local Volunteers.[10] Two-and-a-half-years later, when a press gang in Chester seized a member of the Royal Chester Volunteers for the Royal Navy, his regimental colleagues, who made up one-fifth of the city population, set out to rescue him.[11]

Such problems were not as apparent when the gentlemen of the London Light Horse Volunteers or the Yeomanry cavalry were deployed. The former were warmly praised by London police magistrates for their role in helping to suppress riots against corrupt recruiting agents, known as 'crimps', in July 1795.[12] Yeomanry corps were kept busy by food rioters in their respective counties throughout the same year; the Marquess Townshend was convinced that it was the determination of the Yeomanry which maintained the peace of Norfolk in that year.[13] However, it is also possible that the deployment of the Yeomanry angered and increased the resentment of subsistence rioters; the hungry crowd generally accused farmers of profiteering at their expense and being the real cause of high prices, and they must have found it particularly offensive when farmers and their sons appeared in splendid Yeomanry uniforms as an aid to the civil power.

Fit for Service?

Most Volunteers who saw any kind of action did so as police deployed, most notably, during the food riots of the 1790s and the Luddite disorders of 1811-12; a few of the coast gunners exchanged shots with French privateers, and one or two of the infantry units or Yeomanry troops near the coast clashed with smugglers. Lord Cawdor's troop of the Castlemartin Yeomanry were part of the small force which marched against Colonel William Tate's *Légion Noire* when it landed in Pembrokeshire in February 1797;[14] but the French surrendered without a fight, and the question remains - how would the Volunteers have fared had they been required to engage with a resolute French invasion force?

Units like the London Light Horse Volunteers may well have been dependable against French troops; and other corps, with good, determined leadership and stiffened by regulars may have proved themselves. This was generally the case in Ireland in 1798 when Yeomen faced Humbert's French veterans or Irish rebels: at Castlebar the Galway Yeomanry ran from the French with everyone else; however under the bold leadership of a local landlord, Lord Longford, and a Scottish regular, Major Porter, some 200 Yeomen, stiffened by a hundred or so Scots Fencibles, pursued and then confronted several thousand Irish rebels.[15] It is clear however that many senior officers and politicians wondered about the dependability and efficiency of the British Volunteers should invasion come. These concerns were voiced particularly after the rupture of the Peace of Amiens.

Part of the problem was that the Volunteer corps were jealous of their independence and no professional officer could give orders to such a corps unless it was called out on permanent duty. Some corps employed a regular soldier or a Militiaman to train them, but others were trained largely by their own officers, and by no means all of these had acquired Colonel Herries' knowledge and abilities. There was little regularity about training and much of this was the fault of the Government, particularly in 1803 when, alarmed by the potential cost of equipping and paying all the Volunteers who came forward, they set out to discourage volunteering by reducing allowances and privileges. This meant that men

14. E H Stuart Jones, *The Last Invasion of Britain*, Cardiff (1950) *passim*.

15. Thomas Pakenham, *The Year of Liberty: The Great Irish Rebellion of 1798*, London (1969) pp355-56, 370-72.

enrolled before 22 June 1803 were paid for 85 days' training in a year and were only required to serve in their own military district, while those enrolling after that date were only to be paid for 20 days' training and could be sent anywhere in the Kingdom. There were also problems over the actual days set aside for training which arose specifically out of the nature of late-eighteenth and early-nineteenth century British society. In spite of the advance of industrialization the country remained over-whelmingly rural - indeed the problems of supply created by the French blockade made British farming crucial for survival, and very profitable for the farmer - but as a consequence, it could be very difficult to persuade farmers, or farm labourers, to attend for drill during the harvest. Attempts to organise training parades on Sundays brought forth the wrath of many clergy and created problems for some ardent Christians; the French might be anti-Christ, but that was no reason to break the Sabbath. Robert Hay was expelled from the Morpeth Volunteer Infantry for absenting himself from parade; he excused himself in a letter to the *Newcastle Courant* explaining that training on a Sunday was '…repugnant…to the laws of both religion and good policy'.[16] A degree of improvement in training occurred shortly after the reopening of hostilities in 1803 when the Duke of York, as Commander-in-Chief, was authorised to appoint a body of inspecting field officers to advise the Volunteers. While seeking their advice was not obligatory, it seems that these officers were consulted readily by the commanders of Volunteer units, and early in 1804 the inspectors were writing reports to Horse Guards describing marked improvements in the part-time soldiery. A system of compulsory inspections for the different corps, and the insti-tution of regular staff officers for the Volunteers contributed further to the improvements in training. The most common problems noted by the inspectors early in 1804 were shortages of arms and equipment.[17]

But not everyone had faith in the Volunteers, even after the improve-ments of 1803-04. There continued to be unease in respect of the democratic nature of some of the urban corps, especially those run by committees based on those of the American Revolutionary militia; at least one MP feared them as potential 'armed parliaments'.[18] Significant among

16. *Newcastle Courant*, 15 November 1800.

17. Richard Glover, *Britain at Bay: Defence against Bonaparte 1803-14*, London (1973) pp209-10.

18. Colley, *op cit* p115.

their critics was William Windham for whom they were '...painted cherries which none but simple birds would take for real fruit'.[19] When the Ministry of All the Talents assumed power early in 1806, Windham became Secretary for War. He had plans for training all the able bodied men in the country in annual batches of 200,000; his Training Act (46 Geo.III cap.90) reached the statute book in July 1806, but it was never implemented. However his criticisms of the Volunteers, his cuts in their allowances and abolition of their inspecting field officers, severely reduced their morale and probably also their efficiency. Windham's successor, Lord Castlereagh, repealed much of his legislation and gave some limited support to the Volunteers, but he too wanted an efficient home defence force, more uniform than that provided by the existing Volunteer units, and it was to this end that he established the Local Militia in June 1808. Within a year some 125,00 men of the Volunteer infantry companies had transferred with their units into the Local Militia.

The end of the War with Napoleon meant the end of their military adventures for most Volunteers, though some Yeomanry Corps remained in existence and saw service in police actions through to the Chartist disorders, and, most notoriously, at 'Peterloo' in August 1819. The Volunteers had served two functions. During the 1790s in particular they had been the most visible manifestation of loyalty to Crown and Constitution against the British Jacobins; and during the years when invasion seemed most likely, 1798 and 1803-05, they had provided an additional line of defence to be deployed alongside the regular Army and Militia. While it is impossible to assess how they would have responded in battle, it is probably fair to say that they were at their most efficient when the danger of invasion was at its greatest between the rupture of the Peace of Amiens and Nelson's victory at Trafalgar.

19. Quoted in Glover, *op cit*, p143.

DE WITT BAILEY AND DAVID HARDING

1. The principal secondary sources for this article are; H L Blackmore, *British Military Firearms 1650-1850*, London (1961); D W Bailey, *British Military Longarms 1715-1865*, London (1986); Graham Priest, *The Brown Bess Bayonet*, Norwich (1986). Additional source material is derived from two forthcoming studies by the present authors; D W Bailey, *British Military Smallarms: Board of Ordnance Production 1690-1815* and D F Harding, *Firearms of the East India Company: Smallarms of the British Indian Armies 1600-1856*.

Perhaps the most enduring image of the British Army at Waterloo is that of red-coated infantry in square using their muskets and bayonets to defeat the onslaught of brave and skilled French cavalry - a classic demonstration of the musket as 'the Queen of Battles'. And yet most of the British muskets were of a design adapted quite radically for service in India, and which in 1793 would have been considered inadequate for regular service in Europe. This article examines how it came about that the principal British line infantry weapon at Waterloo was the 'India Pattern' musket.[1] The explanation casts light on the English military gun trade of the period, and on the differing approaches to small-arms design of its two main customers.

The Board of Ordnance and its Small-Arms in 1793

At the outbreak of war the British Army's infantry weapon was the Short Land Pattern Musket with bayonet. This musket, with a 42 inch barrel, had been officially adopted as the standard line infantry musket in 1768. All of these weapons were manufactured by private sector gunmakers working on contract to the Board of Ordnance.

The ten years preceding 1793 had seen all-time low small-arms production by the Ordnance. This was partly due to overstocked storehouses and financial retrenchment at the end of the long war in America, and partly to the reforming zeal of the incumbent Master General, Charles, 3rd Duke of Richmond. Richmond considered the Short Land Musket to be outdated and had encouraged much experimentation in the field of small-arms, but all potential improvements had foundered on the twin rocks of military conservatism and financial stringency. Towards the end of the decade of peace a radically new design of infantry musket, 'The Duke of Richmond's Pattern', based on the combining of a variety of European ideas, was officially adopted as the new infantry weapon. In 1793, the new musket was going through a difficult period of experimental production. Ironically, during the last full year of peace, Ordnance production of small-arms fell to the lowest level since the end of the American War, and, at the same time, 30,000 muskets, 2,000 carbines and 2,000 pairs of pistols were disposed of at auction.

The fog of optimism and aloofness began to dissipate in December 1792. On Boxing Day the contractor Jonathan Hennem was ordered to produce 5,000 Old Pattern (conventional Short Land) muskets at the rate of 250 per week, but Henry Nock received contracts for 10,000 of the New Pattern (Duke of Richmond's) muskets as well as for 5,000 Old Pattern muskets. They were badly needed: the Master Furbisher informed the Board that only 1,962 muskets with steel rammers remained in store at the end of May 1793. In July, contracts were placed in Liège for 10,000 muskets with options on a further 10,000, but barely half of these arms were received before the French seized this major arms-producing centre in July 1794. The Ordnance bought many foreign arms in 1794, but they exhibited an alarming diversity of patterns, calibres and barrel-lengths.

The Board also sought to expand the work-force in England. During 1793, six new contractors for rough-stocking and setting-up were appointed, in addition to ten firms for the supply of barrels and locks. Prices were increased for the various components and production processes. Given the overall nature of the gun trade at this time, the results were impressive: some 31,000 Short Land Muskets were produced in 1793, more than had ever before been delivered during the first year of a new war. However, this was still woefully inadequate for the rapidly expanding requirements of Britain's home and allied forces.

In October 1793 the Master General informed the Home Secretary, Henry Dundas, that the Ordnance would be unable to equip recently raised regiments in a timely manner. The Board had only 5,356 Short Land Muskets in store, and warrants had already been signed for the issue of more than that number. Richmond stated that all efforts to increase the productivity of the work-force had achieved a maximum output of 500 to 1,000 arms per week. He said the contractors blamed their journeymen as idle, and had claimed that standards of work had been raised beyond what they had been recently producing; they had also complained that a higher quality of proof powder was destroying a larger percentage of barrels; and finally, that large orders from Ireland and the East India Company were keeping the largest and least skilled portion of the work-force busy. Richmond blamed the carelessness of workmen rather than stronger powder for the barrel failures, and stated that Ordnance standards had not in fact been raised. But he confirmed the impact of the Irish and East India Company orders on a finite pool of labour.

Richmond suggested an approach to the East India Company, asking them to sell to Government their current output of arms, and to agree to place no further orders until Board of Ordnance requirements had been met. He told Henry Dundas that he was

> '...aware how unpleasant it must be to take such a step, and to deliver out to our Troops these East India Arms, which are considered of somewhat an inferior quality to ours, but...the least important must give way to the most; and you will be best able to judge whether the East India Company can admit of a delay in respect to these arms. And altho' they might not be quite so perfect as ours, they undoubtedly must be serviceable ones, and such as the new Raised Corps must put up with on the present Emergency.[2]

2. Public Record Office, HO50/370/59, Richmond to Dundas, 11 Oct 1793.

Hence was conceived the idea of introducing into British Army service the arms of the East India Company.

The Ordnance's disparagement of the Company's musket masks their own unawareness of the fact that British Army regiments had already used that weapon quite happily in India; some had specifically asked for it in preference to their heavier Ordnance muskets.

The East India Company and its Small-Arms

As Chairman of the Board of Control (the Government watch-dog for Indian affairs) Henry Dundas would have had access to records showing that the East India Company had far more small-arms in store than the Ordnance. The Company's declared reserves in India in mid-1794 amounted to 76,200 muskets, 839 fusils, 8,564 carbines, and 18,090 pairs of pistols, and these figures took account of only the weapons in store at the main arsenals in Calcutta, Madras and Bombay.

The reason why such a discrepancy could arise between the two services' reserves of firearms was, chiefly, that the East India Company had its own independent and very successful procurement system. The Company placed annual contracts for small-arms with a list of selected London gunmakers, and paid just a few specialist examiners to inspect the product before acceptance. Thus, the small-arms procured by the Company could be, and were, different from those of the Board of Ordnance, and were obtained in great quantities. As India was separated from the source of supply by a long and dangerous sea voyage, it was Company policy to aim at having one musket in store in India for every one in use. Thus, in the shipping seasons of 1793 and 1794 alone (a time of peace in India), the Company ordered 47,595 muskets and 14,900 other small-arms. In spite of making such huge demands the Company was never obliged to turn to foreign sources of supply.

There were several reasons why the Company enjoyed such abundant supplies of weapons. The simple design of their musket was well suited to mass manufacture. They aimed for serviceability and availability rather than for sheer quality as the Ordnance did. Thus (in the 1790s at least), the Company applied lower, though adequate, standards of inspection. Not least, the Company paid the gunmakers quickly and reliably. The same tradesmen generally worked for both the Ordnance and the Company, and it would seem that without their steady income from the India work, few if any of them would have been able to remain in business and work for the Ordnance at all. The eventual profits from the Ordnance work were very worthwhile, but a gunmaker risked bankruptcy while waiting for Government warrants or debentures to be cashed, unless he was also working for the East India Company. During periods of peace in Europe, the India work kept the English military gun trade in existence.

Since the Company had become a major power in India during the Seven Years' War it had been almost constantly at war. By 1793 it had armies larger than the peacetime British Army, an ever-increasing portion of which was serving in India, paid for, and often armed by, the Company. For the sake of simplicity the Company's muskets were of the same calibre (nominally .76 inch), as those supplied to the King's regiments and could make use of the same ammunition, but within that constraint there was scope for quite major differences. Since 1760, the Company's musket had been specially adapted for Indian service in the hands of sepoys and European soldiers alike. In that year, the Company diverged from the Ordnance norm by adopting a pattern of musket recommended by Stringer Lawrence, the first Commander-in-Chief in India. It had a 39 inch barrel (seven inches shorter than the contemporary Ordnance Long Land Pattern Musket), and was otherwise of a light construction and comparatively plain in style. The pattern was changed in certain minor details in 1770 and 1771, but remained essentially short, light and of simple manufacture. The short barrel was never found to be a disadvantage: even when soldiers were drawn up three ranks deep a correct manner of 'locking up' avoided any danger to the front rank, and, in any case, a two-rank formation was increasingly used in India from at least 1761 onwards.

Sales of East India Company Small-Arms to Government, 1794-1815

By January 1794, the Duke of Richmond had become convinced that it would be better to keep craftsmen occupied on East India Company orders, and to buy their output from the Company, rather than try to terminate their work in favour of the Ordnance, since many of them could not work to Ordnance standards anyway. Henry Dundas agreed. He was well placed to approach the Court of Directors about selling arms to Government, and did so in February 1794. The Directors replied the very next day that they did 'most readily consent' to selling the Government such arms as they happened to have on hand in England or in course of manufacture. By 7

November 1794, transfers amounted to 28,920 muskets and 5,664 arms of lesser categories. Another 6,560 muskets followed during 1795, 10,000 in 1796 and no less than 42,000 in 1797.

These transfers were not Government requisitions, nor did they represent the Company's entire production of small-arms. The Company demanded, and duly received, full reimbursement for the weapons and all associated costs, and when payment was delayed they charged the Government interest at 4% per annum. Due regard to the national interest would have made it difficult for the Directors to turn down the initial request for help, but the national interest was at stake in India as well as Europe. The Government (through the Board of Control) had its share of responsibility for India, and could not expect the Company to cease sending arms there indefinitely. Thus, in the shipping seasons of 1793-99 inclusive, the Madras Army alone received more than 44,850 muskets.

During this period and on through to 1815, the Ordnance frequently asked the Company to help it arm a specific force or ally, and the Company usually complied and then simply re-ordered the surrendered arms. But the Court of Directors was free to refuse, and did so when it considered its needs to be absolute, as for example in 1803, during the Wellesley brothers' subjugation of the crucial Maratha challenge to British power. By 1815, the Company had sold the Ordnance at least 142,970 small-arms. In addition, the Company helped Government with many other kinds of military and naval supplies in different parts of the globe, and repayments amounted to a million or a million-and-a-half pounds at a time. Correspondence between the two organisations leaves no doubt that the boot was on the East India Company's foot in the matter of warlike stores, and that the Chairman of the Court of Directors could deal on terms of equality with Dundas, even though the latter was a Cabinet Minister.

The Adoption and Manufacture of the India Pattern Musket by the Board of Ordnance

The gun trade required many months to expand its pool of workmen in times of increased demand, and this expansion was more easily achieved at the less skilled end of the work-force. This meant that large orders for the simpler East India muskets were more easily fulfilled than those for the Ordnance patterns. This lesson was not lost on the Board, and by February 1795 it was ordering India Pattern muskets direct from the makers on its own account. Charles, 1st Marquis Cornwallis (of Yorktown notoriety) replaced Richmond as Master General of the Ordnance in January 1795. The new brooms did not take long to sweep away the gilded gingerbread of the Richmond regime: in February the first contracts for the production of more than 42,000 East India pattern muskets by the Ordnance work-force were placed, and the term 'India Pattern' came into use in Ordnance records. The muskets were to be 'Rough Stocked, out of his [the contractor's] own plank, made off, cleansed and set up, and locks tapped, engraved and hardened'. Deliveries were minimal until 1797: only 1,574 in 1795 and 8,435 in 1796. A hierarchy of issue had been worked out: Short Land Muskets for regular British Army troops, India Pattern for the Volunteers and Supplementary Militia, and trade muskets and foreign arms for the foreign troops in British pay.

By 1797, it was clear to the Ordnance that neither the Short Land Pattern nor Richmond's musket could be produced in adequate quantities. Having already bought 82,000 East India Company muskets and having ordered so many more of their own copies of that pattern, the Ordnance now decided to standardize on the Company's musket, with all its advantages in cheapness, simplicity and ease of manufacture. In April 1797, the Board instructed the Birmingham contractors to rough-stock and set-up all remaining Land Pattern musket parts, and the decks were cleared for the large-scale exclusive production of the India Pattern musket. Some 72,600 complete arms, 30,500 barrels and 42,300 locks were delivered during 1797. In contrast, only 2,661 Short Land muskets were produced. The last (500) Short Land muskets were delivered in 1802. Although the traditional Ordnance methods of production were retained for all other types of small-arms, for the India Pattern Musket and the India

Pattern Sergeants' Carbine (also introduced in 1797), the production process was simplified, largely by the reduction and dilution of detailed inspections at each stage of manufacture. Additional contractors were taken on.

Despite this major concentration on the India Pattern musket, the eventual return to a higher quality arm was not lost sight of, and development plans proceeded until in September 1801 the first pilot group of barrels for a 'New Land Pattern' musket were produced. The Peace of Amiens (March 1802 - May 1803) gave the Board its opportunity to put this new pattern into production, but when war broke out again manufacture reverted overwhelmingly to the India Pattern musket until 1814.

In 1804 the gunmakers signed agreements with the Ordnance not to work for anyone else except the East India Company without permission. In the same year the Board adopted a special procedure for procuring the India Pattern musket: the major components only (barrel, lock, rammer and bayonet) were bought in their rough states, and later issued to 'setters-up' who supplied the stock, brass furniture and small pins etc, and made the whole into complete arms. In 1807 the Company followed suit, except that they also bought in the brasswork themselves. Hitherto, they had allowed the setter-up to provide all his own components. During the 1790s, wartime pressures on the gun trade had depressed the quality of the Company's small-arms, but reforms brought in from 1801 (including this new system of musket procurement) raised standards above the pre-War norm.

During the war the Company's musket remained the same in its essentials (barrel-length, calibre, comparative simplicity and lightness) but in some details it converged with the evolving design of the Ordnance copy. The stock became more robust at the 'small' and in the fore-end; the shape of the butt was modernized; in early 1810 the cock was strengthened by being changed to the throat-hole type from the weaker (though more elegant) swan-neck type. By about 1809-13 the muskets of the two services were the same in pattern and quality, and distinguishable only by their markings.

The eventual success of the Ordnance's efforts to supply small-arms during the war can be gauged by the fact that between 1795 and 1815 at least 2,834,485 India Pattern muskets were produced as well as 378,000 other small-arms. In 1814 there were no less than 743,000 serviceable muskets and 75,000 more 'repairable' ones in store, in addition to 554,974 smallarms of all kinds in the hands of troops. Such quantities had only been achieved by suspending the Board's traditional high quality of finish and adopting instead the East India Company's musket and the underlying philosphy of serviceability.

The British Army's Use of the India Pattern Musket

From the commencement of the big deliveries in 1797 the India Pattern musket would have come rapidly into service as pre-war arms wore out. By 1809, it is known that regiments such as the 14th Foot, serving in India, were routinely equipped with the Ordnance India Pattern musket, brought out with them from England, and a committee of officers from the King's and Company's services at Calcutta in that year certified that there was no difference in design or quality between these arms and those of the East India Company.

In 1811, the Directors of the Company remarked that the Board of Ordnance had informed them that '…the Species of Fire Arm, called a Land Service Musket,…has been lately used by the Foot Guards only'. The latter weapon, they pointed out, had a longer barrel and was 'altogether heavier than the Common Musquet hitherto sent you, which is technically called the Indian Pattern [sic], for having been first used in our Armies, although now used by all the King's regiments of the *Line* and the *Militia*'.[3] Specific references confirm that the 4th Foot, the 52nd and 71st Light Infantry, four battalions of Foot Guards and the Light Company of the 1st King's German Legion had New Land Pattern weapons on issue when they fought at Waterloo. The British rifle regiments and companies had the Baker Rifle. But these were exceptions: the British line infantry at Waterloo were armed with the India Pattern musket.

3. India Office Records, L/MIL/3/2071, Letter to Bengal, 16 Oct 1811.

Thus did the India Pattern musket replace the more costly and elaborate Short Land Pattern musket in the mid-1790s, and serve as the standard British line infantry weapon throughout the Napoleonic Wars. It remained in service until the introduction of weapons with percussion ignition in about 1840. Under the pressures of war, small-arms design and manufacturing processes had been simplified to facilitate what we would now consider to be mass production. The East India Company's existing simplified design and relatively streamlined approach to production greatly eased the Government's enforced alterations in its own small-arms procurement programme. There could be no clearer vindication of the Company's approach to this major economic and military component of its commercial function. At the same time, the Board of Ordnance's insistence on maintaining high quality in its small-arms despite wartime pressures served in its turn to improve the quality of the Company's own weapons.

COMPARISON OF ORDNANCE MUSKETS OF THE LINE INFANTRY, 1793–1815				
	Barrel length	Overall length	Reach with bayonet	Weight
Short Land Pattern	42in	58in	76in	10lb 8oz
India Pattern	39in	55in	73in	9lb 11oz
New Land Pattern	42in	58in	76in	10lb 6oz

In all cases the calibre was nominally .76 inch, the size of ball .693 inch and weight of the powder charge 6 drams Avoirdupois.

BRIAN ROBSON

1. Thomas Gill, c1744-1801. See Thomas Gill Junior, 'Recollections of his father, the late Mr Thomas Gill', *Journal of the Arms and Armour Society*, Vol III (1960), pp171-193.

Towards the end of the eighteenth century, the leading English sword-maker, Thomas Gill, of London and Birmingham, was accustomed to marking his blades with the rubric 'Warranted Never To Fail'.[1] It was a bold boast because any sword blade can be bent or broken in certain circumstances, and particularly in the conditions of the battlefield. But it had a deeper significance because it reflected a growing concern with the design and quality of manufacture of English military swords.

The 1788 Pattern Swords

To understand how this came about it is necessary to consider for a moment the nature of the British Army's regimental system at that time. The eighteenth century regiment was, in very broad terms, a cross between a private company and a franchise operation. The colonel of the regiment was responsible for raising, manning and paying it, for arming, equipping, feeding and lodging it. The Government provided certain items of equipment, notably muskets; otherwise, the colonel was responsible for finding the arms (including swords) and equipment, to patterns normally his choice. In return for these responsibilities, the colonel received a series of allowances, usually calculated on a per capita basis. By various devices - some legal, some not - he expected at the end of the day to make a profit.

Whatever the merits of this system from the Government's point of view, it had one outstanding defect in relation to equipment. Because each regiment was largely free to choose its own patterns of equipment (including swords) there was no effective standardization and, in consequence, no real system of war reserves. Thus, if a regiment on active service managed to lose or damage equipment and weapons for whatever reason, it could be months before the regiment was able to replace it and might be operationally crippled in the meantime.

Worse even than the absence of any standardization, perhaps, was the absence of any clearly defined standards of proof and quality. The particular design of sword chosen by a cavalry colonel for his regiment might or might not prove suitable for active service; human nature being what it was, there was an obvious temptation to skimp on quality and to retain weapons in service after they were really worn-out, in the interest of saving money.

In 1788, in the melancholy aftermath of the war against the American colonists, a Board of General Officers of Regiments of Cavalry was set up under General Henry Seymour Conway to consider, inter alia, the problem of the swords of the British cavalry. Each regiment was required to forward a specimen of the swords with which it was equipped so that the Board could settle upon standard patterns for all the cavalry. The Board was also required to decide whether British or German manufacture was preferable.

For the Heavy Cavalry (that is to say, the regiments of Dragoons and Dragoon Guards, but not the Household Troops), the Board recommended a long, straight sword, nearly 47 inches long and weighing some three pounds; the hilt, a half-basket of steel bars, was to be that of the 6th (Inniskilling) Dragoons. For the Light Cavalry (that is to say, the regiments of Light Dragoons), the sword was to have a moderately curved blade, with a steel or iron knucklebow guard. It was some six inches shorter overall and weighed two or three ounces less than the Heavy Cavalry model. In theory, officers were to carry the same swords as the troopers.

It was when the Board went into the question of manufacture that the most interesting facts emerged. Three of the leading English manufacturers, including Thomas Gill, and one German, the celebrated John Justus Runkel of Solingen (then the acknowledged centre of the German sword-making industry), were called in and questioned. Their answers showed that not only were there no official standards of proof for military swords but that there was no real agreement among the experts as to what the tests ought to be. Gill, for example, thought that blades should be tested by bending and then using them to cut iron; he thought striking on a flat surface a fallacious proof. Others thought blades should be struck on flat wood or iron surfaces, while Runkel was opposed to bending. They were united only in believing that other people had made very bad swords in the past. Tests revealed little difference in quality between English and German blades.

The Board ultimately decided that in future all swords for military use should be tested by striking on a flat wooden surface and then being bent to an extent of two inches per foot of blade length. Subject to the Treasury imposing an import duty to even out competition, regiments should continue to be free to purchase their swords where they wished.[2]

It was a worthy effort to introduce some sort of order into a chaotic situation but the results were not, in practice, very satisfactory. The Heavy Cavalry sword was a monstrosity - heavy, badly balanced and generally cumbersome, with a cylindrical grip which allowed the sword to twist in the hand, and a guard which restricted movement. The Light Cavalry sword, by contrast, was better balanced, with a shaped grip, but it was not sufficiently curved to make a really good slashing sword while too curved to be suitable for thrusting. Moreover, the tests laid down were too rudimentary and imprecise to prevent bad manufacture. The fact was that sword blades constituted a complex and taxing metallurgical problem in which the desirable, but opposing, qualities of stiffness and flexibility had to be balanced so as to avoid brittleness on the one hand and softness on the other. It was not for another hundred years that this problem began to be solved consistently in this country.

The Test of Battle

The 1788 Pattern swords received their first real test in 1793. The army which went to the Netherlands in that year, under the Duke of York, has some claims to be the worst-equipped that Britain has sent to the Continent. It lacked transport, its guns were notably inferior to the Continental models, and particularly those of the French on the Gribeauval system, and its ammunition waggons, heavy and unwieldy, were of a design which dated back to the time of Marlborough. The cavalry regiments were brigaded alongside the Austrian cavalry,

2. The proceedings of the Board are contained in Public Record Office, WO71/11.

60

then considered the finest in Europe. To one observer, at least, the Austrian equipment and training were immeasurably superior to that of the British; that observer was Major John Gaspard Le Marchant, of the 2nd Dragoon Guards. 'I have been busily engaged in making drawings of all the articles in the military equipage of our Allies which differ from our own, such as saddles, accoutrements, arms etc.' he wrote. 'I have also paid particular observation to the mode of training the Austrian cavalry to the use of the sabre, in which their superiority over us is incredible'.[3] Not only was their training superior but their swords were equally so. Le Marchant observed that 'The swords then in use in the British cavalry were of various descriptions, scarcely two regiments having the same pattern; but one of the most popular was a wide, long and heavy blade, mounted with a cumbersome, fantastic handle'. Clearly, the process of standardization had not gone very far; the quality also left something to be desired, according to Le Marchant, who noted that the swords were often so brittle that they broke at the first blow, and so heavy and badly balanced that they tended to twist in the hand so that the final effect was more that of a club than a blade. Many of the wounds suffered by the British troopers were accidentally self-inflicted. Nevertheless, it is fair to record that at Villers-en-Couchés and at Beaumont, in April 1794, the British cavalry achieved stunning successes against the French revolutionary infantry. Towards the end of that ultimately disastrous campaign Le Marchant returned home and set to work to try to make use of the knowledge and experience that he had amassed; in particular, he sought to do something about the swords and the sword training of the British cavalry. He had by this time formulated clear views about the weapon for the cavalry. He believed that in the charge the sword was relatively unimportant - it was the sheer impetus of the horsemen which counted. The sword came into its own only when the enemy infantry or cavalry had been broken up and there followed what Le Marchant called, rather curiously, 'desultory encounters' - that is to say, individual, hand-to-hand combats. For that purpose, he believed, a curved, slashing sword was required rather than a long,

3. D Le Marchant, *Memoirs of the late Major General Le Marchant*, London 1841, p13. For Le Marchants's career as a whole, see R H Thoumine, *Scientific Soldier: a Life of General Le Marchant 1766-1812*, London (1968).

heavy, thrusting sword. All types of cavalry should be equipped with the same sword. His advocacy of the curved, slashing sword was based to some extent on the example of the Oriental scimitar used by the Turkish janissaries, the North African Arabs, the Egyptian Mamelukes and the Hungarian 'hussars'.

Le Marchant consulted the leading swordmakers in Birmingham and Sheffield, including, we may assume, Thomas Gill, but the man who most closely shared his ideas about the design of swords was the well-known Birmingham manufacturer, Henry Osborne. Together, they evolved a design for a curved, slashing sword, with a $31^{1}/_{2}$ inch blade which Le Marchant submitted to the Commander-in-Chief, the Duke of York, under cover of a memorial entitled 'A Plan for Constructing and Mounting in a Different Manner the Swords of the Cavalry', early in 1796. No copy of this memorial has so far been traced but it is clear that the proposed sword was very similar to the Pattern 1796 Light Cavalry sword subsequently adopted except that it was slightly shorter. The new method of constructing and mounting cannot be defined precisely in the absence of the original document but almost certainly it referred to the method of riveting the backpiece and grip to the tang of the blade as described below.

The 1796 Pattern Swords

Le Marchant's proposals were submitted to another Board of Cavalry General Officers in 1796, and the results of their deliberations were announced in a General Order of 27 June 1796, as follows;

'[Heavy Cavalry] The swords having been found from long and repeated experience to be unmanageable owing to the length of the blade and the weight of the hilt, a sword 35 inches long in the blade is to be substituted for those now in use, and the rivet which fixes the back of the hilt to the middle of the handle must go through the shank of the blade; and the back to be well riveted near the guard. The shank of the blade to be large and the top of the scabbard made to take off for the easier repairing of the same as pattern sent herewith. [Light Cavalry] The sabre is to be of the same pattern as the one last approved of by His Majesty; and the length of the blade to be from 32½ to 33 inches measured in a straight line from the hilt to the point but not to exceed the latter measure. The scabbard to be the same as that for the Heavy Cavalry.[4]

4. PRO.WO3/29/43-44.

This order is perhaps more remarkable for its imprecision than anything else. As was the custom, it was not accompanied by any drawings; manufacturers were required instead to take their own measurements and details form the sealed patterns of swords deposited with the Comptroller of Army Accounts. It is not in the least surprising therefore that existing specimens show considerable variations of detail. Even the blade length could vary by as much as half an inch in the case of the Light Cavalry sword, and the precise curvature of the blade in that case was not directly specified at all.

The Patterns promulgated in 1796 were those with which the British cavalry was to fight throughout the next 19 years of the Revolutionary and Napoleonic Wars. They are therefore of key importance, not least because of the substantial advance in standardization.

It is clear that Le Marchant's ideas were not accepted in full, since the Board recommended separate designs of sword for Heavy and Light Cavalry. It was probably no coincidence, however, that the Pattern 1796 Heavy Cavalry sword was a direct copy of the Austrian heavy cavalry sword of 1775, the *Pallasche fur Kurassiere, Dragoner und Chevaux-Legers* Model 1775, which Le Marchant had observed in the Netherlands three years earlier.[5] As such, it offended against all Le Marchant's precepts. The long, straight, broad blade with its clumsy-looking hatchet point rendered it almost useless for both thrusting and slashing, but since Le Marchant was almost certainly correct in believing that heavy cavalry achieved its effect through the sheer weight and velocity of the charge, it probably did not matter a great deal. On the credit side, the guard gives good protection and mobility and the way in which the 'ears' on the backpiece are riveted

5. Eduard Wagner, *Hieb-und Stichwaffen*, Prague (1916) pp333, 375; also, A Dolloczek, *Monographie der K. u K. Osterreichisch-Ungarischen Blanken-und Handfeuer Waffen*, Vienna (1896) *passim*.

right through the grip and tang produces an altogether stouter and more rigid construction. It is this riveting through the tang of the blade which is probably Le Marchant's most original contribution. New to British cavalry swords was the very heavy iron or steel scabbard with detachable mouthpiece and two loose rings which reflected the decision that, in future, swords should be carried by means of slings from a waist-belt instead of by a belt hook from a shoulder belt as hitherto. While it gave better protection to the sword than the old leather scabbards, the wooden linings soon disintegrated on active service and rendered the blade very blunt.

Despite criticisms, this heavy sword was capable of great execution in the hands of a skilled swordsman. Afficionados of Bernard Cornwell's Richard Sharpe novels, set in Spain in the Peninsular War, will recollect that the hero, although a rifleman, carries a 1796 Pattern Heavy Cavalry sword by choice - but then Sharpe is a very big man.[6] The first issues of this sword seem to have been to the 1st Royal Dragoons in 1796.

The Pattern 1796 Light Cavalry sword was designed exactly to Le Marchant's ideas. Its broad, curved blade made it a superb slashing sword - indeed, there were complaints from the French side about the horrific wounds which it was capable of inflicting.[7] The simple, stirrup-shaped knuckle-bow guard is fastened through the tang of the blade, as in the Heavy Cavalry sword and the scabbard, although curved, is also identical. The whole sword is some three or four ounces lighter than the Heavy Cavalry sword and much better balanced in the hand. The first issues went to the 15th Light Dragoons in 1797.

In addition to introducing new patterns of sword, the authorities at the Horse Guards moved to tackle the continuing problem of faulty manufacture to which Le Marchant had also drawn attention. In future, the depot at the Tower of London would maintain a stock of proved and tested swords of both cavalry patterns and regiments requiring new swords would, in future, have to draw them from there, the colonel's allowances being suitably reduced. The supply of swords in these cases would therefore cease to be a private regimental matter.[8]

6. Bernard Cornwell's 'Richard Sharpe' series of novels is published by William Collins Sons & Co.

7. To achieve maximum slashing effect, a blade needs to be curved to produce a slicing cut. Most Oriental swords are made to this principle and the curved swords used by European light cavalry were derived from the Turkish scimitar via the irregular Hungarian troops who came to be known as 'hussars'.

8. The Household Cavalry carried on procuring their swords privately until the end of the nineteenth century.

'Yeomanry Cavalry!!'
Coloured etching after George
Woodward, published by S W
Fores, London,
7 March 1796.
This is typical of attacks on the
Volunteers in respect of their
alleged personal stake in maintain-
ing law and order.
National Army Museum   6805-4

**'Temple Bar & St Paul's Asso-
ciation Receiving Their Colours in Front of St Paul's on
7th Decr. 1798'**
Watercolour by Henry Matthews
c1798.
Civic extravaganzas such as this,
with military forces taking a prominent and popular role for the first
time, were a celebration of loyalty
to the King and Constitution in a
time of war and social tension.
National Army Museum   6510-1

**Guidon of The Ringwood
Yeomanry Cavalry, c1802**
The single-troop 'Ringwood Light
Dragoons' were raised in 1798.
National Army Museum   7202-16

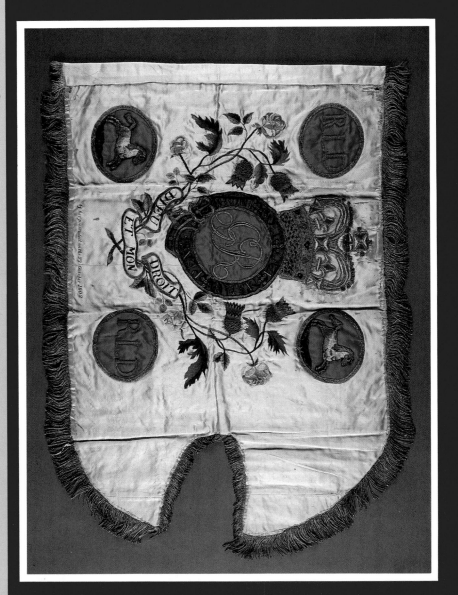

India Pattern Musket

Officially introduced as a temporary expedient, the levels of workmanship, finish and inspection were much reduced when compared with its predecessor, the Short Land Pattern Musket. A shorter 39 inch barrel and simplified and smaller furniture with lower quality lock and stock combined to create what both Ordnance and Army considered to be the minimum acceptable requirement for an infantry musket.

Close up of the India Pattern Musket showing few modifications from the original design adopted in the early 1770's. Its elaborate stock carving and elegant lock design reflect its archaic origins.

Trustees of the Royal Armouries, HM Tower of London

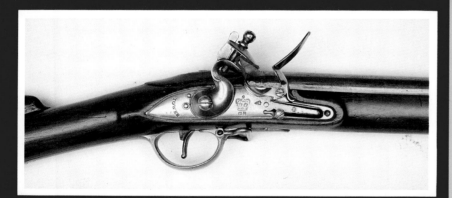

India Pattern Sergeants' Carbine Issued to Sergeants of Line Infantry Regiments

The Sergeants' Carbine adopted for the British Service in 1797 with a 37inch, .65 calibre barrel. The overall design is a reduced version of the India Pattern Infantry Musket.

National Army Museum   6710-45

New Land Pattern Musket

Introduced in 1802, during the brief period of peace, this musket was the direct generic successor to the Long Land Pattern Musket and a weapon for the Foot Guards. Note the simplified stock carving of the lock area and butt with the stronger trigger guard and lack of tailpipe. The flat lock with its raised pan, simplified steel and ring-neck cock represented a great advance in musket lock technology.
Trustees of the Royal Armouries, HM Tower of London

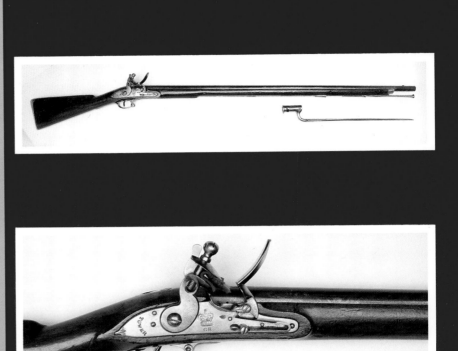

New Land Pattern Light Infantry Musket

Utilising the same lock and general characteristics of the Infantry Musket this weapon has a shorter, 39 inch barrel, improved sights and a trigger guard modified to improve the soldier's grip.
A close up of the lock and breech area showing the salient features of this arm: the backsight and a scrolled trigger guard.
National Army Museum   7407-90

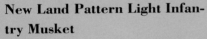

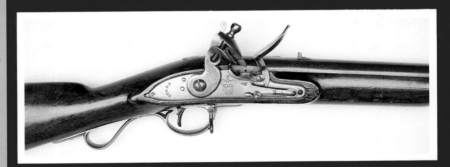

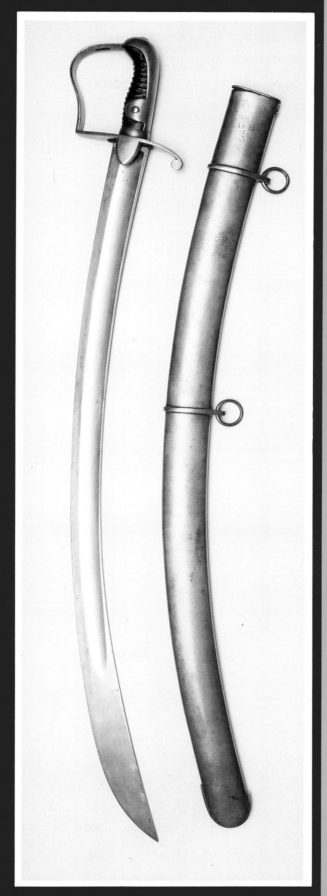

**Pattern 1796 Light Cavalry
Troopers' Sword and Scabbard**
Made by Osborn and Gunby, and
issued to G Troop, 18th Light
Dragoons (Hussars).
National Army Museum   6310-129

Pattern 1796 Light Cavalry Officers' Sword
Blade marked 'Tho Gill's Warranted Never To Fail 1798'. Trustees of the Royal Armouries, HM Tower of London

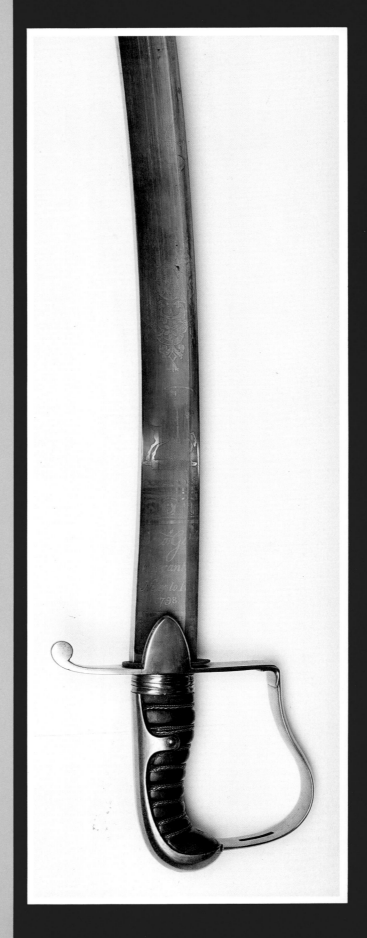

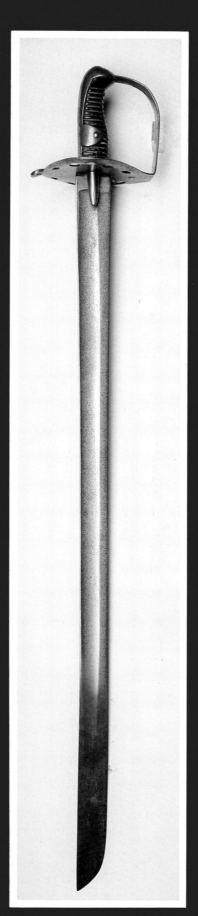

**Pattern 1796 Heavy Cavalry
Officer's Sword (Left)**
With 'Ladder' Hilt.
National Army Museum   6702-9

**Pattern 1796 Heavy Cavalry
Troopers' Sword (Right)**
Made by John Gill.
Trustees of the Royal Armouries,
HM Tower of London

**Pattern 1796 Heavy Cavalry
Trooper's Sword and Scabbard**
Note the 'spear' point, to the blade.
The close-up view shows the langets
removed and inner side of the 'disc'
cut away
National Army Museum   7510-91

The intention was that officers should carry the same pattern of sword as their men. In the case of Light Cavalry officers, this was indeed what happened, although the blade was normally highly decorated and was often worn with a black leather scabbard. Off duty, officers tended to wear a highly ornate, curved sabre of Oriental appearance, which became fashionable after the Egyptian campaign of 1798 and was known as a Mameluke-hilted sabre. For Heavy Cavalry officers, the service sword had the same blade as that of the trooper's sword although it was usually decorated; the guard was quite different, being a half-basket steel hilt of so-called 'ladder' pattern; off duty, officers carried a much lighter sword with a 'boatshell' hilt.

However good the swords in design and quality, they were useless unless the men were properly trained in their use and Le Marchant had observed the superiority of the Austrians in this respect. Staggering as it may seem to modern eyes, the British Army of 1792 had no common system of drill or training. To manoeuvre two or more regiments together was to invite confusion, since each regiment might have different words of command and different evolutions. For the infantry, Colonel David Dundas' famous drill book of 1788, largely copied from the Prussians, and entitled *Principles of Military Movements, Chiefly Applied to Infantry* was adopted as regulation in 1792. His interim *Rules and Regulations for the Cavalry* were introduced in 1795, followed in June 1796 by a full cavalry drill, *Instructions and Regulations for the Formations and Movements of the Cavalry*, with which was associated Le Marchant's famous *Rules and Regulations for the Sword Exercise of the Cavalry*, printed in December that year.

Le Marchant had, in fact, been working on this in parallel with designing his new sword. Most of the drawings were executed by his brother-in-law, Peter Carey, although Carey seems to have come unstuck in producing the mounted illustrations and had to be helped out by a professional artist. Interestingly, the various drawings show the Pattern 1788 Light Cavalry sword but on page 15 there is a drawing of the Pattern 1796 Light Cavalry sword, clearly inserted following the Board of General Officers' recommendation.

All these innovations combined to produce a much clearer distinction between the functions and purpose of the heavy and light cavalry. Hitherto, the distinction in the British Army, such as it was, had tended to come down almost wholly to one of the size of the men and horses. In practice, they had both been regarded as available for shock action against the opposing infantry or cavalry. At Beaumont, for example, in 1794, the British brigade had included both light and heavy cavalry regiments. From 1796 onwards, the roles began to be differentiated more clearly. The heavy cavalry continued to constitute the heavy armour, the eighteenth century version of today's main battle tank. Big men and big horses, they achieved their effect by sheer impetus - and, on the Continent, they were normally heavily armoured, with steel cuirasses and back-plates. By contrast, the primary role of the light cavalry was seen as that of reconnaissance and patrolling, although they were trained for shock action when the opportunity offered. Continuing the analogy, they were becoming the armoured car and light tank regiments of the period.

Thus, when Sir Arthur Wellesley landed in Portugal in 1808 to re-establish a British army on the Continent, his cavalry was better trained, better equipped and with a better thought-out doctrine than its predecessors. Its weakness, which Wellesley was able to do nothing about, lay in the training and amateurishness of its officers who, for the most part, saw war as an extension of fox-hunting, and whose ideas of tactics extended no further than pointing their men at the enemy and charging hell-for-leather.[9] (It was a weakness which was still present in the Western Desert in 1941). Otherwise, man-for-man, the British cavalry were the equals of Napoleon's Imperial troops whose proud boast was that they had stabled their horses in every capital in Europe.

In the eight remaining years of the Napoleonic Wars, the Pattern 1796 cavalry swords were fully tested. The Light Cavalry weapon proved a conspicuous success and remained basically unchanged.

9. One must except from these strictures the cavalry of the King's German Legion who took their profession seriously and were, in consequence, more highly regarded by Wellington.

Apart from the occasional removal of the shield-shaped langets, most remaining swords of the period conform very closely to the original pattern. The Prussian Army adopted the same sword, virtually unchanged, as its Light Cavalry Model 1811.

The defects of the Heavy Cavalry sword, by contrast, led to a number of unofficial modifications which were so common as to suggest that, even if not done with formal official approval, they were done without official *disapproval*. In practice, it was found that the sharp inner edge of the disc guard frayed the clothing as well as being uncomfortable on horseback, so it was frequently filed or cut away. Indeed, swords without this modification are relatively uncommon. In the process, the long, thin langets, which served no very useful purpose, were often removed also. The other major modification which is encoutered is the grinding-down of the original hatchet point to form a spear point. The reason for this was clearly implied by Captain Bragge, of the 3rd Dragoons, writing about the cavalry action at Bienvenida in April 1812; 'It is worthy of remark that scarcely one Frenchman died of his wounds although dreadfully chopped, whereas 12 English Dragoons were killed on the spot and others dangerously wounded by thrusts. If our men had used their swords so, three times the number of French would have been killed'.[10] The fact was that, even if the British troopers could have been prevailed upon to use their swords for thrusting rather than slashing, the weapons were totally unfitted for it. Against heavily armoured cuirassiers, the 1796 Pattern Heavy Cavalry sword was all but useless in its original form. By the time of Waterloo, experience had shown the value of grinding away the point to produce something with which the troopers could attempt to thrust. On the night before the battle, Trooper James Smithies of the 1st Royal Dragoons noted that '…for the first time ever known in our army, the cavalry were ordered to sharpen the backs of their swords'.[11]

John Gaspard Le Marchant died, fittingly if slightly ironically, at the Battle of Salamanca on 22 July 1812, leading the heavy cavalry charge which destroyed two French divisions. Even Wellington, with

10. S A C Cassels ed., *Peninsular Portrait 1811-1814 The letters of Captain William Bragge Third (King's Own) Dragoons*, London (1963), p49.

11. *Journal of the Society for Army Historical Research*, Vol XXXIV, (1956) p20.

his jaundiced view of his cavalry, was moved to say that he had never seen anything more beautiful in his life. There were other great days to come for the cavalry which Le Marchant had done so much to improve - at Garcia Hernandez on 23 July 1812, when the heavy cavalry of the King's German Legion trampled down three French battalions drawn up in square and, even more fittingly, at Waterloo three years later. Perhaps the most outstanding individual feat at Waterloo was that of Sergeant Ewart, of the Royal North British Dragoons, who captured the Eagle of the French 45th Regiment of the Line; '…the bearer thrust at my groin. I parried it off and cut him down through the head. A lancer came at me - I threw the lance off by my right side and cut him through the chin and upwards through the teeth. Next, a foot-soldier fired at me and then charged me with his bayonet which I also had the good luck to parry and then I cut him down through the head. This ended it'.[12] Ewart was a giant of a man, 6 feet 4 inches tall, and probably any sort of sword would have been devastating in his hands, but the sword he is said to have used is preserved, dents and all; it is a plain Heavy Cavalry sword of the 1796 pattern, with a semi-spear point.[13]

The 1796 Pattern Light Cavalry swords were replaced in the regular cavalry starting in 1824 but they lingered on in some Yeomanry regiments until the 1860s. In India, cast-off blades were eagerly sought by native troopers of the Indian regiments for re-blading their swords - a peculiarly delicate tribute to the original design.

The Heavy Cavalry sword was also replaced in the 1820s. Like its Light Cavalry counterpart it had formed part of the renaissance of the British cavalry after 1794.

12. *Ibid*, Vol XLIII (1965) p105.

13. It is in the Scottish United Services Museum, Edinburgh Castle, Accession No. L1956-9.

'I cannot say that I owe my successes to any favour or confidence from the Horse Guards; they never showed me any, from the first day that I had command until this hour. In the first place, they thought very little of anyone who had served in India. An Indian victory was not only no ground for confidence, but was actually a cause of suspicion. Then because I was in Parliament, and connected with people in office, I was a politician, and a politician can never be a soldier. Moreover, they looked upon me with a kind of jealousy, because I was a Lord's son, a sprig of nobility, who had come into the army more for ornament than for use[1].

A S Bennell

1. L J Jennings, ed., *The Croker Papers*, London (1884) Vol 1 p342.

The setting of the apprenticeship of Arthur Wellesley as a political general was the Governor-Generalship in India of Richard Wellesley, his elder brother. Richard, 2nd Earl of Mornington and later 1st Marquess Wellesley, was on his appointment to India in 1797 ambitious and untried. His younger brother Arthur, at 27 the lieutenant-colonel of the 33rd Foot and colonel in the Army, was stationed in Calcutta when Richard arrived. Travelling with Richard as his private secretary was another brother, Henry Wellesley, later Lord Cowley. It was to be an historic encounter of a political family and the diplomacy of India[2].

2. Iris Butler, *The Eldest Brother*, London (1973) pp93-4.

The India to which the Wellesleys came

Richard Wellesley remained in India from May 1798 to August 1805. During that time he transformed the diplomatic situation of the British East India Company, a civil ruler as well as a chartered commercial organisation. There was direct displacement of ineffective Indian governments. There was also a great extension of the subsidiary alliance system. By this, in return for a defensive guarantee, the Company stationed troops within the territory of a country power, paid for by that state, but available for general political purposes. Since the protected state had lost the right to an independent policy, the spread of this system served to create British paramountcy. In this

3. Edward Ingram, *Commitment to Empire: Prophecies of the Great Game in Asia 1797-1800*, Oxford (1981) pp124-5.

mingling of diplomatic and military activity, the brainchild of Richard Wellesley, Arthur Wellesley was to play an important part.[3]

In 1798 the territory of the East India Company included Bengal (the British bridgehead), and enclaves around Madras and Bombay. Closely linked to the British policy and economy were two states in a condition of clientage; Oudh (the modern Uttar Pradesh), and the Carnatic (the modern Tamilnadu). The whole of western India, the northern Deccan and the lands between the Jumna and the Godavari rivers, was dominated by the Maratha Confederacy, a loosely-grouped set of warlords nominally ruled by the *Peshwa* (hereditary Prime Minister) Baji Rao II of Poona, with Daulat Rao Sinde, Rhaguji Bhonsle of Nagpur (the Rajah of Berar) and Jaswant Rao Holkar as effectively independent. There were two Muslim rulers in southern India; the Nizam of Hyderabad and Tipu of Mysore, son of Haidar Ali.

During the year that Arthur Wellesley spent in India before the arrival of his brother, the main event had been an attempted expedition to capture Manila. This had moved as far as Penang before being recalled because the Governor of Madras feared an invasion of the Carnatic by Tipu. Arthur Wellesley had believed that he had legitimate pretensions to command this force. He had also visited Madras, and probably travelled a little way from Fort St George, perhaps in preparation for a contest with Mysore that many thought imminent. So, when Richard sought his informal advice on military and political matters, Arthur was prepared.

The Crisis of 1798-99

Richard Wellesley at once saw the situation of the Company as one of crisis. The Nizam of Hyderabad had come to rely on a French-officered sepoy force. The Maratha confederacy was wracked by a prolonged dispute between *Peshwa* Baji Rao II and Daulat Rao Sinde. Within a few days of his arrival at Calcutta, Richard Wellesley learnt of a proclamation by the French Republican Governor of Mauritius which spoke of Tipu of Mysore as only awaiting the arrival of French troops before setting himself to expel the British from India. It was a foolish proclamation. The island was almost bare of troops. It was in effect a call for volunteers; very few came forward. It had followed from an embassy sent by Tipu, and set in train a series of political initiatives, in some of which Arthur Wellesley was involved.[4]

A treaty arrangement with the Nizam of Hyderabad, at the cost of a full defensive guarantee, increased the British presence within that state. The French-officered force was disbanded; the officers were sent back to Europe, and many of the sepoys re-enlisted with the Company. An attempt to introduce Company mediation into the Maratha confederacy was a failure however, Baji Rao being in no position to respond, and not seeing the dubious alliance of Tipu with the French as a threat. Of these ventures Arthur was an interested spectator, although at one point in August 1798 Richard Wellesley evidently considered installing him as Resident at Hyderabad.[5]

The 33rd Regiment was now moved from Calcutta to Madras, its young commander caught up in preparations for a decisive contest, whether diplomatic or military, with Mysore. He explained his brother's intended policy to the Governor of Madras, the 2nd Lord Clive. The creation of a credible military presence in readiness for the campaigning season was not easy, since Madras was always a deficit Presidency in the economy of the Company. It must have required a combination of firmness and tact for Arthur Wellesley - whose Indian experience was brief and who was the junior in age to Company officers of equivalent rank - to progress his brother's wishes without antagonising the civil and military leaders in Madras. He achieved this however, and was to work in close relation with a number of them for the next six years.

In December 1798, at the urgent suggestion of Arthur Wellesley, Richard Wellesley moved south from Calcutta to Madras. The move was made necessary by the inter-relation of the campaigning season and the prospect of negotiation. An explanation of the Mauritius affair was demanded of Tipu, but the issue was evaded. Richard responded with an ultimatum, demanding that Tipu should accept a representative; the reply was delayed. Richard ordered the army to

4. M Martin ed., *Despatches...of Marquis Wellesley*, London (1836-37) Vol 1 p vii; Malartic Proclamation, 30 Jan 1798.

5. Richard to Arthur Wellesley, 17 Aug 1798; Col John Gurwood, ed, *The Dispatches of the Field Marshal The Duke of Wellington during his various Campaigns in India, Denmark, Portugal, Spain, the Low Countries and France*, London (1837-44) Vol 1 p90.

advance into Mysore. Arthur was placed in command of part of this invasion force. When a belated and frivolous reply arrived from Tipu, Arthur was one of those from whom Richard sought advice. He recommended that an agent should be despatched to Tipu, but that the army should continue its advance, in part because he was not confident of a victory over Mysore in a single season. He was concerned also about Richard's political base in London;

> '...if we should fail, you will stand higher with the public, both here and in Europe, and you will have a better prospect of securing a good peace...than if you send an army into Tipu's country and hold no previous communication with him.[6]

Sound advice; not taken. The ruthlessness of the single campaign against Tipu was that of Richard Wellesley.

The army moved on to the tableland of Mysore. After two engagements, one of them with a Bombay Presidency army moving in upon him from the western coast, Tipu withdrew into his fortress capital of Seringapatam. After a siege had been in progress for some time, Tipu attempted to negotiate. Arthur Wellesley was a member of a political commission devised by Richard to advise the Madras Commander-in-Chief, Lieutenant-General George Harris. He had in his possession discretionary orders which permitted relaxation of terms of peace, which could be used if the situation required.[7] The terms offered to Tipu by the collective advice of the commission were harsh and discussions were rejected. It was the military rather than the political education of Arthur Wellesley that was advanced in the next few days. A night attack that he attempted on an outpost failed, and he did not take part in the storming of the city on 4 May 1799. Later that day he was ordered into the city to restore control, and so was present at the famous scene in which the body of Tipu was found and indentified by former servants.

With the fall of Seringapatam, the militancy of Mysore came to an end. The Company was free, save for the obligations of alliance with the Nizam, to dispose of the territory. In a month of intense activity,

6. Arthur to Richard 16 Feb 1799; Arthur, 2nd Duke of Wellington, ed., *Supplementary Despatches and Memoranda of Field Marshal Arthur, Duke of Wellington*, London (1858-72) Vol I p193.

7. A copy of Richard Wellesley to Harris, 23 Feb 1799 (printed in Martin, *op cit*, Vol 1 p456 in the Wellesley Papers in the British Library, Add. MSS 13,668/40, has written on it '...left in Colonel Wellesley's hands to be delivered if occasion should require, and not otherwise'.

a group of military and political officers, which included Arthur Wellesley, created a settlement. They worked within guidelines prepared by Richard in Madras, brought to them by an accelerated system of runners. The Hindu dynasty was restored, a treaty of alliance established Company supervision, and a partition treaty reduced Mysore to a limited and land-locked state. Colonel Barry Close, a member of the commission, was appointed Resident, and Arthur Wellesley was given the military command in Mysore.[8]

8. A S Bennell, 'Wellesley's Settlement of Mysore, 1799', *Journal of the Royal Asiatic Society*, (1952) pp 124-32.

The years in Mysore were a period of military administration, although there were short intervals of operations against insurgents. In his first independent command, Arthur Wellesley pursued the insurgent chieftain Dhoondiah Waugh to his death in September 1800. Later that year, he was instructed to organise an invasion force to be directed in the first instance against Java, but later intended to capture Mauritius. Once this force had been assembled in Ceylon, orders came from London for it to assist in an attack on the French in Egypt, and Arthur Wellesley, acting on his own authority and with some presumption, transferred the 5,000-strong army to Bombay. Here he was superseded by a senior officer (David Baird) as was to happen to him again in Portugal. He fell ill in Bombay, and the ship on which he was to have travelled to Egypt sank with all hands. His displacement from command on this occasion led to a coolness with the Governor-General which was to last for 18 months.

1803 - Year of Victory

In October 1802 the opening in Maratha politics for which Richard Wellesley had hoped arrived. Jaswant Rao Holkar, a warrior of genius, defeated armies of Baji Rao and Daulat Rao Sinde outside Poona. Baji Rao fled to the Bombay coast, while remaining within his own territories. On the morning of the battle he had accepted in outline the terms of a subsidiary alliance treaty which, as Resident, Barry Close had been pressing on him. This provisional alliance was confirmed by Richard Wellesley, and converted by Close into the Treaty of Bassein, signed in the last moments of 1802. An advance into

Maharastra was prepared. Arthur Wellesley planned the logistics for a detachment which, he hinted strongly in private letters, he felt that he should be asked to command. He had been gazetted a Major-General in April 1802. On policy he was at his most sceptical, speaking of '...taking up a ruined cause if we interfere at all in favour of Baji Rao'.[9]

Selected to lead forward the detachment of British and Company troops intended to restore Baji Rao to his capital (if possible peacefully), Arthur's instructions were also to conciliate the lesser feudal rulers of southern Maharastra. When he had moved to within ten days' march of Poona, and been disappointed in an expected junction with Baji Rao, he realised that he needed a totally new political directive. He resumed personal contact with his brother by analysing the necessary next steps in British Maratha policy. The papers of the Calcutta Secretariat show that this action was greatly appreciated by Richard Wellesley, and that he at once considered giving Arthur full political powers.[10]

Looking beyond the occupation of Poona, Arthur sought to create a defensive position against a possible hostile confederacy of Daulat Rao Sinde and Raghuji Bhonsle. He wished to force Sinde to agree to move northwards, leaving the southern Deccan as a Company protectorate. If this demand was rejected, '...we are ready and the supposed enemy are not'. Captain John Malcolm had explained to him why the Governor-General was 'anxious to bring these questions to a decision as soon as possible'. Richard Wellesley appreciated that his political mandate from London, renewed in September 1802, was limited, and had been extended with specific reference to financial retrenchment.

In June 1803, Daulat Rao Sinde and Raghuji Bhonsle, by moving their armies to a point of junction near Burhanpur, and by refusing to negotiate, threatened an armed confrontation with the Company. They wished not only to reverse the change at Poona; they were also well placed to devastate the lands of the Nizam of Hyderabad. It seemed most doubtful that they would concur in the status which the Company contended that it had gained by the Treaty of Bassein.

9. Arthur Wellesley to Webbe 15 Dec 1802, *Supplementary Despatches*, Vol III p471.

10. BL. Add. MSS. 13,602/4, Shawe to Malcolm, 5 May 1803 (letter misdated).

Barry Close, John Malcolm and Arthur Wellesley, the informal triumvirate attempting to carry through the Maratha policy of Richard Wellesley, were frustrated by their out-of-date political directive. During the march to Poona, Malcolm had earlier hinted to Calcutta the need for delegated political authority.[11]

Arthur Wellesley was conscious that in any confrontation he was dependent on a line of communication which stretched back to Mysore. He faced acute supply and transport difficulties. He had planned to operate against the Marathas during the monsoon; prevarication was threatening these arrangements. Meanwhile, Close and Malcolm had daily experience of the ineffectiveness of Baji Rao as an ally after his restoration to his capital on 13 May. All three feared that British control of the southern Deccan was endangered. Sinde and Bhonsle were seeking to recreate the Maratha confederacy by resuming relations with Jaswant Rao Holkar. The need for a focal point of the Company's political and military authority was very clear to all of them, Arthur Wellesley finally urging directly that there should be 'powers here to act at once'.[12]

Richard Wellesley could not repeat the solution of 1798 and himself move to Madras, for while this would shorten his line of communication with Poona it would lengthen that with northern India, where General Gerard Lake, Commander-in-Chief, was preparing to move an army forward to threaten Agra and Delhi. In late June, after holding back for a month at the recommendation of his senior member of Council and the head of his Secretariat, Richard invested his brother with full delegated political and military authority, including the power to declare war or make peace. The objective was '...to destroy the military power of either or both [Maratha] chiefs'.[13] Territorial concessions were set out by which alone peace with the Company could be secured, or restored if war had been declared. The instructions were framed on the assumption that the two Maratha rulers would shrink from conflict, and be faced down. But they were equally valid if Arthur Wellesley decided, after a final attempt at negotiation, that war was inevitable. By delegating authority in this way, Richard

11. A S Bennell, 'The Anglo-Maratha Confrontation of June and July 1803' *JRAS* (1962) pp 107-31.

12. Arthur to Richard 4 Jun 1803, Gurwood, *op cit*, Vol 1 p614.

13. Richard to Arthur, 26 Jun 1803, Martin, *op cit*, Vol III p149; Gurwood, *op cit*, Vol II p49.

Wellesley must have realised that the probable outcome would be transfer of the confrontation from the *durbar* tent to the battlefield. His political reason for haste, questionable support in Whitehall, was matched by the anxiety of Arthur Wellesley to resolve a diplomatic contest of uncertain duration by the swifter arbitrament of war. His decision to declare war in the first days of August freed his army to seize Ahmednagar and that of Lake to invade the Ganges-Jumna Valley.

Arthur regarded the Deccan as the defensive rather than the offensive front against the Marathas. After a speedy capture of Ahmednagar, he successfully diverted the Maratha armies from a journey of plunder towards Hyderabad. He set himself to clear the northern territories of the Nizam. The result was the encounter-battle of Assaye, fought on 23 September 1803, in which with only half of his force, he defeated part of the French-officered infantry of Sinde. In acting aggressively that day, Arthur fulfilled the political requirement of his brother's Maratha policy by demonstrating the reality of the Company's power to its hesitant allies, the *Peshwa* and the Nizam. It was probably the case, as Barry Close suggested at the time, that Arthur Wellesley at Assaye attacked a position which Sinde had '...selected with the intention of using it for an action: it was particularly secure'.[14] A further series of forced marches averted a threat to Poona, and culminated in the Battle of Argaum on 29 November 1803.

Following the siege of Gawilghar, a hill-fort belonging to Raghuji Bhonsle, and the arrival of news of the substantial victories achieved in the north by Lake, the two Maratha rulers who had not been joined by Jaswant Rao Holkar and had remained in the south, sued for peace. With Elphinstone and (subsequently) John Malcolm to help him, Arthur Wellesley discussed peace terms in detail, first with a minister of Raghuji Bhonsle and subsequently with the chief minister of Daulat Rao Sinde. Bhonsle's central concern was the heavy penalty he faced in a transfer of land title to the Nizam, the Company's ineffectual ally whom the Marathas despised. There were also terri-

14. Close to Webbe, 6 Oct 1803, *Poona Residency Correspondence*, Vol IX Bombay (1951) pp151-3.

torial concessions in Cuttack, where a brief campaign had secured a Company land-route from Calcutta to Madras by a series of agreements with minor feudatories. In two days of discussion, by firmness and patience, a settlement with Raghuji Bhonsle was obtained. That with Daulat Rao Sinde proved more difficult, since Arthur lacked information about the lands seized by Lake, where treaties with lesser rulers had been concluded. By an all-embracing clause covering these agreements, a settlement was reached, but at the cost of leaving some essential matters unresolved and thus liable to cause disagreements later. Arthur Wellesley could however report to his brother;

'...by this treaty...all the important objects detailed in your instructions of 27th June are secured, and the ground is laid for a more complete alliance with Sinde's government. Or supposing that he should omit to take advantage of the terms offered...such an influence will be established as will render it very improbable that his means will ever again be directed against that of the Company.[15]

15. Arthur to Richard, 30 Dec 1803, Gurwood, *op cit* Vol II p616.

But the prospect of a pacified Maratha confederacy accepting British paramountcy, which seemed in January 1804 to be within Richard Wellesley's grasp, eluded him and events so moved as to bring his Governor-Generalship to an inglorious close.

1804 - Year of Failure

After he had read letters from Henry Wellesley, written in London in September 1803, which revealed the limited extent to which Henry Addington, the Prime Minister, felt able to support Richard Wellesley against the Company's Court of Directors, Arthur Wellesley felt bound to caution the Governor-General. He recommended that Richard should plan to leave India in the autumn of 1804. Otherwise there was '...great danger of your being dismissed from your office...you will receive orders to resign the government...if you do not announce your determination to go away'.[16] Richard at first seemed prepared to stay only as necessary '...to the accomplishment and security of the

16. Arthur to Richard, 31 Jan 1804, *Supplementary Despatches*, Vol IV p334.

17. Arthur to Richard, 15 Mar 1804, ibid p355; BL.Add.MSS 13,781/136 Shawe to Henry Wellesley, 8 Mar 1804.

18. University of Southampton, Wellington Papers, 3/3/93, Webbe to Arthur Wellesley 19 Jun 1804; A S Bennell, 'Factors in the Marquis Wellesley's failure against Holkar, 1804', *Bulletin of the School of Oriental and African Studies*, Vol 38 (1965) Part 3 pp553-81.
19. Arthur to Henry Wellesley, 13 May 1804, Supplemen*tary Despatches*, Vol IV p383.

great plan which had now been brought so near to a triumphant and solid conclusion'. But actions taken at the margin of the peace settlement which Arthur Wellesley had secured, in the context of 'the great plan', destroyed the prospect of conciliation which he urged on Calcutta. In March 1804 Arthur sounded another warning: Sinde had not lost all his resources, and would go to war rather than surrender the major fort of Gwalior, which Richard Wellesley was determined to obtain. 'I do not think the possession of this or any other fort is worth the risk of renewal of the war...I should prefer the continuance of the peace, both for the public and for you'.[17] Both warnings, which had within them elements of a flawed forecast of events, failed in their purpose.

Misled by Lake's assessment of the weakness of Jaswant Rao Holkar's army, and wearying of inconclusive negotiations, Richard Wellesley declared war on Holkar in April 1804, wrongly supposing that he had an ally in Daulat Rao Sinde. The setting had been created for a reverse, slight in military terms, but of considerable political significance. To this campaign Arthur Wellesley made no contribution; the army of the Deccan could not move forward in an area stricken by famine. Holkar could be attacked from the south, if at all, only from Gujerat. When Richard ordered the withdrawal of his forces to cantonments to ease the pressure on the Company budget, the Resident attached to Sinde forecast that the consequence would be that 'Holkar will acquire an increase of reputation, and all the unprovided soldiers of fortune will flock to his standard, and produce the very danger that it has been our main policy to avoid'.[18] Arthur Wellesley now responded to an earlier suggestion that he should visit Calcutta; he went in the hope that he could give useful political advice, being convinced that Richard '...has no intention of going home in January'.[19] Once arrived, he quickly appreciated the extent of the reverse.

A veiled crisis in Anglo-Maratha relations followed Holkar's demolition of the Company's victorious reputation; indeed he almost succeeded in re-creating the Maratha confederacy, united in its hostility to the British. The forebodings contained in the letters of brotherly advice of January and March were now being realised. Armed once again with the delegated authority he had held previously, Arthur Wellesley set out on the first stage of the long journey to the Deccan. Meantime, in the north, the Maratha policy of Richard was saved in military terms by the exertions of Fraser and Lake in the battles of Deig and Farruckabad (11 and 17 November 1804). But the opportunity for conciliation that John Macolm and Arthur Wellesley had wished to take had been lost, and in diplomatic terms the achievement of 1803 was in ruins.

In January 1805, after recovering at Seringapatam from '...something very like a fever and an ague', Arthur Wellesley determined that he was justified in not going to the Deccan, since it now seemed probable that Sinde and Bhonsle would not again be actively involved in hostilities with the Company; once again he was half correct in his projection. He now resolved to leave for Europe, exercising the permission he had obtained from Lake the year before, both because he believed that his military career could best be advanced there, and because he could speak as a political delegate. With this the Calcutta Secretariat agreed, for he would;

> '...do more good than all the others who have gone home, both because he has more information, and because his manners and character will enable him to mix with every class of man that it is necessary to reclaim from error.[20]

20. BL.Add.MSS. 13,747/384 Shawe to Malcolm, 23 Feb 1805.

Rumour had it that he was about to be appointed Commander-in-Chief Bombay, but by this time '...there is no situation in India which would induce me to stay'.[21] On the evening of 16 February 1805, he finally resolved to return to England. A letter from Richard, asking him to reconsider, missed his sailing by a few hours. Shortly before he left, he heard that he had been awarded a KCB. We have his written word for it, stated in the context of the grant of his first step in the peerage four years later, that he left India with a personal fortune of £42,000.[22]

21. Arthur Wellesley to Craddock, 25 Jan 1805, *Supplementary Despatches*, Vol IV p483.

22. Arthur Wellesley to William Wellesley-Pole 13 Sep 1809, Royal Historical Society *Camden Miscellany*, Vol 18, (1948) p24.

A Political Apprenticeship

Writing in Marathi almost a century later, the radical leader Bal Gangadhar Tilak reminded his readers that 'God has not conferred upon foreigners the grant to the kingdom of India inscribed on a copper plate'.[23] Richard Wellesley believed that the Almighty had made just such a provision, and had also bestowed upon his family the right to rule. Such confidence can sometimes become self-fulfilling. From the time of Richard's arrival in India, Arthur was enabled to act as if his political as well as his military judgement was of value. This had been so during the campaign against Mysore, in its preparation, execution and settlement. It would have been so also in the expedition to Mauritius, had that taken place. But, centrally, it is the theme of the contest with the Marathas. Here Richard brought military and political responsibility together, and gave it to his brother. There was a marked element of family interest in this; the exploitation of an Indian opportunity to advance the Wellesleys. Ironically, for such is the nature of military fame, Richard had set his brother's foot on the first rung of the ladder that led to the premiership, and not his own.

Arthur Wellesley was always clear that he had learnt his basic trade - that of warfare - in India. Because he had exercised joint political and military authority, he had come to appreciate the inter-relation of deployed military power and diplomatic initiative. He had analysed events from the letters of Residents at the courts of the country powers and acted on his judgement. He had negotiated with Indian agents while uncertain of extent of the territories in dispute. All this his despatches reveal to us, with the immediacy of telephone transcripts. When, as was the early nineteenth century way, a retired staff officer employed by the Duke supervised the printing of the letters from the originals, Arthur was surprised as he read the proofs at the range of topics covered. Today it is possible to set these letters against those of his contemporaries, and from that scrutiny the Arthur Wellesley of the Indian years emerges with enhanced stature. Writing of wartime Washington, Felix Frankfurter has said of political life that it was 'warfare, permeated by people with a zeal to pervert'. The Premier of 1828 had surely been trained in a hard school.

23. B R Nanda, *Gokhale, The Indian Moderates and the British Raj*, Delhi (1977) p248.

Arthur Wellesley's biographers are divided on the value of his Indian experience. Staff College Professor Edward Hamley, in his short study, *Wellington's Career* (1860), devoted very few words to the topic since he considered that it would '…occupy a space disproportionate to its relative importance'.[1] Sir John Fortescue's *Six British Soldiers* (1928), made reference to 'little military exercises',[2] despite the fact that in 1800 Colonel Wellesley's opponent, Dhoondiah Waugh, commanded as many as 40,000 men. General Lord Roberts VC, in *The Rise of Wellington* (1895), looked on Arthur Wellesley's Indian years as progressive military growth in juxtaposition to the Peninsula and Waterloo, while S G P Ward, *Wellington* (1963), has maintained that there was nothing Arthur did after the Indian experience that he had not done already, and it was merely a case of translating the lesson into a European military idiom.[3]

Arthur Wellesley's combat experience in India can be divided into roughly three segments: the 1799 operations against Tipu Sultan's fortress of Seringapatam in the final Anglo-Mysore War, the campaign against the 'freebooter' Dhoondiah Waugh in 1800, and the Anglo-Maratha War of 1803. The Dhoondiah Waugh episode was of particular significance since it was Arthur's first major independent command.

Arthur Wellesley versus The King of the World

There remains considerable confusion over Dhoondiah's actual identity. W H Fitchett in *The Great Duke* (1911), depicted him as a 'nameless man' who had served as a Maratha trooper in the army of Tipu's father Haidar Ali. Upon Haidar's death he was alleged to have established himself as a 'freebooter'. According to Fitchett, Tipu, on assuming power, converted Dhoondiah to Islam and imprisoned him.[4] That story's accuracy withstands question better than most, in the sense that Tipu was known to have forcibly converted a number of his captives, including Englishmen. All the sources seem to agree that, at the time of the storming of Seringapatam in May 1799 Dhoondiah was being held prisoner by Tipu for some unspecified reason. It was in the confusion of the fall, or in the mayhem

Randolf G S Cooper

1. Edward Bruce Hamley, *Wellington's Career: A Military and Political Survey*, Edinburgh and London (1860) p6.
2. Sir John Fortescue, *Six British Soldiers*, London (1928) p232.

3. SGP Ward, *Wellington*, London (1963) p46.

4. W H Fitchett, *The Great Duke*, London (1911) Vol I pp81-82.

during the plundering which followed, that Dhoondiah made his escape. He rallied thousands of Tipu's disbanded soldiers, as well as brigands, and assumed the title of 'King of the World' or 'King of Two Worlds'.

Sir Arthur Bryant in *The Great Duke or The Invincible General* (1971) summarized what we have inherited as the standard wisdom concerning Arthur Wellesley's campaign against Dhoondiah Waugh; 'By it he had proved - something new in Indian warfare - that it was possible for regular, disciplined troops not living on plunder to hunt down the lightest-footed and most rapid armies, instead of only being able, as in the past, to win pitched battles or storm fortifications'.[5] The Revd. Mr Gleig in his *Life of the Duke of Wellington* (1862), had spoken of Dhoondiah as being '...unencumbered by baggage'.[6] However, a review of the data available for the war against Dhoondiah leaves the reader wondering to what extent historians have too casually accepted this familiar interpretation of events. The campaign was certainly a much more serious affair than the mere destruction of a group of highly mobile freebooters. Rather, it was a dual chapter in the evolution of British counter-insurgency strategy in South Asia, and the military apprenticeship of Arthur Wellesley.

Governor General Richard Wellesley, Lord Mornington, had caused great concern by appointing his relatively inexperienced brother as Governor of the late Tipu Sultan's capital of Seringapatam on 6 May 1799. The governorship gave Arthur an unusual chance to obtain detailed knowledge of Dhoondiah and his method of operations without first having to take the field in person. Over a three-month period Dhoondiah unleashed predatory attacks north of Seringapatam and on 17 August 1799 there was a bloody encounter when the British nearly trapped him in a pincer movement at Shikapoor. After a second severe fight on 20 August 1799, Dhoondiah withdrew from the East India Company's possessions, moving on into Maratha country to seek sanctuary from the Rajah of Kolhapur. These initial operations were of little effect other than to drive him into the territory of the feuding Maratha clansmen, from whence he returned a year later to prey upon the British and their allies. It was this second round of depredations that compelled Richard Wellesley to send his brother Arthur into the field to lead an

5. Sir Arthur Bryant, *The Great Duke or Invincible General*, London (1971) p43.

6. G R Gleig, *The Life of Arthur, Duke of Wellington*, London, 'New Edition' (1886) p27.

expedition against Dhoondiah in person. The subsequent campaign proved to be a major component in Arthur Wellesley's command-apprenticeship and it has been argued that it allowed him to perfect the blueprint for his later battles against the Marathas.

SGP Ward's *Wellington* makes this linkage quite explicit; 'No British officer had so far solved the problem of bringing hordes of "skampering Maratha horsemen" to battle and the campaign was a dress rehearsal for all Wellesley's later operations'.[7]

However, viewing the Dhoondiah Waugh expedition as a prototype for subsequent warfare against the Marathas led to some dubious, not to say dangerous, assumptions. Dhoondiah's mode of warfare was neither purely mobile nor typically representative of other Maratha warlord armies. Several officers within the British command-structure deceived themselves by thinking that the Maratha response would invariably be of a light-horse or 'Pindari' type and that victory could be brought about merely by repeating the tactics used successfully against formations of light cavalry. That miscalculation was later to prove costly, as in the case of the Battle of Assaye (23 September 1803) where Maratha regular infantry inflicted 33% casualties on Arthur Wellesley's army.

In advance of taking the field in June 1800 Wellesley profited from the correspondence and other intelligence derived from the 1799 operations against Dhoondiah. Having a great pool of collected wisdom to draw upon and being a prolific letter writer, he took pains to glean the accumulated wisdom of veterans who had spent years campaigning in India. His letter of 21 June to the vastly experienced Lieutenant-Colonel James Dalrymple (officer commanding the subsidiary force attached to the army of the Nizam of Hyderabad) acknowledged, with some humility, that he was setting out on a type of operation or 'species' of war, differing from regular or conventional models. Using hindsight we would now classify it as 'counter-insurgency'.[8]

Dhoondiah Waugh understood very well that he could raid the territories of the East India Company and their ally the Nizam with a certain amount of impunity by slipping back across the river into land which belonged to the Marathas, who for their part remained divided in their

7. Ward, *op cit*, p26.

8. Wellesley to Lt-Col James Dalrymple (written from the camp at Hurryhur) 21 Jun 1800; Arthur, 2nd Duke of Wellington, ed., *Supplementary Despatches and Memoranda of Field Marshal Arthur, Duke of Wellington*, London (1858-72) Vol II p28.

feelings towards the British. The British, on the other hand, did not want to give the appearance of arbitrarily annexing territory, a message they risked conveying if they violated Maratha borders in 'hot pursuit' of Dhoondiah. The chieftain's use of Maratha country for sanctuary gave some Company officials the mistaken impression that he was operating with the approval of the *Peshwa* (the Maratha Prime Minister).

The fact that renewed military activity had the potential to start a second Anglo-Maratha war invested any action taken against Dhoondiah with additional significance. The British were not prepared for a full-scale Maratha War at this time. There was the financial and physical cost of the overthrow of Tipu in 1799 to consider, and plans were being made for possible expeditions to Java and Egypt. Arthur needed an unequivocal mandate to carry out cross-border operations to bring Dhoondiah to heel. In many respects, this was a timeless instance of the doubtful legality of cross-border operations in counter-insurgency warfare. (Historically analogous confrontations have occurred in the twentieth-century arenas of Vietnam-Cambodia, Rhodesia-Mozambique, and Nicaragua-Honduras). On 25 May Jossiah Webbe, Secretary to the Government at Fort St George, Madras, informed Arthur that he had permission to pursue Dhoondiah.[9] This order was sufficiently sophisticated to take into consideration the possible alienation of the Marathas and stressed the need to evacuate British forces from the area promptly once the campaign was at an end. At the same time he received permission to offer a reward for the capture of Dhoondiah.[10] This was a major breakthrough, since it put the chieftain's actions '...in no other light than that of a robber and murderer'. As implemented in mid-July 1800, the plan embodied a legal mechanism justifying Dhoondiah's public execution. This proviso hinged on the assumption that Dhoondiah's guilt was pre-determined by his criminal activity rather than by any acts of war. As such, the order amounted to a threat of summary execution without the necessity for a trial.

Although Colonel Wellesley's endorsement of summary execution has been down-played by his numerous biographers, it is clear that he realized the need for decisive measures in counter-insurgency warfare,

9. Webbe to Wellesley, 25 May 1800, *ibid*, pp1-2.

10. *Loc cit*.

whether physical or psychological. On discovering that a party of the enemy was holding a fort at Budnaghur he told the officer commanding at Soonda to '...make arrangements immediately for driving them out...Every man found in the fort must be put to death'.[11] The offer of a reward for Dhoondiah's capture was considered by Wellesley to be an effective means of driving a wedge between 'The King of two Worlds' and his followers. He speculated that, at the very least, it would give Dhoondiah cause to think twice about the loyalty of his subordinates.[12] Yet there were also strict limits to what Arthur considered appropriate or justifiable action. According to Fitchett, he turned down an offer by one of Dhoondiah's ex-associates to assassinate his former master. Wellesley was alleged to have said; 'To offer a reward in public proclamation for a man's head, and to make a private bargain to kill him are two different things'.[13]

Counter-insurgency operations often entail a blurring of civil and military jurisdictions in the interests of the restoration of order. In the East India Company framework, the development of a military infra-structure parallel to the civil government could take place without any extraordinary changes in legislation or the chain of command. In this instance, a declaration of martial law, legitimising either a military trial or summary execution, was facilitated by the fact that the Company's jurisdiction combined the components of civil and military administra-tion under one authority.[14]

The Nature of the War

Dhoondiah had found it an easy matter to build an army of up to 40,000 men by gathering demobilized soldiers and brigands from the land. A considerable number of the insurgents had formerly belonged to the armies of Mysore, and even the East India Company itself. Some sources state that he had absorbed Tipu's Mysore cavalry, but this would seem to be an exaggeration, since several of those units had been incorporated directly into the Company's forces or had joined the various Maratha clans.

It has been tempting for authors, (Richard Aldington for example, in

11. Wellesley to the Officer Command-ing at Soonda, 11 Jun 1800, *ibid*, pp10-22.

12. *Ibid*, pp57-58.

13. Fitchett, *op cit*, p84.

14. Wellesley to Lt-Col George Mignan, 21 Jun 1800, *Supplementary Despatches*, Vol II p27.

15. Richard Aldington, *Wellington: Being an Account of the Life and Achievements of Arthur Wellesley, 1st Duke of Wellington*, London (1946) p72.

his *Wellington*, 1946), to classify Dhoondiah's men as guerrillas[15] but that term poses problems of its own. The modern application of the word 'guerrilla' is derived from the voluminous writings of Mao Tse Tung, who has become in effect this century's leading authority on guerrilla warfare. The guerrilla scenario, as described by Mao, is one of constant evolution. In his argument guerrilla warfare leads to irregular warfare, which is destined to become conventional mobile warfare and, ultimately, conventional warfare of position. In this context, 'guerrilla warfare' is characterized by a dearth of sophisticated weapons-systems such as artillery. Moreover, the term 'freebooter', used interchangeably with the indigenous term *Pindari*, has become synonymous with lightly-armed bands of horsemen who ravaged the land in search of plunder. Yet, in order to characterise Dhoondiah's forces as 'freebooters', we would also have to gloss over the fact that his army contained several units of irregular infantry and a substantial artillery component. The mere possession of artillery in a region where monsoon rains could quadruple the size of rivers and turn the black cotton soil to a viscous mass negates the claim that Dhoondiah's army was notably fleet of foot. There is also the matter of Dhoondiah's utilization of fixed fortifications to consider. His soldiers had been capable of taking the fort at Dummel and he had established a stronghold in the mountain fortress of Chittledroog. Such a willingness to indulge in positional warfare (in the context of fixed fortifications) further lessens the appropriateness of statements that this was purely a guerrilla war. Since Dhoondiah's force was equipped with artillery, fought from fixed positions on a number of occasions, and was partly made up of former soldiers of the Kingdom of Mysore, it would seem that 'irregular' would be a more appropriate term for it than 'guerrilla'.

Arthur's despatches confirm that Dhoondiah continued to make use of infantry for garrison duties, while his field-army included numerous artillery pieces. The regaining of the fort at Dummel by escalade on 26 July 1800 resulted in the capture of a 1,000-strong garrison. Elements of Dhoondiah's field artillery proved to be a great liability, and contributed to a second reverse less than a week later at Manauli on the Malpurba River, not far from Dummul. Dhoondiah's men, under the command of

Babur Jung, attempted to extricate their guns when the British attacked their camp. In addition to the 5,000 casualties inflicted on the enemy, a quantity of elephants, camels, bullocks and cannon fell into British hands. Accounts of the action indicate that many of the enemy drowned in the river across which they had been struggling to move their ordnance.

By this time Dhoondiah's days were numbered and his resources were dwindling. Desperately, he divided his forces and attempted to flee. In response Arthur Wellesley split his troops into three columns. It was a four-regiment, all-cavalry force,[16] headed by Arthur in person, which charged the enemy at Konagull on 10 September 1800, routing Dhoondiah's 5,000-strong column and slaying the insurgent chief. One of the most significant factors enabling Arthur to catch up with his prey was the fact that Dhoondiah's progress was impeded by a considerable baggage train.

16. Sir John Fortescue, *Wellington*, London, 3rd Edition (1960) p33.

In seeking to unravel the real significance of Arthur Wellesley's military experience in India, the historian encounters numerous problems associated with a larger-than-life character, operating in an environment which, to the Western mind, has always been exotic. In later years, Wellington confirmed that his Indian combat experience had provided a wealth of understanding analogous to his European endeavours. In contrast, however, it can be argued with equal force that his Indian years were a period of highly specialized military activity. Wellington's genius was expressed in his growing ability to read the mind of his enemy and assess his strengths and weaknesses in the context of a battlefield environment. His plans were formulated to deal with a specific threat at a specific time. Rather than search for 'military maxims' which, supposedly, run as common threads through his life, we should, perhaps, in future consider the Duke's apprenticeship as providing him with the opportunity to experiment with differing solutions to a diverse range of military problems.

KENNETH FERGUSON

Although the outbreak of previous French wars had brought apprehensions of invasion and rebellion in Ireland, the circumstances of 1793 seemed at the time reassuringly different. It was believed, in both cases wrongly, that France had been weakened by its internal dissensions, and Ireland appeased by timely concessions to the conquered Catholic population. That there was '...very little probability of any external attack upon Ireland' was the view of the British Government communicated by the Home Secretary, Henry Dundas, to the Lord Lieutenant of Ireland in a despatch of February 1794. Consistent with this complacent judgement, the island was required to yield up its pre-war garrison for service overseas. All 24 of the battalions serving in Ireland in 1793 had gone overseas by the middle of 1795, together with half of the regiments of cavalry (some of which had not been abroad since 1715). Recruitment and the despatch of regiments overseas dominated military business in 1793 and 1794. Kilmainham - that is to say, the Irish command, with its seat at that splendid memorial of the reign of Charles II, the Royal Hospital, Kilmainham - presided in these years over the creation of 30 new regiments, including illustrious corps such as the 88th Foot, the Connaught Rangers. There was intensive recruiting, attended with the same circumstances of alcoholic regalement, desertion, mutiny at the prospect of going to the West Indies, and (on the part of the officers) peculation, as characterised recruitment in the sister kingdom. The scale of the effort of these years is revealed by a memorandum prepared by Thomas Pelham, Chief Secretary, for the Duke of York in November 1796 which showed that over 50,000 soldiers and some 15,000 recruits for the Royal Navy and Marines had by then embarked from Ireland, as against some 30,000 soldiers who had been landed there.[1]

The wholesome preoccupation with recruitment in support of the larger war effort, which characterises the early years of the conflict, soon yielded to less happy activities at home. There were clouds on the horizon already in 1795, but the year of the watershed was 1796. That

1. British Library, Add.MSS.33,113/6, 'Return of the number of men furnished by Ireland for general service, including the army and navy, from the commencement of the war in 1793 to 1 November 1796', Thomas Pelham to Frederick, Duke of York, Commander-in-Chief, 14 Nov 1796, ; see also, D A Chart, 'The Irish levies during the Great French War', *English Historical Review*, Vol XXXII (1917) pp497-516.

autumn the Irish Parliament suspended the Habeas Corpus Act (the effect of which in modern parlance was to introduce internment), and passed the Insurrection Act, a measure which provided for the registration and safe storage of arms, and authorised searches for concealed weapons. It allowed those found in unlawful assembly or hawking seditious papers to be summarily despatched to the Army or Navy; and it introduced the idea of proclaimed districts, where a curfew could be imposed. This formidable statute provided the legal context in which the Army embarked on the pre-emptive disarming of Ulster in the spring of 1797. Other notable events in an eventful last quarter of 1796 were: the announcement on 19 September that the Government would proceed to raise a force of Yeomanry; the appointment on 10 October of a new Commander-in-Chief, Henry Lawes Luttrell, 2nd Earl of Carhampton; and, not least, the arrival at Bantry Bay on 22 December of the storm-battered French fleet bearing General Lazare Hoche and the 9,000-man remnant of a significantly larger force that had set out from Brest. Had not a 'protestant wind' `interfered with the plans of General Hoche, 1796 would have been the resonant year that 1798 afterwards became.

To understand the changes which had occurred in the political circumstances of Ireland between 1793 and 1796, it is helpful to turn to the correspondence of Edmund Burke, whose epistolary observations on Irish affairs are no less sage than his reflections on events in France. In a letter of 1792 which from the hindsight of 1798 seems prescient, Burke had written;

'Suppose the people of Ireland divided into three parts; of these (I speak without compass) two are Catholic. Of the remaining third one-half is composed of dissenters. There is no natural union between those descriptions. It may be produced. If the two parts Catholic be driven into a close confederacy with half the third part of Protestants, with a view to a change in the constitution in Church or State, or both, and you rest the whole of their security on a handful of gentlemen, clergy, and their dependants; compute the strength *you have in Ireland* to oppose to grounded discontent, to capricious innovation, to blind popular fury, and to ambitious turbulent intrigue.[2]

Burke recognised all the factors that made for the disaster of 1798: the inherent weakness of an Irish polity where power reposed with an élite of landed Protestants, who, outside Dublin, their Augustan capital, lived in vulnerable isolation; the smouldering grievances of the Catholic majority; the political ambitions of the Protestant Dissenters; and the danger of a union between these and the Catholics. He saw that Jacobinism had cast 'deep roots' amongst the Dissenters; he feared that the Catholics who were intermingled with them would be tainted; and that 'the strong republican Protestant faction', which had persecuted the Catholics 'as long as persecution would answer their purpose', might now, through conspiracy, 'dupe them to becoming accomplices in effectuating the same purposes'. Burke's insistent advice to his correspondents was to effect a reconciliation with the Catholics so as to preclude the latter from thinking '…that they have no hope to enter into the constitution but through the dissenters'. Burke's views on conciliating the Catholics found support in England, and English ministerial prompting had been responsible for the important Relief Act of 1793, whereby Catholics regained the franchise and entry to professions, such as the Army, from which they had long been excluded. The same ministerial policy had triumphed in the matter of the new Militia established in 1793. This force, constituted by statute on the English model, was recruited by ballot on the basis of parochial lists of the eligible manhood. Its composition accordingly reflected the local religious balance; and this meant that Catholics predominated in the ranks of the regiments of all the counties outside Ulster. This was a remarkable development considering that the bearing of arms had until so recently been an exculsively Protestant privilege. Colonel Maurice Keatinge, author of *Remarks on the defence of Ireland* (1795) aptly observed by way of analogy that the planters in the West Indies had been 'obliged to adopt the desperate resource of arming their negro slaves'. Considering the tensions of

2. This passage, and the numerous other references in this essay to Burke's views, will be found in his *Irish Affairs*, edited by Matthew Arnold, with a new introduction by Conor Cruise O'Brien, London (1988). The passage cited here is on page 267. The later references are at pp437, 425, 266, 418, 436, 423, 243 and 337.

1798 the Irish Militia was a force eminently exposed to the threat of subversion; yet, although it yielded to its critics many instances to fortify their distrust of it, this force, with an establishment after 1795 of 21,660 men, became the bulwark of the garrison.

The Failure of Conciliation

Burke, who died in 1797, did not live to see the outbreak of the Rebellion; but he witnessed 'the system of military government' which preceded it; and he had no hesitation in placing the blame for the 'truly unpleasant situation of Ireland' jointly on 'that unwise body, the United Irishmen' and on the incapacity of the Irish Government. The society of United Irishmen was a radical political movement founded in Belfast in 1791 amongst the Dissenters. It spread to Dublin where it attracted those who became its most conspicuous leaders, Theobald Wolfe Tone and Lord Edward Fitzgerald, both nominally Protestants, exact contemporaries, and both men with military flair. Tone, who as a boy had 'mitched' from school in order to watch the parades and reviews of the Dublin garrison, had once seen himself as the instrument of annexing the Sandwich Islands (Hawaii) to the British Crown. Tone's proposal for an expedition of conquest was ignored by Pitt and his destiny was to become instead a French soldier, the friend and adviser of Hoche on his expedition to Bantry Bay in December 1796. Lord Edward Fitzgerald, a younger son of Ireland's premier nobleman, the Duke of Leinster, was a former holder of the King's commission. This renegade officer, who had risen to be major of the 54th Foot, planned an urban insurrection in Dublin in which his followers would unpave the streets, form barricades and 'dreadfully gall' the soldiers from the house-tops. 'An officer of any skill', he reckoned, 'would be very cautious of bringing the best disciplined troops into a large city in a state of insurrection...the apparent strength of the army should not intimidate, as closing on it makes its powder and ball useless - all its superiority is in fighting at a distance'.[3] It was the leadership in revolution provided by men of the calibre of Tone and Lord Edward Fitzgerald which made the conspiracy so very formidable.

3. 'Copy of a paper found in Lord Edward Fitzgerald's writing box', *Journal of the Irish House of Lords*, Vol VIII p163.

Although the authors of the Revolution were Protestants, whether Dissenters of pious hue or men whose protest was more against religion itself, the odium of the Rebellion subsequently fell on the Catholics, who, though willing and fearsome collaborators, were not its prime instigators. The Irish Catholics, who in Burke's early memory had been looked upon as 'enemies to God and man...a race of bigoted savages who were a disgrace to human nature itself', emerged from the 1798 rebellion with this damning character revived and reinforced, as the Cruikshank caricatures which illustrate Maxwell's *History of the Rebellion*, published as late as 1845, amply demonstrate.

It is a moot point whether the Irish Catholics, whom Burke so fervently wished to rehabilitate, could have been conciliated. The Dublin Castle officials, whose views were shared by a considerable body of Protestant opinion in Ireland, thought they could not. It suffices to say that, if there was a slim chance that conciliation might have worked in the early 1790s, it soon disappeared. The judgement of Sir Arthur Wellesley, who served in Ireland as Chief Secretary before he went to the Peninsula, was that '...no political measure would alter the temper of the people of this country', who would rise in rebellion if the enemy arrived in sufficient force. By 1796 the lower classes of the Catholics were already committed to such a rebellion, and a pre-existing Catholic conspiratorial movement, the Defenders, had been absorbed into the United Irishmen, whose leaders had by then obtained the promise of French assistance.

It was in this context that Dublin Castle called on the Army to disarm the conspirators. Thus began what Burke called 'the system of military government' or 'Luttrellade'. This last expression was a reference to General Henry Lawes Luttrell, 2nd Earl of Carhampton, who, having employed rough methods in Connaught in 1795, became Irish Commander-in-Chief in the autumn of 1796. Luttrell - to Burke a man 'universally odious' - was a bluff cavalry officer who had already earned his footnote in history as the opponent of John Wilkes in the famous Middlesex election of 1769. According to Sir Ralph Abercromby, Luttrell's successor as Commander-in-Chief, he was wont to precede the judges with his troops, opening the gaols as he went and sending the prisoners on board a tender and thence to the Navy. These measures he adopted with conviction. As he put it in a pamphlet published in 1798, '...if it shall please [Lord Camden, the Lord Lieutenant] to permit them to go to war with us, and to permit us only to go to law with them, it will not require the second sight of a Scotchman to foretell the issue of the contest'. There was a logic in Lord Carhampton's point, and deteriorating circumstances made coercion inevitable; but, as Edmund Burke had discerned, there was no future in military government;

> '...where the hearts of the better sort of people do not go with the hands of the soldiery, you may call your constitution what you will, in effect it will consist of three parts (orders, if you please) - cavalry, infantry, and artillery, - and of nothing else or better.

The Disarming of Ulster

In the winter of 1796 the strength of the Army in Ireland stood at some 35,000 men. These Carhampton had disposed in five military districts. The most important district was the northern, where Major-General Gerard Lake, a 52-year-old widower who had joined the 1st Regiment of Foot Guards at the age of 14, commanded 11,000 men. Elsewhere, Dalrymple had 7,400 men in a southern district; Smith had 6,500 in the west; Crosbie had 7,000 men in the east; and Ralph Dundas had 3,500 in the centre. These troops were predominantly made up of Irish Militia (of whom there were 18,152 effectives in January 1797), and of British Fencible infantry (9,141 effectives). A handful of line battalions sent to Ireland to recruit mustered between them only 1,906 effectives. The cavalry force, the only substantial element of the Regular Army that was left, mustered 3,684 regulars and 664 Fencibles. It was these forces which would have had to contend with the French, had Hoche succeeded in landing at Bantry; and it was they who were now to' be the instruments of military government, first in Ulster and then in the other provinces.[4]

4. The figures for troop numbers come from the National Archives, Dublin Castle, File 620/50/56.

The task in hand was to search for concealed arms. The extent of the conspiracy is shown by the enormous quantities of weapons collected. The total seized during 1797 and 1798 in all parts of the country amounted to 48,000 guns and 70,000 pikes. At first sight an archaic weapon, the pike became the characteristic military implement of the insurgents, and much to be feared. A hard-won lesson of the early days of the Rebellion in Leinster in May 1798 was that cavalry charged pikemen at their peril. The 9th Dragoons were to lose 24 men in three charges against pikemen assembled behind the walls of Old Kilcullen churchyard on the morning of 24 May; and the 7th Dragoon Guards lost 20 men by making a similar mistake at Rathangan five days later.

The difficulty of finding weapons by conventional searching was destined to bring the Army into disrepute. The campaign to seize arms began in earnest in Ulster on 13 March 1797, when Lake issued a proclamation. After the experience of a few days he concluded that his notices were 'of very little use'. It was Lake's colleague, Brigadier-General Knox, an Ulsterman, commanding at Dungannon, who came to the stark realisation that 'the country can never be settled until it is disarmed and that is only to be done by terror'. Beatings and house-burning, and the cultivation by means of rough manners of a general awe for the soldiers, showed better results than Lake's notices had done. It was a policy, however, which hurt the tender consciences of many officers, and which was destructive of discipline and prone to lead to excesses. The worst of these reported during Lake's tenure of the command in Ulster was an incident near Newry at the beginning of June 1797. The Ancient Britons, a regiment of Welsh Fencible cavalry, and members of the Yeomanry appear to have murdered some 20 people. The Ancient Britons had the worst reputation of any corps in Ireland at the time. A Government supporter went as far as to describe them as 'human devils'.

If the disarming of the Scottish Highlands after the '45 and certain incidents in the American War of Independence are put aside, the period of Lake's command in Ulster marks the initiation of the British army into the techniques of counter-insurgency. The system began with a curfew, outposts on the approach roads, and a requirement for written passports. Men who were suspect 'from character or the circumstances of the moment' were detained. Then came the realisation that indulging the troops' natural inclination to treat the population roughly bore results. Sir John Moore, describing his orders in Munster in 1798, put the matter thus: the policy was 'to excite terror' by treating the people 'with as much harshness as possible, as far as words and manners went', whilst practising sufficient supervision 'to prevent any great abuses by the troops'. In the spring of 1798 the device of 'free quarters' was adopted, a calculated perversion of the royal prerogative of quartering. The troops were allowed to 'supply themselves with whatever provisions were necessary to enable them to live well', the reasoning being that those afflicted with the billeted troops would influence public opinion so as to compel a propitiatory surrender of arms.

In later times, nationalist writers came to accuse the Government of having made the Rebellion 'explode'. The popular image of 1798 is of pitch-capping and half-hanging conducted by soldiers. How frequent these refined cruelties may have been is difficult to judge; but there is sparse contemporary mention of them, save in *The Press*, the organ of the revolutionaries. This journal took the view that the Army brought with it 'fire and sword, slaughter and devastation, rape, massacre and plunder'; and in the six months before it ceased publication in April 1798 it printed 30 alleged instances of military misconduct, of which the most serious was a charge that the Wicklow Regiment of Militia, whilst stationed in county Westmeath, had killed 72 persons. Not all that *The Press* alleged inspires credence; but it remains the case that there are numerous complaints about the conduct of the soldiers in sources which were friendly to them. The Marquess Cornwallis, Lord Lieutenant and Irish Commander-in-Chief, writing privately at the end of 1798, referred to the 'coercive measures which so totally failed last year', and to the 'flogging and free-quarter' which were no opiates.[5]

5. Cornwallis to his son, Viscount Brome, 27 Dec 1798; Charles Ross ed., *Correspondence of Charles, First Marquis Cornwallis*, London (1859) Vol III p24.

Seducing Soldiers from their Allegiance

The strangely-inverted nomenclature of the 16th/5th Lancers bears witness to a mishap which befell the 5th Dragoons at Loughlinstown Camp in 1798 and to the wider attempt by the revolutionaries to seduce the soldiers from their allegiance. In the case of the 5th Dragoons, seven private soldiers had been tried and shot for plotting, at the very height of the Rebellion, on the night of 10-11 July 1798, to deliver over to the rebels the hutted camp at Loughlinstown south of Dublin, which had been established three years earlier to guard the capital from attack from the south. The regiment had other sins to its discredit, and George III, accepting the view that it was 'radically bad and depraved', directed in 1799 that it be disbanded. For the next 60 years a gap in the numbering of the regiments of cavalry testified to the fight for the allegiance of soldiers generally in 1798.

This had been a formidable struggle extending over several years. As early as June 1794 handbills had been thrown into the barracks at Belfast. In the following year there were sundry prosecutions for treason of persons accused of administering the Defenders' oath to soldiers. In August 1795 at Dublin, and in September at Cork, disaffected persons exploited mutinous situations which arose when regiments learned that they were to be drafted overseas. The National Army Museum Collections include a handbill from the Cork mutiny that would appear to be the work of the United Irishmen.[6]

6. National Army Museum, 6807-370-42.

The authorities became alarmed about the spread of disaffection in the ranks, and in the spring of 1797 took decisive action. Some dozens of soldiers were tried and shot, notably at Blaris, the hutted camp near Lisburn which was Lake's headquarters. These executions seem to have had a salutary effect, and the regiments in Ulster appear thereafter to have been immune from subversion. Elsewhere, however, the threat remained. A paper found in the possession of Lord Edward Fitzgerald at the time of his arrest shortly before the Rebellion established the existence of cells in several regiments. Captain J W Armstrong of the King's County Militia, who was approached to join the United Irishmen because he regularly browsed and chatted politics in a Grafton Street bookshop, had the strange experience of being enrolled into the United Irishmen's cell in his own regiment, where he encountered 13 or 14 soldiers including three sergeants. He duly relayed all he heard to the Government.

During the Rebellion the great majority of soldiers held firm, but the fruit of the conspirators' work was seen in desertions by individuals and by groups. The most notorious group desertion was after the Battle of Castlebar (28 August 1798), when 146 of the Longford Militia and 42 of the Kilkenny Militia were returned as missing, the 'greater part' believed to have deserted to the enemy. Some individuals were guilty of amazing duplicity. A Yeomanry officer, John Esmonde, lieutenant in the Clane corps, led the insurgent attack on Prosperous (Co. Kildare) on 24 May, and afterwards returned to his Yeomanry unit as if nothing had happened. For this crime he was duly hanged.

The Rebellion

The Rebellion for which the United Irishmen had so long prepared broke out in the Leinster counties on 23 May 1798, inauguarated by a concerted attack on the mail-coaches leaving Dublin for the provinces. The number of troops on the eve of the event had reached 42,390 full-time soldiers and almost as many Yeomanry. Since the Bantry Bay emergency 18 months earlier there had been a net increase of 9,000, half coming from an augmentation of the Militia and half from new arrivals. These numbers were already great, and the exchequer was becoming overburdened with debt to meet the cost. In the spring of 1798, in an extraordinary display of loyalty, nearly 30 regiments were prepared to offer a week's pay to a fund established for the 'exigencies of the state'. With the outbreak of the Rebellion, and later with the French landing in Connaught, the Army was still further enlarged, reaching (according to an Army Medical Board return dated 1 October 1798) a peak of no fewer than 70,000 men.[7]

7. BL. Add.MSS. 35,919/88 Army Medical Board Return, 1 Oct 1798.

Half of this reinforcement arrived in June and the remainder in September. In the light of the over-stretched state of the British Army and its global commitments it is instructive to examine how these troops were gathered. The first arrivals were in the North, responding to the short-lived rising in Antrim and Down. Major-General Campbell and a brigade of Fencible cavalry began to disembark at Carrickfergus on 13 June. Four units - the Lancashire, Dumfries, Berwick and Durham Regiments - were involved and they numbered about 1,000 men. On 18 June some 1,500 infantry reached Belfast: these were the Scotch Royals and the Sutherland Fencibles, the latter a battalion 1,100 strong. On the same day the 100th Foot (to be renumbered in the future the 92nd Foot), reached Dublin. This regiment of over 800 men had come from Portsmouth on board naval vessels. The Royal Navy played an important part in transport arrangements worked out during the first week of June. Admiral Sir Charles Thompson, commanding six ships of the line, took on board at Portsmouth on Sunday 10 June three battalions of Guards together with General Hunter's brigade (the 2nd and 29th Regiments) and landed them at Passage and Ballyhack, near Waterford, the following Saturday. The Guards went into garrison at Waterford, whilst Hunter's men went on to join Major-General Johnson at Ross on 19 June, two days before the Battle of Vinegar Hill. On 17 June the Nottingham and Glengarry Fencible Battalions reached Passage after a voyage from Guernsey; and on the following evening the Cheshire Fencibles arrived from England. These shipments brought between four and five thousand men direct to the theatre of war in County Wexford. A week later, in the last of this series of troop movements, two very strong battalions of English Militia embarked at Liverpool for Dublin. These, the Buckinghamshire and Warwickshire Regiments, respectively 1,400 and 1,300 strong, were the largest battalions to serve in Ireland at this time.

The reinforcements sent in response to the French landing in Connaught on 22 August were composed entirely of English Militia. The Royal Navy transported four regiments, and the Commissioners of Transports procured shipping at Liverpool for another seven. The arrival of these English Militiamen brought the total number of troops in the country to its peak level of 70,000. This high number does not include the Irish Yeomanry, who were perhaps half as numerous as the regulars, and who, with their local knowledge and local interests to protect, were also diligent soldiers. 'God and the Yeomanry saved the capital', maintained Lord Carhampton.

With such large numbers of troops in pay, the odds might appear to have been stacked against the rebels. The generals, of whom at one time there were 43, were nevertheless decidedly apprehensive. The numbers free to take the field were but a fraction of the paper strength. General Francis Needham fought the critical Battle of Arklow (9 June 1798) which marked the northern limit of the Wexford rebels' advance, with a motley force of only 1,137, drawn from nine battalions. Lake, in planning the assault on Vinegar Hill on 21 June, disposed of a field army of about 10,000, but this force had taken several weeks to assemble, and the rebels had prevailed in Wexford for a month. In the autumn the enterprising young French general, Joseph Humbert, was roaming in Connaught for 18 days before Cornwallis took his surrender at Ballinamuck on 8 September. The French force was barely 1,000 strong; yet at Castlebar it had put to an ignominious flight a force of 1,600 soldiers. Cornwallis, east of the Shannon with 8,000 men, and Lake, west of the river with 2,000, proceeded with the greatest caution. Strength and caution remained the cornerstones of military policy in Ireland thereafter.

The rebellion was costly in human life. Thomas Newenham, writing in 1805, calculated that there had been 30,000 deaths during the Rebellion, of which 1,600 were military deaths. His figure included losses among the Yeomanry. Official figures available in the Dublin Public Record Office before its lamentable destruction in 1922 show the deaths of 1,060 soldiers in the five-month period from May to September. These figures do not include the Yeomanry.

The figure for all deaths of 30,000 is an index to the ferocity of the fighting. Sir Ralph Abercromby, Commander-in-Chief in Ireland for the brief period from December 1797 to April 1798, had come to grief by reason of his famous General Order of 26 February 1798 declaring the Army to be in a 'state of licentiousness which must render it

8. Cornwallis to the Duke of Portland, Home Secretary, 28 Jun 1798; Ross, *op cit* Vol II pp 356-57.

formidable to every one but the enemy'. Lord Cornwallis, discreet in his public utterances, well knew that '...any man in a brown coat...found within several miles of the field of action' was liable to be 'butchered without discrimination', and that such ferocity 'was not confined to the private soldiers'.[8]

The Rebellion was for all parties a tragedy. The Catholics and Dissenters, whom Wolfe Tone had briefly succeeded in uniting in rebellion, knew defeat. The Dissenters were in a few short years solidly ranged on the other side of the Irish religious and political struggle, their disastrous past suppressed. The Protestants of the Ascendancy kept their estates, but they lost their own peculiar nationhood. The Rebellion taught them the limits of their own strength. So completely did it dispel the old colonial self-confidence that in 1800 refuge was sought in an Act of Union with Great Britain, a measure that was the very antithesis of the legislative independence that Grattan had won for Anglo-Ireland in 1782. The 'Irish nation', reverted to being a term primarily descriptive of the Catholics. An era that had begun for Ireland a century before with resounding military triumph in the war of William III, inaugurating a lustrous century for the victors, ended in an orgy of savagery which ushered in a prolonged period of political stalemate and smouldering violence.

On the morrow of his first great Peninsular victory at Vimeiro (21 August 1808), Sir Arthur Wellesley praised his army in glowing terms in a letter to the Duke of York;

> 'Their gallantry and their discipline were equally conspicuous…this is the only action I have ever been in, in which everything passed as it was directed, and no mistake was made by any of the officers charged with its conduct.[1]

The truth was that, whatever his later disparagement of his troops, Wellington was from the very outset of the Peninsular War commanding the steadiest and perhaps the best-trained infantry in Europe.

Forging the Instrument

But where had they sprung from? Eight years earlier it is inconceivable that a British commander could have written in such terms about his army. In 1800 Lord Cornwallis was not alone in describing the British Army as 'the laughing stock of Europe'. For a generation the Army had known little but adversity, and in 1800 its misfortunes touched bottom. Driven out of Holland in the autumn of 1799, it went on to the fiascos of the attempted landings at Belle Ile, Ferrol and Cadiz. These reverses could be blamed on adverse circumstances or faulty planning; nevertheless the Army's discipline and training were dubious, its tactical doctrine still uncertain and incomplete. From a naval hero, Lord St Vincent, came the most damning indictment - '…the whole infantry of the country is…totally unfit for a service of hardy enterprise'.[2]

Yet only a year later the picture was changed totally by the victory in Egypt. During a single fortnight in March, 1801, Sir Ralph Abercromby made good an assault landing, dislodged the French from an intermediate position in the offensive Battle of Mandara, and smashed their counter-offensive in the battle of Alexandria. 'We appear', Lord Buckingham commented, 'to have broken that magical invincibility…of the great nation'.[3] The great student of war Baron

PIERS MACKESY

1. Col John Gurwood, ed., *Selections from the Dispatches and General Orders of Field Marshal the Duke of Wellington*, London (1851) p213.

2. Sir Julian S Corbett, Sir Herbert Richmond, eds., *The Private Papers of George, 2nd Earl Spencer, 1794-1801*, London (1913-24) Vol III p346.

3. Historical Manuscripts Commission, *Report on the Manuscripts of J B Fortescue, Esq, Preserved at Dropmore*, London (1905-08) Vol VII p19.

Jomini saw the Eyptian operations as a turning point for the British Army - *l'époque de sa regénération*.

Underlying those battles of regeneration lay months of preparation, which had begun in June, 1800, with the arrival in Minorca of Sir Ralph Abercromby as Commander-in-Chief in the Mediterranean; a soldier whom Sir Henry Bunbury was to recall as 'respected and beloved by all who served under his command'.[4] Sir Ralph had learned to know adversity, in the campaigns of the 1790s in Flanders, the West Indies and Holland; and always he had commanded ill-prepared scratch forces with no opportunity to train them. At Minorca he once again inherited a force of mixed quality, with a long history of disappointment and defeat. Sixteen of his eventual 26 battalions were the usual ragbag: four foreign, and three newly recruited from the Militia, while most of the remainder had the typical profile of the infantry of the day, with a record of fluctuating strengths, heavy wastage, indifferent recruits and spasmodic training.

But Abercromby had two advantages at Minorca which he had not enjoyed in his previous commands. He had several months to train his force; and its nucleus consisted of ten seasoned battalions from the Mediterranean garrisons, better in John Moore's judgement than any he had seen in the recent Dutch campaign. Sir Ralph grasped his opportunity. He was determined to forge an instrument fit to face the veterans of Bonaparte's old *Armée d'Italie* in Egypt. In adverse circumstances, with much of the next eight months spent floating round the Mediterranean in leaky transports, he created perhaps the most coherent British striking force to take the field in eight years of war. Every opportunity was seized to put the troops ashore for training and exercise; and officers remarked on his 'close and detailed inspection' of the regiments and the emulation which he fostered.[5]

'Emulation' suggests a hint of the new-style discipline associated later with Moore's training of the Light Brigade at Shorncliffe. Abercromby's views on discipline were balanced and humane. He insisted, for example, on punctilious saluting; but he believed that obedience should be instilled with 'prudence and sense'. This was

4. Sir Henry Bunbury, *Narratives of Some Passages in the Great War with France (1799-1810)*, London (1927) p29.

5. Scottish Record Office, GD45/4/16, Journal of Lord Dalhousie, 3 Dec 1800; E Stuart Wortley, *A Prime Minister and his Son*, London (1925) p337.

especially true of the volunteers from the Militia, the best of material but unused to strict discipline: '...to this they must be led by degrees, they must not be treated with too much harshness and severity. It is well worth while to bestow some time on such men...'. He emphasised the officers' duty of 'care and attention', a doctrine not always honoured in the Army of the day.[6] The results of his training began to be seen even in the abortive Cadiz expedition of September, 1800. When the flat-boats were being loaded Lord Dalhousie saw cheerfulness in every face, the troops in excellent spirits and physical condition and with confidence in their commanders.

The Regeneration of Tactics

Pioneer though he was in discipline, how competent was Abercromby to train his army in tactics? And what did he teach his regiments?

The infantry tactics on which Wellington was to rely in the Peninsula combined two elements: one the legacy of Frederick the Great, eighteenth century battle-drill executed to a high standard; the other, the use of light infantry on a large scale, not merely for outpost duty but to overcome French skirmishing tactics in battle. This synthesis of elements had had no place in British tactical thinking at the beginning of the wars in 1793. On the contrary, the two concepts were polarised.

Since the end of the Seven Years War a distinction had been remarked in the British Army between a 'German' and an 'American' school of officers: the one typified by rigid close-order infantry drill designed for open plains and a strong cavalry threat; the other characterised by a looser order, faster marching and more emphasis on light infantry, practices developed to meet the needs of small forces in close country against an enemy skilled in aimed fire but without cavalry. The line as practised in America was very different from German usage, two instead of three-deep and the files more open. British officers returning from the American War in 1783 were tenacious advocates of the loose, shallow line and emphasis on light infantry and skirmishing.

6. SRO, Hope of Luffness MSS., Sir Ralph Abercromby to Col Alexander Hope 20 Nov 1799; Brodie of Brodie MSS., Journal of Col George Brodie, Vol I p35, 16 Aug 1800.

But these lessons were of dubious relevance to the warfare of Europe; and the British Army of 1793 was no longer capable of the manoeuvres which Frederick's Prussians had brought to perfection. During the ten years of peace British tactical doctrine had fallen into chaos. The habit of manoeuvring in loose order was exacerbated by the absence of a uniform drill manual; nor were training areas available in peacetime where battalions could exercise together in brigades. The result of this disorder was seen in the opening campaigns of the French Revolutionary Wars, when the British infantry's performance was mixed, to say the least, and made worse by hasty recruiting and expansion. 'We were ashamed of our service', General Sir Herbert Taylor baldly recollected.[7]

The foundations of recovery, however, had already been laid, with the publication in 1792 of a new official drill manual by Colonel David Dundas, based on his *Principles of Military Movements* of 1788. Dundas emphatically belonged to the 'German' school. His book was an explicit rejection of American experience; his aim, '…to put an end to the prevalence…of loose desultory movements,…of want of solidity etc'. Dundas' work brought British battle-drill back to Frederickian practice. The battalion was formed in three ranks, one pace apart, with the files closed up elbow to elbow; and the drill step was only 75 paces to the minute. It was a system designed to deliver shock and withstand cavalry. Dundas's answer to cavalry was 'superior order, regularity and weight of fire': a truth which was to be proved in Egypt.[8]

The flaw in Dundas's doctrine was his neglect of light infantry work, to which he allotted only a few sketchy pages. The timing of this downgrading was unfortunate; for in the early years of the Revolution, skirmishing came to dominate the fighting in Belgium, for reasons not all of which Dundas could have foreseen. To meet this new form of warfare the British Army was unprepared. Its battalion light companies were not properly trained to subdue enemy skirmishers; nor had it any specialist light infantry regiments to match the dozen battalions of *chasseurs à pied* which the French had raised before the

7. Quoted by C M. Clode, *The Military Forces of the Crown*, London (1869) Vol II p355.

8. Col David Dundas, *Principles of Military Movements, Chiefly Applied to Infantry*, London (1788) p11.

War. As late as 1799, a Highland officer reported from the dunes of Holland that the British infantry were 'perfectly unacquainted with the system of sharpshooting'.[9]

9. C Greenhill Gardyne, *The Life of a Regiment: The History of the Gordon Highlanders from its Formation in 1794 to 1816*, Edinburgh (1901) Vol I p67.

Generals of the 'American' school, like Cornwallis and John Simcoe, rightly deplored the lack of light infantry; but they sometimes spoke as if what was needed was the total overthrow of the 'German' system. In fact the need was to strike a better balance; and the outcome of British tactical developments was not the overthrow of the 'German' system by the 'American', but a synthesis of the two. When the Duke of York became Commander-in-Chief in 1795 and acquired the power to enforce the new *Regulations*, he did begin to redress the balance towards light infantry training, for he had seen the new French armies in action.

Thus, when Abercromby went to the Mediterranean in 1800, some progress had been made towards establishing a common tactical groundwork. What was needed was a commander who could train a prototype force in the new *Regulations* and test it in battle. And this Abercromby was singularly fitted to do.

One must admit that Abercromby was not one of the great battle-field commanders. He did not control his battles with flair and boldness, and by stationing himself too far forward in the fighting he tended to lose sight of the general picture. Yet as a trainer of troops he was in the forefront. As a friend told him, 'You have experience of the modern manner of warfare, which the grandees of our army lack'.[10]

10. Lord James Dunfermline, *Lieuten-ant-General Sir Ralph Abercromby, KB, 1793-1801: a Memoir by his Son*, Edinburgh (1861) p138.

He belonged neither to the 'German' nor to the 'American' school. As a General Officer all his experience had been in the most recent campaigns against the French Revolution, in the hedgerows and plains of Flanders and in the forests and hills of the West Indies. He had learned the value of light infantry, and at Minorca in 1800 his training programme placed considerable emphasis on light infantry work. At that time he was expecting to fight in European hedges and vineyards or tropical forests rather than the sandy plains of Aboukir. He showed particular interest in the light infantry battalion drill of the

90th Regiment, which had been trained under the inspiration of the 'American' General Sir Charles Stuart by the future General Kenneth Mackenzie. Even on the voyage to Egypt, Abercromby was putting his regiments' ordinary battalion companies through light infantry exercises.

But Egypt would not be prime skirmishing country; and the enemy would have a strong and excellent cavalry force while Abercromby had virtually none. In these conditions, efficient close-order drill was essential; and the basis of that would be Dundas' 1792 *Regulations*. Abercromby had always been an admirer of Dundas' work, and years earlier he had twice written urging him to publish his *Principles*. At the same time he was aware that Dundas's 18 basic manoeuvres were too complex for the battlefield; and on field days in Minorca the 1792 *Regulations* were simplified to a few straightforward evolutions. The cavalry threat was also prepared against: brigades were rehearsed in forming a variety of squares, and trials were conducted with a new way of marching in square to maintain mobility in the presence of enemy cavalry. In the event the well-drilled line proved to be capable of seeing off cavalry without resorting to squares; and in Egypt Abercromby used flanking columns to protect the exposed ends of his line, recalling the *ordre mixte* of French doctrine.

The final element in his training programme was the assault landing. He was determined to allow no repetition of the muddles he had witnessed on the Dutch beaches and at Cadiz. A series of brigade landing exercises were held on the coast of Asia Minor, with competition stimulated by recording the time taken to complete the forming-up on the beach. New joint-staff arrangements were made with the Navy to ensure that boat movements were co-ordinated with precision. When Abercromby sailed for the assault he was confident in his army, 14,000 strong, and looked forward to testing it with the task of destroying Bonaparte's oriental dreams: '...defeating the most splendid project of modern times'.

The Test of Battle

The assault landing in Aboukir Bay on 8 March 1801 was an astonishing military feat and a triumphant vindication of Abercromby's programme of training and rehearsal. Boats with 5,000 infantry moved in line through a storm of cannon shot and musketry, delivering nine battalions to their correct stations on the beach where they instantly formed, loaded and beat off French attacks. The effect on the army's confidence was electrifying; and in the next fortnight the British commanders praised their troops' performance in unison. Moore, Coote, Oakes, Anstruther and Abercromby himself emphasised not merely the courage of the troops, but a coolness which was the product of discipline and training. The troops had formed on the beach 'as if on parade', an image that constantly recurs in the coming days and marks the role of the parade-ground in preparing troops for the battle-drill of the flintlock era.[11]

11. Dundas of Beechwood MSS, care of National Register of Archives, Scotland, Col Robert Anstruther, DQMG, to Lt-Gen Sir David Dundas, 17 Mar 1801.

Abercromby's next task was to advance west and capture Alexandria, a dozen miles away along the narrow peninsula, a mile to a mile-and-a-half wide, which separated Lake Aboukir (or Maadieh) from the sea. On 13 March he dislodged a French covering force from an intermediate position in the Battle of Mandara, and in the early morning of 21 March his army smashed a French counter-offensive and decided the victorious outcome of the campaign. The Battle of Mandara might be singled out as the pivotal moment when the regenerated British Army came of age. The precision of its manoeuvres was matched by its steadiness under fire and under attack; and for the first time its light infantry acted as an integral element in a general action.

The advance to contact on 12 and 13 March was made in two parallel columns, which deployed into line when they encountered the main body of the enemy. On the first of these days Major Hudson Lowe of the Corsican Rangers witnessed 25 battalions deploying '...in a more perfect manner than I have seen it at any review'.[12] The advance continued in two lines through a broken terrain of scrub and ruins, with the companies constantly forced to break the line and file

12. British Library, Add. MSS. 20,107/50, Major Hudson Lowe, Corsican Rangers, to his father.

round obstructions; yet when the army halted at the end of the day scarcely any correction of the line was necessary.

Next day, the advance in two columns was resumed, in order to manoeuvre and turn the French right. The French, however, took the offensive, leading with their cavalry, which first struck the 90th Foot as it emerged from a palm grove. The battalion deployed at the double, and beat off the attack with a rolling volley which ran down the line from the right 'like a rattling peal of thunder'.[13] The French dragoons veered to their right, where the 8th and 18th Regiments were deploying. Their second charge was repulsed like their first. 'No impression', a witness recorded, 'was to be made upon infantry which coolly waited for the words of command, ready, present, fire, and this the 18th Regiment did; much greater proof of steadiness, coolness and discipline could not be given'.[14] In this manner the British infantry met their first charge by the reconstituted cavalry of France. The French infantry attacks which followed were duly smashed by the British line, and the enemy fell back to Alexandria.

The defeat of the French dragoons confirmed David Dundas' contention that the answer to cavalry was 'superior order, regularity and weight of fire'. And indeed the day was an affirmation of the soundness of his *Regulations*, as tested by trained and disciplined troops. Moore's brigade had remained in open column to protect the right flank; and though under heavy cannon fire it preserved its correct intervals throughout the day. There was not a moment when Moore was not confident that he could halt and wheel his companies to a flank to form a continuous line. Colonel Edward Paget remarked that the column's precision would have gladdened General Dundas' heart at a Phoenix Park review.

Light infantry also played an integral part in the battle. In the initial advance the heads of the columns were shielded against French sharpshooters by skirmishers, furnished by regimental light companies, the Corsican Rangers and the 90th with its specialist training. In the Battle of Mandara, Moore's column was protected in the French fashion by the Corsican Rangers in skirmishing order to ward off enemy *voltigeurs* and hussars.

13. Quoted by S H F. Johnston, *The History of the Cameronians (Scottish Rifles)*, Vol I, *1689-1910*, Aldershot (1957) p186.

14. Bodleian Library, North MSS, c18/3, Account of the Battle of Mandara by an unidentified eyewitness.

On 21 March Abercromby fought his last battle, in which he was mortally wounded. The Battle of Alexandria was a confused action in poor light, controlled on the British side for the most part at brigade and battalion level. In small combats the infantry displayed its high confidence; turning a rear rank about to repel cavalry, refusing to panic (as Paget said the Austrians would have done), when battalion flanks were turned, and getting to their feet to fight individually when caught and ridden over in the open by cavalry. Such heavy losses were inflicted on the enemy that their troops never again showed willingness to fight seriously in Egypt.

The moral effect of the fortnight's operations was immense. 'This is the Army of Italy!', Moore exclaimed triumphantly of the enemy. The army now knew that with sound regulations and thorough training it could combine bravery with 'system'. 'Our people', wrote Colonel Robert Anstruther, 'now feel as they used to do, and have the utmost contempt for the French, and especially for their cavalry'.[15]

15. HMC *Fortescue*, Vol VI p476; Dundas of Beechwood MSS, *loc cit*.

Training had been shown to be relevant: the drills performed at reviews and field-days could be performed in battle. And the soundness of David Dundas' training manual had been demonstrated, as officers wrote from the battlefield to tell him. 'You have formed the British army', Anstruther wrote: 'Regiments of all kinds, collected from all places, have met in one body…following one system, one military language…All this we owe to you'.[16] Not quite all: for it was Abercromby who forged the instrument and tested the system. He had always been Dundas' supporter; and he too sent his acknowledgment: 'The principles you have laid down have begun to operate'.[17]

16. Dundas of Beechwood MSS, *loc cit*.

17. Dundas of Beechwood MSS, Abercromby to David Dundas, 18 Mar 1801.

Moore went home from Egypt and formed the nucleus of the future Light Division, remembering the skills of the Corsican Rangers and the 90th at Mandara, the latter living proof that specialist light infantry could perform all roles. It was the officer who had trained them, Mackenzie, whom Moore chose to command the 52nd when he re-formed that regiment as light infantry at Shorncliffe.

Just as significant as these lessons in the new warfare was the reaffirmation of an old system. The French Revolution may have changed the political and social atmosphere of war, and shaken Europe's confidence in old military practices. Yet the flintlock and bayonet were virtually the same weapons for which Frederick and his drillmaster von Saldern had perfected their tactical system half a century earlier: the combination of columns of manoeuvre and fighting line which Abercromby used at Mandara. From the Prussian example Dundas had derived his *Regulations*; and when Colonel Paget extolled the 'system and regularity' of Moore's brigade at Mandara he had no doubt about what he meant. He could not know that he had seen the future warfare of the Peninsula, in which he was to play a distinguished part; and he looked backwards for a comparison. The brigade, he wrote, had manoeuvred 'with all the system and regularity of a Berlin review'.[18]

18. Eden Paget ed. *Letters and*

A Good Man at Falmouth: Captain Philip Melvill, Defender of Pendennis Castle, 1796-1811

Alan J Guy

On Monday 4 November 1811, the port of Falmouth was the scene of a patriotic, civic and military extravaganza typical of a period when glamorous public ritual was used increasingly to bind up social wounds inflicted by war and economic hardship. This time the occasion was a solemn one - the funeral of a much-loved inhabitant, Captain Philip Melvill, Lieutenant-Governor of Pendennis Castle, one of the two fortresses guarding the town's 'capacious and commodious' harbour.

At 10am, the coffin was carried from the Castle House by men of the Royal Artillery and placed upon a trestle on the Grand Parade. Nearby, in front of the storehouse, the Royal Monmouthshire and Brecon Militia were drawn up two-deep, the men resting on reversed arms. At the firing of the first minute gun, the battalion broke into open column of sections and filed past on either side of the coffin to the strains of the Dead March from *Saul*. When the last division had passed by, the coffin was placed upon the funeral car, drawn by four horses, and the cortège moved out through the main gate, receiving the honours of the guard, escorted by the scarlet-coated cavalry of the Loyal Meneage Yeomanry (their swords drawn), two brass 3 pounder guns of the Pendennis Artillery Volunteers and followed by a train of mourners which included the chief civic, religious, naval and military dignitaries of the region. The route to the parish church was thronged with citizens, in particular the poor and the children of the charity schools which the Captain had helped to found and maintain.[1]

Melvill's ceremonial departure from human sight, like so much else of his service in Falmouth, casts light not simply on measures taken to defend a neglected fortification and a vulnerable harbour against the threat of invasion but, much more importantly, on the ideologies that sustained local leaders of opinion during the long struggle against the Godless power of Revolutionary and Napoleonic France.

1. Susan E Gay, *Old Falmouth*, London (1903) p30; *Royal Cornwall Gazette* (abstracted by Mr Rex Hall), 2 Nov 1811. The three troops of the Loyal Meneage Yeomanry (129 all ranks) were formed from the amalgamation, *c*1804, of the Helston Yeomanry Cavalry and two troops from Trelowarren and Penryn; Charles Thomas, 'Cornish Volunteers in the Early Nineteenth Century, 1803-08' Part One, *Devon and Cornwall Notes and Queries*, Vol XXVII (1959-61) pp48-49.

From Pollilur to Pendennis

It is fair to say that Philip Melvill would hardly have chosen to end his military career in a run-down Cornish garrison, but his term of genuinely 'active' service had been brief and unfortunate. Born on 7 April 1762, he was the fourth and youngest son of John Melvill, Collector of the Customs at Dunbar. When Philip reached the age of 16, his father obtained for him a commission in Lord Macleod's 73rd Foot, conditional on his raising a quota of recruits, which he did by journeying on foot to a remote part of the Highlands. There was no immediate military tradition in the family and, as he later admitted, '...his choice of this profession...originated in those feelings, and propensities, which comprise the substance of our corrupt nature, and seek their particular gratification in the outward shew of respect, the ambition to command, the noisy pomp and desultory habits of a military life'.[2]

In March 1779, the regiment sailed from Spithead for India. The transports were ravaged by jail fever as far as the Cape of Good Hope and Melvill, who by this time had been promoted lieutenant of the light company, caught it with such violence that for a time his life was despaired of.

The Highlanders disembarked at Madras in January 1780. Their arrival greatly heartened the East India Company's officials there, who by diplomatic ineptitude had already involved themselves in war with the Marathas and were about to add to their list of enemies the formidable Haidar Ali of Mysore. That summer, Haidar took the field with an army of 90,000 men, 15,000 of whom were thoroughly trained in the European fashion, and raided up to the suburbs of Madras itself. An inept attempt to concentrate the King's and Company's troops at Conjeeveram, an exposed position 35 miles south-west of Madras, resulted in the destruction at Pollilur, on the morning of 10 September, of a 3,000-strong detachment, commanded by Lieutenant-Colonel William Baillie, just nine miles short of the rendezvous. In the opinion of Sir John Fortescue this disaster came close to accomplishing the ruin of British power in India.[3]

2. Sources for Melvill's life are; *Memoirs of the late Philip Melvill Esq. Lieutenant-Governor of Pendennis Castle, Cornwall; with an Appendix, containing Extracts from his Diaries and Letters: selected by a Friend, together with Two Letters and a Sermon occasioned by his Death*, London (1812); Revd John Wilcox, *The True Christian Exemplified: being the Substance of a Sermon occasioned by the Death of Philip Melvill, Esq., Deputy Governor of Pendennis Castle, Cornwall*, London (1811); G C Boase, *Collectanea Cornubiensia: A Collection of Biographical and Topographical Notes relating to the County of Cornwall*, Truro (1890); British Library, Add. MSS. 58,438, Letters to his Wife, (1804-05); Cornwall Record Office, AD 132, Letter-Book of Capt Melvill, 1803-05, microfilm copy in the National Army Museum, London.

3. For the origins and conduct of the war with Haidar Ali, see Sir Penderel Moon, *The British Conquest and Dominion of India*, London (1989) pp187-210 and Sir John Fortescue, *History of the British Army*, Vol III, London (1911) pp428-99.

The 73rd's light company, commanded by Captain David Baird,[4] formed part of a thousand-strong detachment of picked troops which had joined Baillie's column the previous day. In the terrible onslaught which followed, the bone of Melvill's left arm was shattered by a musket ball. Moments later, as he turned to utter a word of command, a second ball passed through the same arm and pierced his left breast. As Haidar's innumerable cavalry broke into the European ranks, the muscles of his right arm were severed by a cut from a *tulwar* and he was knocked off his feet. The victors stripped him of his uniform, dragged him across the ground, his head striking on every stone, and nearly finished him off with a lance-thrust in the back.

For two nights he lay upon a bank of scorching sand, his pillow the corpse of a fellow officer, with nothing to eat but a few herbs and grasses and nothing to drink but his own urine. He tried to stab himself, but his maimed arms lacked the strength to strike home. On the morning of the third day, he was bundled into Haidar's camp by bounty hunters claiming a bounty of ten rupees for every European brought in alive. From there he was taken to the fortress of Bangalore, where, confined in a wretched shed, denied proper medical care and loaded with manacles, Melvill and his companions became objects of curiosity and amusement for visitors of rank, and were treated with 'contempt, abhorrence and tyranny' by their guards.[5]

Melvill's captivity lasted for nearly four years, when he was repatriated following the Treaty of Mangalore. He was promoted captain, but his painful wounds and generally precarious health disqualified him from further active service. He wore his left arm supported by a scarf for the remainder of his life, and his right arm was damaged to the extent that although he could still move his fingers, he could neither raise his right hand nor, if it was raised by some external force, keep it in position.

Early in 1786 he embarked for home, arriving months later at Falmouth;

'On entering the harbour he was struck with the elevated site, and noble aspect of Pendennis Castle, which made such an

4. Lt-Gen Sir David Baird, as he later became, '...honoured [Melvill] with his friendship and esteem, and with a generous ardour endeavoured on every occasion to promote his interests'. He subscribed for five copies of old comrade's biography, and Lady Baird for another five.

5. For the action at Pollilur (also known as the Battle of Conjeeveram) and the fate of the captives, see the *Memoirs* pp35-59; Capt Innes Munro (73rd Foot), *A Narrative of Military Operations on the Coromandel Coast against the combined Forces of the French, Dutch and Hyder Ally Cawn from the year 1780 to the Peace of 1784, in a Series of Letters*, London (1789), especially an account almost certainly derived from Melvill on pp162-64; *Memoirs of the Late War in Asia, with a Narrative of the Imprisonment and Sufferings of our Officers, by an Officer of Colonel Baillie's Detachment*, London (1788); Alexander William Crawford, Lord Lindsay, *Lives of the Lindsays, or a Memoir of the Houses of Crawford and Balcarres*, Wigan (1840) Vol 4, *passim*.

impression on his mind that he often spoke of it as a desirable residence, bearing some resemblance in its situation to Dunbar, and where if free to choose, he would prefer to settle. This the Lord, in the course of his good providence, brought to pass...

He was appointed almost at once to the captaincy of a company of Invalids (the usual posting, as Rifleman Harris was to remark, for men who were 'more or less shattered') in Guernsey. Here he remained until 1793, when the outbreak of the war with Revolutionary France resulted in Castle Cornet being considered far too exposed a post to be entrusted to a near-cripple. During this period, he reflected at length upon the providential circumstances of his preservation at sea, on the battlefield, and in prison, coming at last '...to a simple and absolute reliance on the strength and righteousness of his great surety and foederal head, Christ Jesus'. 'When I lay a miserable wounded outcast on the field of battle', he wrote, 'thy hand, O gracious Saviour, was still upon me for good. But what am I, a sinful worm, that such care, such watchful care, should have been taken of my life?'

The fruits of his conversion, characteristic of a phase in Church history when piety went hand in hand with outgoing moral earnestness, were seen in a heightened concern for the domestic circumstances of the veterans under his command and their families, for whom he established a charity school, as well as a Sunday school at his own house. In the wider Christian community of the island, he took part in establishing a series of evening theological lectures.

The Key of Cornwall

For a time it seemed that Melvill's Army career had come to an end, for soon after his transfer to an Invalid company at Portsmouth in June 1793 he fell dangerously ill and petitioned to be allowed to retire on full pay. He removed himself and his growing family[6] to the healthier (and more economical) climate of Topsham in Devon;

'But happy as his present state was, he could not acquiesce in a retirement which precluded him from sharing, according to his

6. Melvill had married Elizabeth Cary, daughter of Peter Dobrée of Beauregard, Guernsey in 1787. Three of his nine children pre-deceased him. One of the latter, Lt John Fall Melvill, Royal Artillery, was drowned during the occupation of Madeira in 1807. One of his grandsons, Lt Teignmouth Melvill of the 24th Foot, was killed at Isandlwana in 1879, defending to the last the Colours, which were found wrapped around his body.

ability, in those active and patriotic measures of internal defence, which the safety of the country required, and in which so many thousands of his compatriots were engaged.

Accordingly, on 1 November 1796, he took over command of the Invalid company at Pendennis Castle from the absentee Captain Roger Pomeroy Gilbert.

At that time, the regular duty of the fortress '…seemed to require no exertion to which the health of a valetudinarian might not be equal'. Soon however, and not for the first time in the eighteenth century, Falmouth was to assume the character of a frontier town. Its harbour, trumpeted the author of *A Falmouth Guide* was, '…justly considered by the first naval characters as the best in the kingdom' and although not every mariner would have agreed so positively, there was a deep-water anchorage for up to 500 sail and vessels of the greatest burthen could easily tie up at the quay.[7] There had been invasion scares in 1744, 1759 and, most dramatically, in 1779 when a Franco-Spanish armada rode unopposed in the Channel and the inhabitants made haste to pack up their valuables.[8] Falmouth's situation (immediately opposite to Brest), and the western orientation of the latest French invasion projects (Hoche at Bantry Bay in December 1796, the *Legion Noire*'s filibuster at Fishguard in February 1797 and Humbert's campaign in insurgent Ireland during August-September 1798), generated fresh anxieties.

The two principal fortifications defending the Fal both dated from the 1540s. The smaller work, St Mawes Castle, still retained its elegant Henrician trefoil lay-out - it had but one 24 pounder fit for service in the summer of 1796. Pendennis, girdled by its Elizabethan bastioned front, mounted 55 pieces of ordnance; two 24 pounders, fourteen 18 pounders, twenty-five 9 pounders and nine 6 pounders, with a generous supply of roundshot, grape and cartridge and 10,052 pounds of gunpowder stored in casks. It was considered that more heavy guns were needed.[9]

During the Civil War, a 900-strong Royalist garrison had maintained a very creditable defence against the New Model Army; in-

7. *A Falmouth Guide, containing a Concise Account of the History, Trade, Port and Public Establishments of Falmouth*, Falmouth (1815) pp17-21.

8. Gay, *op cit*, pp91-92; A Temple Patterson, *The Other Armada: The Franco-Spanish Attempt to Invade Britain in 1779*, Manchester (1960) *passim*.

9. Public Record Office, WO30/66/151/53, Report of a Survey of the Coast of Cornwall, Aug-Sep 1796, (Pendennis and St Mawes).

10. Report, Sep 1796, enclosed in PRO.WO30/74/14, Defence of the Western District, 1803-04, Lt-Gen John Graves Simcoe to the Quarter-master-General, 14 Oct 1803.

11. PRO.WO30/66/153, Survey Report, Aug-Sep 1796; PRO. WO17/797, Return, Pendennis Castle, 1 Nov 1796.

12. Major Poole had been Lieutenant-Governor since October 1776; Melvill's commission was dated 29 June 1797. His salary as Lieutenant Governor was £84 per annum (the absentee Governor, Gen Felix Buckley, was paid £284:3s:6d). In addition, Melvill received a pension of £50 per annum from the East India Company, and during 1803-05 an additional £80 per annum as Commissary of Stores in return for allowing some of his own quarters to be used as a store. He also received captain's pay of £182.10s per annum, fees from the men's canteen, dues from passing vessels and interest from £500 stock in the three per-cent consols.

13. PRO.WO30/66/153, Survey Report, Aug-Sep 1796.

formed opinion held that 2,000 was the optimum number needed to hold the place, although 900 might still be sufficient 'to resist and defeat an insulting enemy'.[10] When Captain Melvill took over his command, it consisted of Ensign Smith, 'not able to Join on Account of Old Age' (there was no lieutenant in post) four sergeants, two drummers and 36 private men, some of advanced age and all unacquainted with the service of the great guns. Also in the fort were a Master Gunner, five Invalid Artillerymen and 80 officers and men of the Wiltshire Militia,[11] whose commander insisted that during the absence of the Lieutenant-Governor, Major Nevinson Poole, he was the garrison's senior officer. (This dispute simmered on even after Melvill bought Poole out in June 1797).[12]

Further investigation revealed that there was a serious shortage of entrenching tools in the Castle, likewise of provisions for a siege - the soldiers purchased fresh produce in the local market. The cisterns were in urgent need of repair, a number of moribund defensive works required levelling, and 4,000 yards of enclosures needed to be stripped away to open up fields of fire and deny cover to an attacker. As things stood, '...if the enemy was once to force a passage by [Pendennis and St Mawes] any number of Guns, Men or Stores might be landed in any part of these Harbours with great ease, as there are no other fortifications hereabouts and the landing places are numerous and extensive'.[13]

In July 1801, Lieutenant-General John Graves Simcoe, GOC Western District, observed that;

'Pendennis has in all Ages but the present been held in the highest Estimation - it secures the Harbour of Falmouth, the Key of Cornwall, and which in the possession of an Enemy, might lead to the most disastrous consequences.

As a Military Arsenal it ought to be considered that it affords (or rather should afford) a safe deposit for Artillery and Stores of all kinds, ready for an Army to take the Field and attack an Enemy in the Rear. Or by holding out a Siege to narrow their operations and waste their resources. At the same time from hence such a Depot might be distributed by Water to any parts that might be requisite.[14]

Two years later, Simcoe again insisted that Pendennis was;

'...a place of the first importance and is most shamefully neglected. It cannot hold out twelve hours and this arises from the old works that *crossed* the Peninsula being half destroyed, so that at night the Enemy may now surround the whole of the Fortress; and from all its old ditches being left, from its thick enclosures of earth which have not been destroyed and which to a discerning Enemy would render the approach by Parallels in a great measure unnecessary.[15]

As late in the day as April 1804, Simcoe was still urging that the Castle was less tenable than it had been under Cromwell.[16]

Meanwhile, within the gates, Captain Melvill had discovered that the slack hand of his predecessor had encouraged all the vices usually attendant on the want of discipline, '...habitual drunkenness, swearing, profanation of the Sabbath and the like'. Convinced both from the military and the spiritual points of view that idleness was at the root of most mischief and discontent, he not only enforced garrison standing orders with a new rigour but also parcelled out a tract of uncultivated ground close to the fort and provided the men with tools to work it. So successful was he that a number of them built huts for their families among the flowers and vegetables they grew there. A sterner test of his leadership skills came early in 1798 when he received a draft of 63 men (bringing his company to an effective strength of 98), some of whom, it was thought, were tainted by the recent naval mutiny at the Nore.[17] Ordered to work one morning, the men refused to obey. Melvill hastened to the spot, put himself at their head and told them that he would take his share of the labour as far as his strength would carry. The instant he set his shoulder to the task, they gave him three cheers, promising absolute obedience for the future.

By now, greater manpower had become available for the defence of

14.   PRO.WO55/797, Engineer Papers, Plymouth District, Simcoe to the Duke of York, Commander-in-Chief, 28 July 1801.

15.   PRO.WO30/74/5, Paper by Lt-Gen Simcoe 'Respecting the Defence of Plymouth & weighing the propriety of *Strengthening* Pendennis Castle', 30 July 1803.

16.   PRO.WO30/74/4, Simcoe to the Quartermaster-General, 20 April 1804.

17.   PRO.WO17/797, Return, 2 Feb 1798.

the Castle and the town as the urban élite of Falmouth channelled the energies of the subordinate population into the Volunteer Movement. At a town meeting on 8 March 1797, organized by the Mayor (Dr Stephen Luke), Melvill, Captain Isaac Burgess (late of the North Devon Militia), the gentlemen of the Corporation and other principal inhabitants, the call went out for all citizens capable of bearing arms (reckoned to be nearly 500), to come forward and man the guns at Pendennis. Within four days, 350 of them, chiefly 'Artificers, Seafaring Men and Labourers', had volunteered to '...assist in Pendennis Castle at a Minute's Notice'. Grouped, for the time being, in seven independent and disunited companies, it was proposed that they should be '...trained by a few lessons to the management of the great Guns and be divided into Companies each officer'd by Gentlemen in the Neighbourhood to whom they are to Repair on the Signal being fired'. An additional 30 men enrolled as a troop of Volunteer Cavalry under the command of Dr Luke, while 60 more formed themselves into two companies of light infantry. On 30 April 1797 the entire force was accepted for service under the generic title of 'Falmouth Independent Volunteers'. During the summer, this unwieldy organization divided into the 'Falmouth Gentlemen and Yeomanry', the 'Falmouth Infantry Volunteers', and a 450-strong regiment of 'Pendennis Artillery Volunteers', which united the existing seven independent companies under Isaac Burgess as Captain-Commandant, his commission dated 14 August 1797. On 13 December, he was advanced to the rank of Major-Commandant, becoming Lieutenant-Colonel-Commandant of the Corps on 13 September 1798.

The non-commissioned officers and private men were armed with pikes, which, it was maintained, would enable them to repel an attack on the Castle by escalade, and they were occasionally exercised in pike-drill and infantry evolutions, but the 'practice of the great guns' was at all times considered to be their most important and fundamental duty. They fired ball from the heavy ordnance on an average of once a month at marks moored in the sea or in the harbour entrance, and small prizes were occasionally awarded to encourage emulation among the gun-crews. They also practised with the Castle's howitzers, '...in the use of which they are so expert, as to have fired with powder eight times in a minute'.[18]

Stood down at the Peace of Amiens, the Regiment was re-raised in 1803 with an additional company, and mustered 504 effectives by the close of the year. They were drilled in the service of infantrymen and gunners (this time including the service of field artillery) and were described in April 1803 as being '...extremely well trained and very useful for the Defence of Pendennis Castle'. Throughout 1807-08 the Corps was returned as being 'Fit to act with Troops of the Line', either as artillery or infantry. The officers were 'very regular and attentive' and the unit as a whole was reckoned to be 'A stout active body of Men under Arms'. With effect from 14 September 1808, the Volunteers were absorbed into Castlereagh's centrally-controlled Local Militia as the 6th or Pendennis Regiment (Artillery) - one of only a few artillery Local Militia corps. During 1810, Lord William Bentinck put them through their paces as infantry, as a 'car brigade' (riding upon military wagons of the horse-bus type, which enabled them to keep pace with mobile artillery) and on the great ordnance. 'The evolutions and firings were made with all the steadiness and exactness of regular troops', he reported, 'Lieut-Col Burgess, his officers and men, are entitled to the highest praise'.[19]

Professions of Faith and Sinews of War

The triumph of civic leadership and patriotic unanimity represented by the formation and growth of the Pendennis Artillery Volunteers came at a time when Falmouth was becoming increasingly hard-hit by the War. It was Cornwall's most populous settlement; by 1811 there were 719 houses in the town and its suburbs, inhabited by as many as 6,000 souls. The number of resident families increased from 1,218 to 1,346 in the decade 1801-11 alone. Falmouth's chief claim to fame was its armed Post Office packet-boat service, plying to the Americas, the West Indies, Iberia and the Mediterranean, but in time of peace there was abundant trade also. From America came tobacco,

18. PRO. HO50/332, Dr Luke to Richard, Earl of Mount Edgecumbe, Lord Lieutenant, 11 March 1797; same to same, 22 March 1797; Capt Isaac Burgess to the Duke of Portland, Home Secretary, 24 Oct 1797. (Burgess had served in the embodied North Devon Militia during 1781-83 and again during 1792-93). PRO.WO13/4242, Muster Rolls and Pay Lists; PRO.WO17/1035, Returns; PRO.HO50/331, Edgecumbe to Lord Hobart, Secretary of State for War, 6 April 1803; National Army Museum, 6807-178, Papers of Lt-Gen Sir George Nugent Bart., Letters and Returns, Western District, pp46, 67, 143; C Tomkins 'The History and Establishment of the Pendennis Artillery Volunteers', *The British Volunteer, or a General History of the Volunteer and Associated Corps enrolled for the Defence of Great Britain*, Whitehall, (1799-1800); C Thomas, 'Cornish Volunteers in the Eighteenth Century, continued (1794-1807)' Part Two, *DCN&Q*, Vol XXVII (1956-58) p327.

19. NAM. 6807-178 p168; C Thomas, 'The Royal Cornwall Local Militia and the End of the Napoleonic Volunteers, 1808-1836', *DCN&Q* Vol XXVIII (1959-61) pp206-07.

20. *Falmouth Guide*, pp14-16, 32-41; J Rowe, *Cornwall in the Age of the Industrial Revolution*, Liverpool (1953) *passim*.

21. PRO.HO50/331, Dr Luke to Lord Mount Edgecumbe, 22 March 1797. During the invasion alert of 1803-05, 15 men per company - 120 men in three detachments - were on permanent duty in the Castle.

22. 'Parson Hitchins' and Melvill both resided for a time at 'Mount Sion' and it was said the area owed its name to their piety. It was equally likely that the place had been the site of a synagogue; Gay, *op cit* p179.

23. *Falmouth Guide* pp49-62. In 1810 the Misericordia Society united with a pre-existing and smaller Dissenting charity to form the Falmouth Misericordia and Benevolent Society. Melvill was instrumental in forming a similar body, the Ely Chapel Humane Society, in Holborn at the end of his life. The minister of Ely Chapel, John Wilcox, preached the memorial sermon for Melvill and profits from the text were dedicated to the Humane Society.

wood, wheat, flour and Indian corn; from Spain, Portugal and the Mediterranean came fruit, oil, silk, wool, salt, brandy and wine; grain, fruit, salt, wine and brandy arrived from France, while from the Baltic lands came hemp, tallow, pitch, tar, iron, timber, linen and sail-cloth. Exports included Cornish pilchards and tin, leather and cotton goods. In wartime, this commerce 'suffered a great declension'. Foreign markets were effectively closed from 1798 to 1801 and again from 1807 to 1810.[20] Only the smugglers thrived, and only a glut of fish kept many of the poor from starving, while the payment of a shilling a day to the Volunteers when they turned out for training or service was in part conceived as relief for the families of the poorer men.[21]

There was also a heavy demand on the town's philanthropic agencies, in which Captain Melvill was, once again, prominently engaged. There were no fewer than 20 charitable organizations at work in Falmouth during the war, the majority founded since 1801. These included Church of England charity schools for girls and boys, founded in 1801 and 1804 respectively, an Anglican Sunday School for 300 pupils founded by the officiating Minister, Richard Hawkin Hitchins with Melvill as his coadjutor[22] (1809); a Methodist Sunday School catering for another 250 children (1805); a Public Dispensary founded in 1806 '...to afford advice and medicines to suffering industrious persons'; Melvill's particular project, the Misericordia Society (1807), '...which has for its object the relief of poor strangers, who are not otherwise able to obtain it; and of distressed persons in the town who have been reduced from comfortable circumstances'; a Charitable Society (1810), for the benefit of widows, fatherless and orphaned children; Almshouses for ten poor widows (1810); a Lying-in Charity (1810), which provided poor women with linen during their accouchment, and several societies of ladies who devoted themselves to needlework and making clothes for the destitute, '...while a gentleman reads to them for their amusement'.[23]

Sudden emergencies called forth additional ad hoc charitable giving, notably in the spring of 1805 when Melvill's company (which, since December 1802, had been incorporated in the 2nd Royal Garrison Battalion, re-designated the 2nd Royal Veteran Battalion in July 1804) was removed from Pendennis to Plymouth Citadel. The veterans embarked on the morning of 16 May;

'...such a scene I hardly ever experienced', reported Melvill to his wife, 'I never saw a more moving one - it was more like a funeral than anything else - Thanks be given they went off on the whole well satisfied - & I believe every thing considered they had great reason, for the Inhabitants of Falmouth behaved very handsomely to them - They subscribed nearly fourteen Pounds in their behalf - it came when divided to 3/6 for every Woman & child - you will perhaps say, My dear Husband bore the brunt, No indeed, I only gave 10/6 & others gave a Guinea & some more - so be easy, it is a comfort to have had any thing in our power to do for these honest and faithful creatures...[24]

In addition to his involvement in local charities, Melvill also took a lead in distributing the publications of the Tract Society, founded in 1799 to develop the work of Hannah More by circulating cheap and wholesome literature aimed at counteracting the effects of vicious ballads and Tom Paine's *Rights of Man* on the mass-readership. The Captain routinely doled out the Society's texts to troops leaving from Falmouth for active service overseas. He was also involved in the work of the British and Foreign Bible Society, an interdenominational organization founded in 1804 to distribute economically-priced Bibles and New Testaments and, towards the end of his life, the Naval and Military Bible Society, founded in 1780 to distribute Bibles among the lower ranks of the armed forces. 'The maintenance of our laws, liberty and religion, our freedom from attack, invasion and civil tumult; and our very existence as a nation are all preserved to us by their valour, the dangers, the wounds the blood, and the lives of these brave and generous men' argued the Society's charge to its members - the gift of a Bible would prepare a man for the worst that might befall him. More revealingly perhaps, senior officers had testified '...from their own observation...that the Holy Scriptures, which teach men to

24. BL.Add. MSS.58,438, Melvill to his wife, 16 May 1805. For the history of the Garrison Battalions see A S White, 'Garrison, Reserve and Veteran Battalions and Companies', *Journal of the Society for Army Historical Research* Vol 38 (1960) pp156-67.

be faithful servants to God, would teach them also to be faithful servants to their king and country' - a not inconsiderable dividend at a time of potential military disaffection. One passage in particular must have struck a chord with Captain Melvill;

'Imagine a valiant Soldier or Sailor, after the labours of battle, taken prisoner in an enemy's land, or sorely wounded, or dying in the service of his country; with no eye to pity, no hand to relieve, no voice to soothe or administer consolation in his expiring moments. What a melancholy scene of agony and distress.[25]

25. *Report of the Proceedings of the Naval and Military Bible Society MDCCCXII*, London (1812) pp4-6. The Society distributed Bibles and New Testaments '...according to the authorized version, without note or comment'. The subscription was one guinea per annum. Nearly 50,000 Bibles and a greater number of Testaments had been distributed by 1812; during that year 2,135 Bibles and 518 Testaments were handed out, 49 of the Bibles to the Pendennis Garrison. For the (greatly exaggerated) fears of disaffection in the military at this period, see Clive Emsley, 'Political Disaffection and the British Army in 1792', *Bulletin of the Institute of Historical Research*, Vol XLVIII (1975) pp230-45.

Such a conjunction of prudential and ethically inspired social action took place against a back-drop of religious enthusiasm of which, by now, Melvill had become a notable product. The county of Cornwall, which had enjoyed considerable economic prosperity before the war and was inhabited by independent-minded seafarers and tin-miners had been in the forefront of the Methodist revival, and the town of Falmouth itself, it was suggested, '...contained a greater proportion of persons adhering to different religious sects than any other place of the same population in the kingdom'. The building record tends to confirm this claim - the parish church was considerably enlarged in 1813 to accommodate a burgeoning congregation, an Independant Chapel was created in 1790, a Baptist Chapel in 1803 (enlarged in 1807), the Methodist Chapel built in 1791 was enlarged in 1814, a Society of Friends Meeting House was built in 1805 and a Unitarian Meeting commenced in 1812. These foundations, like the philanthropic societies and the Volunteers, created countless opportunities for service and self-distinction within an essentially conservative framework, channelling energies away from radical, subversive activity.

Melvill himself was staunchly Anglican, on the Evangelical wing of the Church and, like many of the leading Evangelicals and Methodists of his day, conservative in his politics, intensely loyal to the King and Constitution, yet far from blind to what he saw as the low moral condition of the nation. His beliefs were summed up in a conviction of original sin, salvation by grace, justification by faith and the necessity for good works. He was anti-Catholic, but otherwise tolerant in his churchmansip; he did not hesitate to engage a Dissenting minister to conduct Divine Service in the garrison when the vicar was too hard pressed to do the job. His favourite author was the mid-Georgian Dissenting divine Dr Philip Doddridge, whose stress on domestic pietism and tenderness in devotional life appealed greatly to him. In the hero of Doddridge's spiritual odyssey, *Some Passages in the Life of the Honourable Colonel James Gardiner* (1747), a veteran of Marlborough's wars slain at Prestonpans in 1745, Melvill found a character whom, '...both as a christian and a soldier, he deemed a fit model for imitation, and with whose conduct he compared his own, point by point, in the many parallel circumstances of their lives, remarking with great contrition on his own inferiority'.[26]

Ultimately, his confidence in Falmouth's ability to resist the French rested neither upon its ordnance nor the exertions of its defenders, but on the power of the Almighty;

> 'It is very uncertain if Bonaparte will be permitted to carry his threats into execution', he told his wife in September 1804, 'If the Lord is with us, we need not care who is against us - Let us with the Pious David, under the same Divine guidence, be enabled to say "Tho an Host of Men encamp against me I will fear no ill.[27]

When he heard in 1805 that the French Fleet had joined with the Spanish at Cadiz in the prelude to the campaign of Trafalgar, he informed his wife '...people here are of course anxious to know what will be the end of all this - of this we may be satisfied that all is working together for those who love and fear God - Put thy whole trust in Jehovah Jesus!'[28]

Pendennis Castle itself, for all General Simcoe's unease, was by now thought to be in very respectable state of defence against an assault - the ditches had been deepened where the sections were low and newly fraized and palisaded; fields of fire had been greatly

26. Dr Doddridge's *Gardiner* was first published in 1747 and quickly established for itself a sure place in the history of conversion. The British Library contains reprints of 1748, 1764, 1772, 1778, 1782, 1785, 1798, 1808 and 1812. Like Melvill, Gardiner had been dangerously wounded (at Ramillies in 1706) but his conversion did not take place until 1719. For Doddridge and his wider influence on eighteenth century piety, see Geoffrey F Nuttall, ed, *Calendar of the Correspondence of Philip Doddridge DD*, Historic Manuscripts Commission/Northants. Record Office, London (1979) and Alan Everitt, 'Springs of Sensibility: Philip Doddridge of Northampton and the Evangelical Tradition' in *Landscape and Community in England*, London (1985) pp201-45.

27. BL.Add.MSS.58,438, Melvill to his wife, 4 Sep 1804. The reference is to Psalm XXVII, v3; 'Though an host should encamp against me my heart shall not fear: though war should rise against me in this will I be confident'.

28. *Ibid*, same to same, 5 May 1805.

29 PRO.WO55/797, General State of the Works in the Western District, 3 July 1804; K W Maurice-Jones, *History of Coast Artillery in the British Army*, Woolwich (1959) p19. A 'Return of Ordnance' in the Nugent Papers, NAM. 6807-178 pp80-82, dated 7 Oct 1807 and signed by Melvill, lists four 68 pdr. carronades, eight 24 pdr. carronades, twenty-two 24 pdr. guns, fourteen 18 pdr. guns and two 8in howitzers in the Castle's 'Great Ordnance' and a field train comprising two 5^1/2 in mortars, two 4^2/5 in mortars, four brass 6 pdr. guns and two brass 3 pdr. guns.

30. *Royal Cornwall Gazette*, 6 May 1809.

31. In a similar action in 1812 in aid of the civil power, the Royal Monmouthshire and Brecon Militia marched from Pendennis to Redruth to overawe starving tin miners who were seizing stocks of grain; Rowe, *op cit* pp180-83.

32. His successor, Capt James Considine, was appointed on 2 Nov 1811. He died in 1814 and was succeeded by a maimed veteran of the recent conflict, Lt-Col William Fenwick, who had been '…severely wounded in the Maya Pass in the Pyrenees, July 25, 1813; when he suffered amputation very high in the right thigh', *Gentleman's Magazine*, Vol CII, Part 2 (1832) p181.

33. The story of the virtuous Hezekiah, King of Judah, whose span of life was lengthened by fifteen years, is told in 2 Kings, XX.

improved by the levelling of old works and enclosures and the fort was well armed. Among its 48 guns were twenty-two 24 pounders and twelve carronades.[29] As the threat of invasion swiftly receded, tension was lowered to the extent that the desecration of 49 young walnut trees on the Board of Ordnance land adjacent to the fort was a notable event,[30] and the most significant military transaction of the last years of Melvill's government was the sending of a Militia detachment into Falmouth at the request of the Mayor to quell unrest arising from a dispute between the packet boat crews and the port Revenue officials (1810).[31] In January 1809 shock-waves from a distant conflict beat upon the town when many sick, wounded and destitute soldiers were landed there from the Corunna evacuation. Melvill was instrumental in raising a subscription for their relief in Falmouth, Truro and Penryn. When a typhus epidemic broke out among them, Melvill remained at his post in the Castle, dispensing medicines and warm clothing, while others fled.

It had always been his intention to stay at the Castle for the duration of the War, 'reserving to myself the hope of retiring from the service if the Lord should send peace'. Bouts of severe illness conspired to weaken this resolve, and as he was forced to admit, Pendennis was a 'bleak place' in the winter gales. At the end of 1810, he removed to London to be near his eldest surviving son, returning to the Castle in 1811 to put his affairs in Cornwall in order. While there, he contracted a fever 'of the typhus kind' and on 27 October 1811 he died, aged 49.[32] Just over a month previously, on the anniversary of his maiming at Pollilur, he had written;

'Who ever experienced such mercies? What a spectacle of complicated human misery did I on this day, thirty-one years past, present to the eye of a merciless foe? The Lord saved me on that day, and has added to my years more than twice the length of his grant to the good Hezekiah.[33] How small a portion of this noble gift has been dedicated to the munificent donor! what hours, nay days, have I squandered! what opportunities have I neglected! what advantages have I misimproved! how striking is the difference, between what I am, and what I ought to be…

A small memorial tablet in Falmouth parish church, placed by his friends near the place where his body was interred, recorded that,

'In him were united

Exalted piety - unaffected humility -

diffusive benevolence -

Enriched with every grace that can adorn the Christian character,

he gloried only in the

Cross of Christ.

PETER B BOYDEN

1. This is a revised version of an essay, 'A System of Communication throughout each County', first published in the *National Army Museum Annual Report 1978-1979*, pp9-13.

2. Public Record Office, WO17/2787, Distribution of Troops in Great Britain, 1 Sep 1803-1 Jun 1804.

3. *Volunteers of the United Kingdom, 1803*. Ordered by the House of Commons to be printed, 9, 13 Dec 1803. The August 1803 instructions for Volunteer Corps in Kent referred to the use of beacons and other signals to order their assembly, PRO.WO30/65 No. 14, Papers relating to the state and distribution of the Forces, 1796-1804.

In May 1803 the fragile peace, which had followed the signing of the Treaty of Amiens on 25 March 1802 by Britain and France, collapsed and hostilities between the two nations were renewed.[1] This resumption of war was accompanied by preparations for a French invasion of England, for which Napoleon began to assemble landing craft and other vessels and stores at Boulogne. Meanwhile, on this side of the Channel, considerable effort was being expended to ensure that the country was prepared to resist the invaders, should they slip through the naval patrols and effect a landing. The zones regarded as the most vulnerable were the Southern District - Kent, Surrey and Sussex, and the Eastern District - Essex, Suffolk, Norfolk, Huntingdonshire and Cambridgeshire. By 1 September 1803, 19,868 soldiers, 13,798 of them Militiamen, were stationed in the Southern District, with 26,677 in the Eastern District, 21,413 of whom belonged to Militia regiments. By 1 June 1804, these numbers had increased to 37,002 in the Southern District and 27,520 in the Eastern, approximately 43% of all the regular soldiers and Militiamen in Great Britain and the Channel Islands.[2]

In addition to these units, which may be considered the front-line troops, there were also many Volunteer formations of cavalry, artillery and infantry - a 'Home Guard', which would have formed the last line of defence to protect homes and families from any French troops who had evaded or defeated the regular and Militia forces. A total of 380,193 men in Great Britain had offered to serve in Volunteer units by 9 December 1803, of whom 59,123 (or 15.5% of the total) were based in the Eastern and Southern Districts.[3] In order successfully to fulfill their intended role it was essential that the Volunteers should enter the field in the shortest possible time after the enemy had landed. However, the sounding of the alert to the Volunteer units' headquarters (usually one in each town or large village), or the individual Volunteers, who were engaged in non-military occupations, would have been a lengthy process, even using mounted couriers. It was the desire to accelerate this process that led to the establishment of the network of fire-beacons in the summer and autumn of 1803. According to *The Times* of 8 Oct 1803 these beacons were to be;

'...fired on the near approach, or actual landing of an enemy on the Coast..., and on which signal, every one [in a Volunteer unit] is to assemble at his known place of rendezvous, and there expect and receive orders from the general officer, under whose command the several Volunteers and other Corps may be placed, and to whose quarters, on the first alarm of such an event, the Commanding Officer of every Corps is to dispatch a mounted Officer, or non-commissioned Officer, to receive such orders as may be thought necessary.

Establishing and Administering the Beacon System

The methods by which the sites for the beacons were fixed upon, and the cost of constructing them met, were somewhat involved. First of all, the General Officer Commanding a Military District had to convince the County Lieutenancy that it was desirable to erect beacons in the shire. Having done this, the several Lieutenants of the Divisions into which counties were divided were responsible for selecting the sites of the beacons in their areas and having them constructed.[4] Each then forwarded the bill for the work to the Quartermaster General's office at District Headquarters, where it was paid from the Field Work Account, administered by the Commissariat.[5] Exceptionally, in the North and East Ridings of Yorkshire the cost of the beacons was met by the County Lieutenancy.[6] The beacons themselves do not appear to have been very substantial, and the details of construction were left to the Lieutenants of Division responsible for erecting them. Those in Kent were described by *The Times* on 8 October 1803 as being '...stakes of wood, and other materials, with a pole passing through them, in the top of which is a small white flag, to make their situation more visible. When the alarm was given in the day, means will be taken to make a great smoke, accompanied by fire'.

4. For a detailed survey of the beacon network in one county see P B Boyden, 'Fire Beacons, Volunteers, and Local Militia in Napoleonic Essex - 1803-11', E*ssex Archaeology and History*, Vol 15 (1983) pp113-18.
5. *Eleventh Report of the Commissioners of Military Enquiry*, 1810, pp106-07.
6. National Army Museum, 6911-4-14, Quartermaster General's Department Papers, Yorkshire District Field Works Account for year ending 31 Dec 1809.

7. *The Times*, 12 Oct 1803.

8. Essex Record Office, D/Dke F9, Boreham and Wakering Estate Papers, H Pattison to Col Tyrell, 21 Oct 1806.

9. PRO.HO50/68, Military Correspondence, Durham and Edinburgh 1803, William MacFarlane to Charles Yorke, Home Secretary, 25 Nov 1803, enclosing details of the system, issued by the Lord Provost on 17 Nov.

10. G C Guilbert, 'A Napoleonic Fire Beacon on Moel y Gaer, Clwyd', *Post-Medieval Archaeology*, Vol 9 (1975) pp188-202.

11. NAM.6612-25-2, General Order Book, Gosport 1805-06, South-Western District Orders, 27 Oct 1805.

12. NAM.6911-4-19, Deputy Quarter-master General, North Britain, to Brownrigg, 4 Nov 1805.

13. NAM.6911-4-7, Monthly Return of Dover Garrison, 19 Mar 1810.

14. NAM.6911-4-12, Thomas Dal-Hesketh to the Quartermaster-General's Department, 6 Jul 1804.
15. Buckinghamshire Record Office, D/DHV/26, p12, Howard-Vyse Papers; Letter Book copy of Gen George Murray to Gen Richard Vyse, 21 Aug 1804.

A highly developed specimen near Colchester consisted of straw, faggots, and tar barrels,[7] although one in the south of Essex was 'composed of Bean Straw'.[8] The most sophisticated system yet identified was that erected in Edinburgh to give warning of the appearance of the enemy in the Firth of Forth.[9] This involved the use of signal-balls (by day) and fire (by night), with a flag to cancel and amend the day-time signals. Not only was the system designed to bring about on assembly of Volunteers, but also to signal the destruction of mills and the driving of cattle in the County of Edinburgh. However, it seems unlikely that the remains of two large and sophisticated structures excavated at a known beacon site in Flintshire are Lieutenancy fire-beacons.[10] If they are signals posts at all, they are more likely to belong to a chain of naval telegraph stations. More documentary research is needed before definite conclusions can be drawn on this point.

Adjacent to each beacon a hut was erected to accommodate the men watching over it. In some areas beacons were manned by soldiers, while in others local civilians were employed. From 1 November 1805, only 'one careful married soldier' was to be stationed at each beacon in the South Western District, for which he would be paid an extra shilling a day.[11] In Scotland up to the same date beacons were manned by a sergeant from a Veteran Battalion and three privates from neighbouring Volunteer corps[12], while in March 1810 a squad of four privates from the Royal Perth Militia was stationed at each of the beacons at Pluckley, Minster, Westwell, and Lenham in Kent.[13] In areas where the Army was hard-pressed for men, the employment of civilians as beacon-minders had the added advantage of creating work for the poor, although the inability of the complicated administrative machinery to ensure that the men recieved their pay regularly seems to have caused difficulties for many of them. Near Preston, two soldiers minding the beacon on Caddaly Moor were threatened with eviction, unable, because of arrears in their pay, to pay the rent,[14] and in desperation the men posted at Hendingham Beacon near Hull petitioned Horse Guards in an attempt to get their wages.[15] Perhaps the worst case of bureaucratic intransigence is to be found in the attempt by Lewis Majendie of Hedingham Castle, Essex to obtain money owed to

'Richard Wellesley, Marquis Wellesley, KG'
Line engraving by G Adcock after Sir Thomas Lawrence, published by the London Printing and Publishing Company Limited c1830.
Richard Colley Wellesley Earl of Mornington, Arthur Wellesley's elder brother, was appointed Governor General of India in 1787. A brilliant, if erratic, proconsul, his patronage was crucial to his brother's early advancement. His service in India was acknowledged (inadequately in his view) by advancement as Marquess Wellesley of Norragh in the Irish peerage (1799).
National Army Museum 6012-321-15

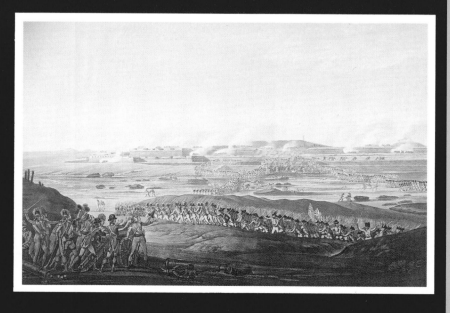

'...The Assault of Seringapatam...'
Coloured aquatint after Alexander Allan, published by Anthony Cardon, London, 1 February 1802. Seringapatam, fortress-capital of Tipu of Mysore, was taken by assault on 4 May 1799. The artist, Captain Alexander Allan, was Deputy Quartermaster General to the expedition.
National Army Museum 7102-33-382

'The Head of the Advanced Guard of the Mahratta Army, Coming to Join Earl Cornwallis, Near Seringapatam, May 28th 1791'.

Coloured engraving, artist unknown, published by James Rennell, 30 March 1792.

This engraving gives a good impression of the appearance of Maratha light horse.

National Army Museum 7403-106

'Marquis Cornwallis'

Mezzotint by James Ward after Sir William Beechey, published by A C de Poggi, London, 1 January 1799. Charles, 1st Marquess Cornwallis, the defeated general at Yorktown in 1781, went on to a brilliant career as Governor General and Commander-in-Chief in India from 1786-93. In May 1798 the Irish situation was considered so desperate that he was begged to accept the two offices of Lord Lieutenant and Commander-in-Chief in Ireland. He retained both appointments until May 1801.

National Army Museum 9011-1

'Battle of Vinegar Hill, June 21st 1798'

Coloured etching by Henry Brocas after Lieutenant Peter Carey, 17th (Light) Dragoons, published by William Allen, Dublin c1798.

National Army Museum 7102-33-411

AN ADDRESS

From the 105th and 113th Regiments to the Public, and their Brothers in Arms.

Citizens and Fellow Soldiers.

IT is no longer time to sport with our Lives and trifle with our Credulity—We, too, have been Industrious Citizens till a dreadful and atrocious War had dried up the channels of our Manufactures and caused us to Roam at large, Idle and Dependent!—Necessity, dire necessity induced us to embark in a cause which our souls abhorred; but hunger has no Law; sooner than perish, we had been tempted by large Sums (badly paid) to enrol ourselves—We did so, on condition of returning to our homes at the approach of Peace; but what now is the case? All faith is broken with us! We are led to be incorporated with Regiments that will never be reduced, except by a formidable enemy and the more formidable climate of the WEST-INDIES! And you, unfortunate and inslaved Natives of Africa, are you to feel our Steel? Are we to be made shed your innocent blood with our Murderous Arms? Forbid it Heaven! Forbid it Justice! No, no, perish first the man who dare embark for so horrid a purpose; Generous Citizens of Cork, do you not sympathise with us? Do you not pity us thus Crimped and Sold by unfaithful Officers? You surely must; for you cannot be hardened to misfortunes.

As to our Brothers in Arms, they cannot, they will not unsheath the Sword to enforce an Aarbitrary and Unjust Measure, Our Fellow Soldiers, are fellow men, and cannot forget what they owe to themselves—they must *think,* and then we are all right. Yes, we will defend our Country, our Homes, our Wives and Children, to this we are pledged, and from this we shall never Flinch.

CORK, September 4, 1795.

'Sir Ralph Abercromby KB Giving the Word of Command'
Mixed method engraving by and after John Kay 1801, originally published by Hugh Paton, Edinburgh, 1837.

To Abercromby can be given much of the credit for the revival of the British Army during the Revolutionary War period. After service in Germany during the Seven Years' War, his professional advancement was postponed by his opposition to the war against the Americans. War with France recalled him to active service and he greatly distinguished himself in Flanders, the Caribbean and North Holland (1799). Extreme short-sightedness contributed to the recklessness in battle which eventually cost him his life at the Battle of Alexandria.
National Army Museum 7504-21-51

SIR RALPH ABERCROMBY. K.B.

51

'The Landing of the British Troops in Egypt on the 8th of March 1801'
Engraving by Lewis Schiavonetti after Philip de Loutherberg, published by Anthony Cardon, London, 1804.
National Army Museum 5702-30-5

**A Regiment Breaking Camp,
Egypt 1801**
Watercolour by Private W Porter,
61st Regiment, c1801.
It is exceptional to find works of art
produced by private soldiers at such
an early date.
National Army Museum   7106-6-1

**A Camp, With Troops Drilling
by a River, Egypt 1801**
Watercolour by Private W Porter,
61st Regiment, c1801.
National Army Museum   7106-6-2

Captain Philip Melvill
From an oil painting (untraced),
illustrated in Susan E Gay, *Old
Falmouth* (1903).
By permission of the British Library

**'Soldiers Attending Divine
Service'**
Coloured aquatint by Schutz after
Thomas Rowlandson, published by
Rudolph Ackermann, London, 1
August 1798.
National Army Museum   8804-23

**'The Song of The Gentlemen
Volunteers of England'**
Coloured, etched music cover by
and after Thomas Rowlandson,
published by E Jones, London,
1798.
National Army Museum   7410-95

**'A Distant View of Ciudad
Rodrigo'**
Coloured aquatint by Charles
Turner after Major Thomas St.
Clair from 'A Series of Views of the
Principal Occurrences of the
Campaigns in Spain and Portugal',
published by Colnaghi and Co,
1812-15.
One of a cadre of British officers
selected to train and command the
Portuguese Army in the Peninsula,
St. Clair led a regiment of
Cacadores (Portuguese riflemen).
The prints produced from his
drawings are some of the best
contemporary views of the Peninsu-
lar War. Note the troop of Spanish
guerrillas in the foreground.
National Army Museum
7102-33-507-14

James Burket of Gosfield for attending the beacon there during 1809. After seven months' correspondence payment had still not been received, and in the meantime, Burket had died, leaving a widow in poverty.[16]

The Effectiveness of the Beacon-System

Having outlined the administrative aspects of the beacon system, it remains to consider its effectiveness, and the military potential of the Volunteer units it would have brought into action in the event of a French landing. Both the East Riding of Yorkshire and the Essex Lieutenancies decided to put their beacons to practical tests of their intervisibility. In the Yorkshire experiment, launched at 8pm on 7 October 1803, it was found to be possible to ignite beacons across the 60 miles between Spurn Point and Whitby in eleven minutes.[17] In Essex, Guy Fawkes Night bonfires for 1803 were suppressed in order to avoid the alarm which might have been caused by people thinking that the beacons had been fired.[18] Sadly, these precautions were insufficient to prevent uproar in Chelmsford at about 10pm on 1 November, when the burning of some weeds to the south of the town was thought to be the firing of a beacon on the coast.[19] Lieutenant-General Sir James Craig, General Officer Commanding, Eastern District, reported to a meeting of the Essex Lieutenancy in January 1804 that his experimental firing of beacons the previous November had revealed serious gaps in the network, which he proposed to improve by the erection of 'about 24 Flag signals' of large size, 'in various parts of the county'.[20]

Further north, Lieutenant-General Sir Hew Dalrymple, GOC Northern District, reported to the Quartermaster General in September 1803 that in his opinion it would be impossible to communicate between Tynemouth and Newcastle using fire-beacons, given the terrain and the fires and smoke that constantly issued from the collieries in the area.[21]

When the Essex beacons were de-commissioned for the first time, the Lord Lieutenant, Baron Braybrooke, recalled that he had '...made & attended the largest beacon & watched in my neighbourhood the corresponding one at Sewers End, & notwithstanding a great flame & smoke our beacon was not seen by our neighbours neither did we distinguish

16. ERO/L/C 2/8, Lieutenancy Correspondence; Majendie to Parker 6 Sep, 13 Oct, 4 Nov, 17 Dec 1809, 30 Apr 1810; H France to Parker 2 Feb, 31 Mar, 3 Apr 1810.

17. *The Times* 13 Oct 1803.

18. ERO/D/DHA 0/13 f6, Hanson Papers, Braybrooke to Hanson, 26 Oct 1803; *The Times*, 31 Oct 1803.

19. *The Times*, 5 Nov 1803. For an account of a similar incident in Yorkshire in August 1805 see T G Manby, *The Doncaster Yeomanry*, Doncaster (1972) pp7-8, a reference I owe to my colleague Elizabeth Talbot Rice.

20. ERO/L/M 40, 90-1, Minutes of Lieutenancy Meeting, 27 Jan 1804.

21. PRO.WO30/62 No 7, Papers relating to defence, 1795-1812, Dalrymple to Brownrigg 26 Sep 1803.

22. BRO/D/DHV/26, Letter-Book copy of Assistant-Adjutant General Yorkshire District, to Dollond & Son, 30 Oct 1805.

23. ERO/L/C 2/8, Braybrooke to Parker, 8 Dec 1807.

24. NAM.6911-4-14, Yorkshire District Field Works Account, 1809.

25. *Loc cit.*

26. NAM.6911-4-14, Vyse to the Quartermaster General, 9 Nov 1809.

27. NAM.6911-4-12, Account of expenses of manning the beacons in Flintshire, 21 Mar-30 Apr 1805.

28. NAM.6807-178, Papers of FM Sir George Nugent Bart.; Letters & Returns, Western District pp37-39, 46-47, 63-65, 67, 132, 143, 155 and 167.

theirs'. (Perhaps he should have procured one of the telescopes which were issued to each beacon by the Quartermaster General's Department)[22]. Braybrooke also noted that '...the soldiers who watched (or rather who were ordered to watch at ye signal houses) behaved disorderly ran in debt in the neighbouring villages & never were seen in their duty - but were heard of as poachers'.[23]

Furthermore, there is no denying that the beacon network as a whole was very expensive to maintain. The beacons themselves were fairly cheap to build - the 28 positions in the West Riding of Yorkshire only realised £42 : 1s :1½d when they were sold-off in 1809.[24] Manning expenses, however, were considerable - in Yorkshire and Lincolnshire it cost £980 : 10s to pay 'military attendants' at the beacons during 1809,[25] although how much of this money actually reached the soldiers concerned is quite another matter. On 9 November 1809, General Richard Vyse complained to the Quartermaster General that the sum of £558 : 9s was owed to the men in back-pay, and that they were 'very much distressed for want of the same'.[26] In Flintshire, the cost of paying and providing fuel for the twelve men watching over the three beacons in the county was £48 : 7s : 6d per month,[27] which works out at over £3,500 for the period that the beacons were probably in existence.

Press accounts of the false invasion alarm in Chelmsford on 1 November 1803, show that in that town at least everyone was well acquainted with his duties in the event of the alert being sounded. But how effective would the Volunteers have been against French regulars? It is possible to begin to answer this question by studying inspection returns for Volunteer corps, and the following remarks are based upon reports on Cornish units between September 1805 and May 1809.[28] In general terms, none of these corps suffered from a shortage of recruits, although up to 25% of the men were absent from inspection parades. Their clothing was usually passable, their arms and accoutrements less so, while the horse-furniture of the cavalry was mostly unsatisfactory. The chief problem for the cavalry was the shortage of decent-sized horses; the available mounts were variously described as indifferent, very small, very awkward, and unsteady. None of the six mounted units were thought to be fit to act with troops of the line, and indiscipline and the ignorance of their officers seem to have been serious problems.

The record of the nine Cornish artillery units was rather better, five of them being at various times passed as fit for active service. Indiscipline was less of a problem with them, although one or two were short of men. A total of eight of the 15 infantry units were from time to time passed as fit to act with troops of the line, although others had discipline problems, mainly caused by the indifferent quality of some of their officers.

The table below shows the efficiency of the Cornish Volunteer units as registered on six dates during 1807-09. It can be seen that at best, in late 1807, only 50% of them were likely to have offered any serious military opposition to a French invasion, whilst in 1808 and 1809, as the better Volunteer units were being re-formed into Castlereagh's Local Militia corps, the quality of the remaining units deteriorated sharply.

	Jul 1807			Sep 1807			Nov 1807			Jul 1808			Nov 1808			May 1809		
	F	A	D	F	A	D	F	A	D	F	A	D	F	A	D	F	A	D
Cavalry	0	3	3	0	5	1	0	3	1	0	3	3	0	6	0	0	3	2
Artillery	4	4	1	6	2	1	3	2	1	5	2	2	2	1	1	0	1	1
Infantry	8	1	4	8	4	1	7	2	1	6	3	4	3	0	0	0	1	1
Totals	12	8	8	14	11	3	10	7	3	11	8	9	5	7	1	0	5	4

F - Fit to act with troops of the line

A - Advancing in discipline

D - Deficient in discipline

By 1809 the threat of a French invasion had receded, and so the beacons were abandoned in many areas at the end of that year.[29] In some cases they continued to be manned on reduced establishments until 1 August 1811, when they were given up for good.[30] How effective the beacons and the Volunteers they were to have summoned to fight the French invaders would have been if put to the test is, perhaps happily, one of the unanswered questions of history.

29. NAM.6911-4-14, Yorkshire District Field Works Account, 1809.

30. ERO/L/C 2/8, Lt-Col Birch to Parker, 26 Jul 1811.

CHARLES ESDAILE

For many years it has been conventional to argue that the Allied victory in the Peninsular War of 1808-14 was the result of the application of a combination of regular and irregular warfare, or as Sir Charles Oman put it, of 'the inexhaustible endurance of Wellington and his army, and the perpetual worry and distraction caused to the French by the spasmodic efforts of the Spaniards'.[1] Writing at about the same time as Oman, Basil Liddell Hart argued that Wellington's ability to maintain his position in the Peninsula in the face of overwhelming numbers and ultimately to achieve final victory over his opponents was due solely to the continued defiance of the Spanish guerrillas. For him the fact that the French armies succeeded in defeating every attempt on the part of the Spaniards at regular resistance was entirely providential for '…it ensured that the main effort of the Spanish [*sic*] was thrown into guerrilla warfare, that an intangible web of guerrilla bands replaced a vulnerable military target, and that enterprising and unconventional guerrilla leaders conducted operations instead of hide-bound Spanish generals'.[2] Furthermore, for Liddell Hart, the operations of the guerrillas, which he appears to have regarded as having been undertaken under Wellington's instigation and direction, came to be '…the predominant influence…on the issue of the struggle'. Although he was prepared to accept that the presence of the Anglo-Portuguese army was crucial in spreading and perpetuating the guerrilla war, in the last resort, 'Wellington's battles were perhaps the least effective part of his operations'.[3]

The Guerrilla Warfare Phenomenon

These arguments, which were taken up by many later writers, have come to form the basis of much current thinking on the Peninsular War. In some respects this preoccupation with the guerrilla struggle will never be unjustified, for there is ample evidence to suggest that the widespread and unceasing Spanish resistance made a deep impression on the French. Marshal Suchet, for example, wrote of a '…new system of resistance…which defended the country in a far more effectual

1. Sir Charles Oman, *A History of the Peninsular War*, Oxford (1902-30) Vol VII p516.

2. Basil Liddell Hart, *The Decisive Wars of History: a Study in Strategy*, London, (1929) p104.

3. *Ibid*, pp105, 115.

manner than the regular war carried on by disciplined armies, because it was more consistent with the nature of the country and the character of its inhabitants'.[4] In a second passage he remarked;

'The armed and disciplined youth sustained with steady constancy a national struggle against the French armies on fields of battle and especially in besieged towns. But the greater part of the population, sometimes without any distinction of age or sex, embarked in that active and obstinate species of contest which brought enemies upon us in all directions and exhausted us far more than regular engagements...Peasants, landowners, fathers of families, priests and monks, unhesitatingly abandoned their dwellings...in order to swell the guerrilla bands that were forming against us. Prepared to undergo every sacrifice...they met in irregular bodies...never failed to attack when...a favourable opportunity promised them success, fled without disgrace when they were weakest, and occasionally, by a general dispersion...disappeared so that it became difficult to discover any trace of them...Their isolated efforts were sufficient, seriously, to molest the third corps in its occupation of Aragón.[5]

Writing in similar vein, Masséna's aide-de-camp, Jean Jacques Pelet, described how the *partidas*, or guerrilla bands, impeded the communications and provisioning of the French armies, provided the Allies with detailed intelligence of every sort, made it 'almost impossible for us to obtain the least notion about the armies that opposed us', and 'brought forth vengeance and reprisals, which in turn fomented the insurrections'. Moreover, he is quite specific as to the mutual interdependence of Wellington and the guerrillas;

'Thus, the bands of insurgents and the English army mutually supported each other. Without the English the Spaniards would have been quickly dispersed or crushed. In the absence of the guerrillas, the French armies would have acquired a unity and strength that they were never able to achieve in this country, and the Anglo-Portuguese army, unwarned of our...projects, would have been unable to withstand concentrated operations.[6]

4. Louis Gabriel Suchet, *Memoirs of the War in Spain from 1808 to 1814*, London (1829) Vol I p44.

5. *Ibid*, pp52-54.

6. Donald D Horward, ed., *The French Campaign in Portugal 1810-1811: An Account by Jean Jacques Pelet*, Minneapolis (1973) pp29-32.

Moving away from the level of grand strategy, it is clear the endless struggle against the guerrillas spread demoralisation among the rank-and-file of the invaders. George Simmons of the 95th wrote of encountering enemy deserters from Masséna's Army of Portugal '...who all speak with horror of prolonging the war in Spain, as they dare not individually leave their camp'.[7] In a letter that must itself have been captured by the guerrillas as it reposes in the Wellington Papers, an officer of the same force complained bitterly of the guerrilla war and the disastrous efects which it had upon the army's discipline, exclaiming, 'I truly cannot bear it any more, my health cannot stand it, and I shall have to be invalided home'.[8]

So far, so good, for there would seem to be ample evidence to support the conventional view. Recent research on the Spanish aspects of the Peninsular War, however, has suggested that the guerrilla war is a far more complicated phenomenon than has generally been thought. In particular, doubts have been cast upon the efficacy of guerrilla warfare *per se*, in that the Spanish regular armies have been shown to have played a major role in sustaining the operations of the *partidas*. A further tendency of this fresh research is to suggest that the guerrillas themselves were by no means an entirely spontaneous civilian phenomenon, for although some of the *partidas* did spring solely from the local inhabitants, others are known to have been led by regular officers and formed upon the basis of, or even entirely composed of, units of the regular army[9]. It is increasingly apparent that the common identification of regular resistance with the Anglo-Portuguese army and irregular resistance with the Spaniards, not to mention of the guerrillas with the civilian population, is an oversimplification.

A Wider View of Warfare

This is not, of course, sufficient to undermine the basic premise that the Spaniards and the Anglo-Portuguese army were mutually interdependent. Rather than talking about the guerrilla war as if it was something separate from the operations of the much maligned Spanish generals, it will certainly be necessary to develop a wider picture of the

7. Lt-Col Willoughby Verner ed., Major George Simmons, *A British Rifleman: Journals and Correspondence during the Peninsular War and the Campaign of Waterloo*, London (1899) p68.

8. University of Southampton, Wellington Papers, 1/313, J R to Jouillé, 19 Jul 1810.

9. See the extended discussion in Charles Esdaile, 'Heroes or Villains? The Spanish Guerrillas in the Peninsular War', *History Today*, Vol XXXVIII April 1988 pp29-35; 'Wellington and the Military Eclipse of Spain, 1808-1814', *International History Review*, Vol XI, No 1 (February, 1989), pp55-67.

Spanish struggle, but doing so will not alter the basic fact that the British presence in Portugal was as vital to Spanish survival as the continued Spanish resistance was to Wellington's victories. There is, however, another area of the subject that will bear further discussion, this being Liddell Hart's contention that the guerillas came to form an integral part of Wellington's strategy. Here, too, it may well be that some revision is necessary, although it is clear that from the earliest days of the war some British observers were highly aware of the potential of combining popular resistance with conventional military operations. Great faith was expressed in the courage and devotion of the Spanish people by many of the liaison officers who were hastily dispatched to Spain by the British government following the uprising of May 1808. As Captain Philip Roche put it;

'...as to [the French] ever conquering Spain, it is in my judgement as much out of the question as their ever conquering England...Would [the British Government] *as fast as it is possible*...put a musket into the hands of every male inhabitant of Spain, France, if they have arms - I would risk my life upon it - will never conquer them.[10]

10. Public Record Office, WO1/233/519-20, Roche to Castlereagh, 16 Oct 1808.

Having entered Spain at the head of a British army, moreover, Sir John Moore recognised that popular resistance was the *sine qua non* of a successful British role in the Peninsula, writing to Lord William Bentinck;

'I have no objection to you or Mr. Frere [the British Ambassador] raising the necessity of as many more British troops as you think proper...I differ from you only on one point, when you say the chief...resistance to the French will be afforded by the English army. If this be so, Spain is lost. The English army I hope will do all which can be expected from their numbers, but the safety of Spain depends upon the service of its inhabitants, their enthusiasm in their cause, and in their fixed determination to die rather than submit to the French....[11]

11. University of Nottingham, Portland Collection, PwJc 141, Moore to Bentinck, 13 Nov 1808.

Even the succession of crushing Spanish defeats that followed was not enough to extinguish Moore's faith in the possibility of guerrilla warfare, for, although many of the letters that he wrote in the course of his campaign are larded with complaints at Spanish apathy, on 16 December he wrote to Castlereagh, 'The fugitives…are spread over the whole country. They have in general their arms, and will be troublesome subjects to the French and we may expect to hear of continual insurrections in the different parts of Spain'.[12]

This faith did not perish with Moore at La Coruña, but it is important to recognise that there was also another strand in British thinking. The dead general had been a man of markedly progressive views, as witness the reforms which he had either instituted or encouraged in the training of the British Army, and many of his brother officers did not share either his trust in, or his enthusiasm for, an appeal to the populace. In October 1808, for example, we find Colonel Sir Thomas Graham, who was no die-hard Tory but for many years a Whig MP, and who was at that point the British representative at the headquarters of the Spanish Army of the Centre, decrying suggestions that attempts should be made to induce the population of the regions occupied by the French to revolt on the grounds that '…prudence as well as humanity should recommend caution to them till the enemy can be driven out for otherwise they become useless sacrifices to his resentment and terror of such punishments may produce bad effects in other provinces'.[13]

Such views left no room for the concept of a 'people's war' whose motor would be patriotism rather than discipline - which is, of course, the only possible basis for the sort of guerrilla war so much admired by Liddell Hart - but it is clear that they were shared by the very general who is supposed to have placed such store by it. By the summer of 1809, much as Moore had predicted, guerrilla bands had emerged all over occupied Spain, and their deeds were becoming common knowledge.[14] Yet in planning his first incursion into Spain - the ill-starred campaign of Talavera - Wellington (then still plain Sir Arthur Wellesley) took absolutely no account of the contribution which they might make, an absence which is repeated in the long and

12. PRO. WO1/236/207-08, Moore to Castlereagh, 16 Dec 1808.

13. UN. PC, PwJc 79, Graham to Bentinck, 30 Oct 1808.

14. *Archivo Histórico Nacional, Madrid, Sección de Estado* 41E, p224, Junta of Cuidad Rodrigo to the *Junta Central*, 13 Feb 1809; PRO. Foreign Office Papers, FO72/73/247-53, Frere to Castlereagh, 26 Jun 1809.

gloomy exchange of views which followed the subsequent retreat. To the extent that popular involvement in the fighting appears at all, it is in a wholly negative sense, Wellington's opinions being encapsulated by a letter that he wrote to Sir John Anstruther on 6 October 1809:

'As to the enthusiasm, about which so much noise has been made even in our own country, I am convinced the world has entirely mistaken its effect. I believe that it only creates confusion where order ought to prevail, and disobedience of orders and indiscipline among the troops...and I fancy that, upon reflection, it will be discovered that what was deemed enthusiasm among the French, which enabled them successfully to resist all Europe at the commencement of the revolution, was force acting through the medium of popular societies and assuming the name of enthusiasm, and that force, in a different shape, has completed the conquest of Europe and kept the continent in subjection. Really, when a Spaniard has cried out vivat [sic] and has put everything in confusion in his...village, he sits down quietly and thinks he has done his duty till the first French patrol arrives, when he shows his activity in packing up his goods and running way, and there is no authority either to set them or keep them right.[15]

15. US.WP.1/284, Wellington to Anstruther, 6 Oct 1809.

It will be here objected that at the very time that he was writing this letter, Wellington was organising a scheme for the defence of Portugal that placed great reliance on the operations of irregular forces as a means of restricting the invaders' capacity to support themselves. Unlike in Spain, however, these forces, based on the Portuguese militia and the traditional home guard known as the *ordenança*, were a part of the historic military structure of the state and thus were subject to formal direction, the *sine qua non* of their incorporation into a plan of campaign. Nor did he believe that the British could maintain their position in the Peninsula if the indigenous contribution was limited to irregular operations, a proposal that reached him in the autumn of 1809 for the entire armies of both Spain and Portugal to be converted into indpendent legions of light troops being dismissed on the grounds that they would be helpless unless their operations were coupled with those of a regular army, and, indeed, that there were some objectives that could not be achieved except by such a force.[16]

Wellington's mistrust of the guerrillas is further suggested by his somewhat lukewarm reaction to the growing resistance of occupied Spain. In the course of 1810 the activity of the *partidas* grew apace, and Oman has shown that their efforts considerably hampered Masséna's invasion of Portugal.[17] The British commander was well aware of the extent of Spanish intransigence, admitting to Anstruther that the Spaniards were 'cordial haters of the French', and telling Lord Liverpool, Secretary for War, that, although Spain might be all but completely occupied, '...there will be no obedience, and there will remain an universal disposition to revolt, which will break out upon the first, and every opportunity...and, in the end, the French yoke must be shaken off'.[18] Yet as late as 11 July 1810 Wellington was writing of the guerrillas that '...the enemy has been in some degree distressed by their operations; but I do not find that they have weakened their corps employed in the operations against the place [Ciudad Rodrigo]'.[19] Not until 19 August did he state his belief that '...in consequence of the operations of the guerrillas...the enemy cannot conquer Spain without employing a force still larger; and that they cannot increase their force in the Peninsula...without increasing their pecuniary and other difficulties and distress'.[20]

It was, then, only gradually that Wellington became aware of the potential of the Spanish guerrillas. In the second half of the war, however, during which he drove the French back from the frontiers of Portugal, and eventually expelled them from the Peninsula altogther, it might appear that he made more use of them in that the Anglo-Portuguese offensives of both 1812 and 1813 were accompanied by elaborate schemes for diversionary operations intended to neutralise the great French numerical superiority. In the period between 1811 and 1813 steps were certainly taken to encourage and strengthen the *partidas*, as, for example, by the dispatch of gifts and mountain guns

16. PRO.WO1/242/416-22, Memorandum of 20 Nov 1809.

17. Oman, *op cit*, Vol III p489.

18. US.WP.1/284, Wellington to Anstruther, 6 Oct 1809; *ibid* 1/304, Wellington to Liverpool, 1 Mar 1810.

19. PRO.WO1/245/61-62, Wellington to Liverpool, 11 Jul 1810.

20. PRO.WO.1/245/357-58, Wellington to Liverpool, 19 Aug 1810.

to their commanders.[21] However, a close look at Wellington's plans still does not reveal wholehearted reliance upon the guerrillas. Although it may fairly be argued that he was only prepared to advance into Spain at all in 1812 precisely because so many of his opponents were neutralised by occupation duties, a large part of the diversionary work was entrusted not to the guerrillas but to the Spanish regulars, most notably the infantry divisions of Ballesteros and Morillo and the cavalry brigade of Penne Villemur. Only in northern Spain did the guerrillas play a prominent role, the plan being for them to work in conjunction with an amphibious raiding force commanded by Rear-Admiral Sir Home Popham so as to give full occupation to Caffarelli's French Army of the North. The fact that these irregulars could be incorporated into Wellington's plans was not unconnected with their recent organisation into the Seventh Army commanded by Gabriel Mendizábal, which achieved their incorporation into a hierarchy of command. Of the numerous guerrillas of Navarre and Aragón, who at this point still retained their independence, there is no mention.[22]

Much the same is true of the campaign of 1813. If Wellington ever trusted in the guerrillas, it appears that he was more than somewhat disillusioned by the events of October-November 1812 when the Spaniards failed to prevent the French from concentrating against his forces, with the result that the Anglo-Portuguese army was ignominiously bundled all the way back to the frontiers of Portugal. During the autumn he had on several occasions expressed his doubts with regard to those irregulars who were co-operating with his forces, and had explicitly informed Lord Bathurst, 'The guerrillas are almost useless in serious operations, even with our troops...'[23] Following his retreat his comments had become positively vitriolic, the *partidas* being dismissed as 'a few rascals' who 'attack one quarter of their number, and sometimes succeed and sometimes not'.[24] For all their undoubted failings, the Spaniards remained an essential part of Wellington's calculations, but thereafter it was primarily as regular troops that he sought to use them. In September 1812 the Duke had been offered the command of the Spanish army, and now sought to use

21. See, for example, PRO.WO1/261/475-76, Collier to Gambier, 20 Aug 1811; US.WP.1/346, Liverpool to Wellington, 8 Apr 1812; US.WP. 1/364, Bourke to Wellington, 26 Jan 1813.

22. Oman, *op cit*, Vol V pp334-5.

23. US.WP.1/351, Wellington to Bathurst, 21 Sep 1812; US.WP.1/3251, Wellington to Popham, 2 Oct 1812.

24. US.WP.1/351, Wellington to Cooke, 25 Nov 1812.

this command, at considerable cost to the smooth running of Anglo-Spanish relations, to get his new subordinates into a state in which they were fit to take the field. In planning the subsequent Vitoria campaign, Wellington certainly took advantage of the fact that a large part of the French forces that were supposed to be containing him had been called away to help deal with the ever more daring and powerful guerrillas of Navarre and the Basque country. Furthermore, the absence of these forces and the complete collapse of the French communications as a result of the insurrection were to prove decisive factors in the victory of Vitoria (21 June 1813). Yet no attempt seems to have been made to co-ordinate the operations of the guerrillas with those of the Anglo-Portuguese army until quite late in the campaign: it was not until 14 June, for example, that Wellington ordered the chief of the Spanish general staff to send a staff officer to Soria to contact the guerrillas of that province in order to discover their state and position and instruct them to move on Tudela and Zaragoza.[25]

Following the Battle of Vitoria, with the exception of Catalonia where desultory fighting continued until 1814, the French forces retreated into and across the Pyrenees. With most of Spain liberated there was no longer any call for guerrilla warfare, and the bulk of the *partidas* disbanded or were incorporated into the regular army: Mina's forces, for example, became the eighth division of the Fourth Army, and in that capacity served throughout the fighting in the Pyrenees and southern France. For the last campaigns of the war, then, the *guerrilla* played no part in Wellington's plans, although, in a backhanded compliment to the havoc that had been wrought by the *partidas*, he did pay much attention to ensuring that the French inhabitants were not provoked into similar activities. As to his attitude to the guerrilla war in Spain, it would appear that Liddell Hart's belief that this formed an integral, and even the most important, part of his strategy is open to considerable reinterpretation. The fact that Wellington was a man of property, a regular officer, and a staunch conservative, is itself enough to cast doubt on theories that he aimed to defeat the French through guerrilla warfare, whilst his

25. US.WP.1/370, Wellington to Wimpffen, 14 Jun 1813.

correspondence shows beyond doubt that he had no faith in any form of people's war, believing neither that patriotic enthusiasm was sufficient basis for a successful war effort, nor that irregular operations could ever produce dependable and lasting results. Although he seems to have been slow to accept the veracity of the reports of widespread irregular resistance emerging from occupied Spain, once convinced of its existence he was prepared to profit from it, and where he could, to turn it to his advantage. What he was not prepared to do, however, was to trust to it entirely: even in Portugal in 1810 one suspects that he was only prepared to place as much reliance upon it as he did because its failure would not endanger the existence of his army, for whom there always existed the haven of evacuation. Nor still less would he have subscribed to Liddell Hart's view that battles were ineffective: as Wellington well knew, the Peninsula could in the last resort only be liberated by conventional military operations, and it was with this end in view that, when he became Spanish commander-in-chief in 1812, he concentrated not on fomenting popular resistance, but on re-building the army as a disciplined, regular force.[26]

None of this, of course, undermines the general conclusion that the Peninsular War was won by a combination of conventional and iregular methods of waging war. Indeed, in later years Wellington himself was generous enough to admit the important role which the *partidas* had played in his success. There is, however, room to doubt that the Duke ever expected that contribution to be as important as it in the event turned out to be. Moreover, to identify the Spanish war effort wholly with the guerrillas, or to believe that guerrilla warfare *per se* was its most effective aspect, is insufficient. Not only was the distinction between the guerrillas and the regular army often highly blurred, but, for all the Anglo-Portuguese presence in Portugal, the *partidas* could not have continued to operate without the support of the regulars. As Wellington himself understood, the Spanish war against Napoleon needs to be seen as a whole, rather than just in terms of its most well-known and dramatic manifestation.

26. Charles Esdaile, *The Duke of Wellington and the Command of the Spanish Army*, London (1990) pp81-82, 85-93, 108-14.

An Artist's Road to Waterloo: The Sketch-book of Ensign Robert Batty, 1813-14

Michael Ball

1. *Army List*, 1814. Batty was commissioned on 14 January 1813, but returned to Cambridge on leave to take his degree before going to Spain.

2. National Army Museum, 9007-50, Sketch-book of Ensign Robert Batty.

3. *The Art Journal*, London (January 1849) p20; *Gentleman's Magazine*, London (February 1849) pp207-8.
4. Algernon Graves, *The Royal Academy of Arts: A Complete Dictionary of Contributors*, London (1905, reprinted 1970).

5. Robert Batty, *Campaign of the Left Wing of the Allied Army, in the Western Pyrenees and South of France, in the Years 1813-14*, London (1823) p16.
6. For a recent one-volume overview of the Peninsular War see David Gates, *The Spanish Ulcer*, London (1986).

On 30 September 1813, a convoy of 15 transports arrived at the port of Pasajes, on the northern coast of Spain, carrying 700 reinforcements for the Foot Guards serving in Wellington's army. Among them was Ensign Robert Batty, newly appointed to the 3rd Battalion of the 1st Regiment of Foot Guards.[1] A keen amateur draughtsman, Batty was to record his experiences in the ensuing months in a unique series of 82 sketches depicting the harbours, shipping, towns and countryside he encountered.[2] The sketches were purchased in July 1990 by the National Army Museum. Eye-witness drawings of any aspect of the Peninsular War are rare and Batty's work, although restricted in its scope, constitutes an important contribution to our understanding both of the terrain over which the British Army fought, and of some of the difficulties which Wellington faced in bringing the war to a successful conclusion.

Batty was born in 1789, the son of Robert Batty MD of Hastings, a physician who was himself a noted amateur artist. At the age of 15 the younger Batty had travelled to Italy to further his education, and it was probably there that he developed his artistic tastes.[3] 1813 had been a momentous year for him. Not only had he been commissioned into the 1st Foot Guards, he had also taken a degree in medicine at Cambridge and exhibited two works at the Royal Academy.[4]

The Situation in the Peninsula

Batty had arrived in Spain at the beginning of a critical phase of the Peninsular War, reflected at Pasajes (or 'Passages' as it was referred to by the British) where the harbour was '… a scene of indescribable bustle and noise, of endless variety of costume and confusion of languages'.[5] Recent Allied victories at Vitoria and Sorauren had broken the French hold on Iberia. The subsequent surrender of the French garrison of Pasajes had enabled Wellington to transfer his line of communications from Lisbon to the north coast of Spain, thereby improving the Anglo-Portuguese Army's transport and supply position.[6]

Victory at the Battle of San Marcial (31 August 1813) and the fall of the important fortress of San Sebastian the same day (a garrison in the citadel excepted) had consolidated this success, but although there was now a possibility of carrying the war into France for the first time, Wellington remained cautious. He was reluctant to invade southern France until the military situation elsewhere in Europe became clear. News of Napoleon's victory at Dresden had reached him in mid-September. Another success in the east might enable the Emperor to divide the Allies and dictate peace terms, leaving him free to strike at Wellington's isolated forces.

The Passage of the Bidassoa

Following the disaster at Vitoria, the demoralized French forces had been re-organized under the command of Marshal Nicolas Soult, the Peninsular veteran who had pursued Moore to Corunna, and one of Napoleon's most able subordinates. Soult now disposed of roughly 60,000 men, spread thinly across a 23-mile front behind the line of the River Bidassoa, which separated Spain from French soil. The tardiness of Wellington's advance had enabled Soult to fortify his position along the river line, but his lateral communications were difficult because of the mountainous terrain and he had insufficient forces adequately to defend the whole position. This lack of numbers and the static nature of the French defence was a weakness which Wellington was quick to exploit, and which was to influence his strategy in the coming months;

> 'These fellows think themselves invulnerable, but I will beat them out and with great ease.... It appears difficult, but the enemy have not men to man the works and lines they occupy...I can pour a greater force on certain points than they can concentrate to resist me.[7]

7. Wellington to Lt-Col John Colborne, quoted, Gates, *op cit*, p437.

The estuary of the Bidassoa was considered by Soult to be the safest sector of his front. The river at this point was 1,000 yards wide and 20 feet deep at high water, and Reille's corps of two divisions was considered sufficient to hold the position. Soult concluded that Wellington's most likely attack would be further upstream, where he had posted six divisions behind earthworks and redoubts.

In the early morning of 7 October, after a night of violent storms, Wellington launched 24,000 troops across the river. Low tide in the estuary had reduced the water level to about four feet and the British 1st and 5th Divisions crossed by means of fords revealed to their intelligence officers by local fishermen. The operation was a calculated risk, since the attacking troops would have been prevented by the rising tide from re-crossing the river if the attack failed. In the event, they were opposed by a single weak division which was easily swept aside. Further upstream, the Light Division, supported by Spanish troops, assaulted and captured the heights of La Rhune. The French found themselves heavily outnumbered at all critical points and offered little resistance. Wellington had achieved his objective of a bridgehead on French soil at the cost of about 1,600 casualties, and with his position breached, Soult ordered a general withdrawal to the line of the River Nivelle.

The subsequent pause in operations, while Wellington waited for the fall of Pamplona and for news of Napoleon's situation in Saxony, gave Robert Batty the leisure to produce a series of views of the Bidassoa valley. Sketching with a pencil on paper approximately 10 by 7 inches in size, and later embellishing his drawings with a fine nib and black ink, he recorded in meticulous detail the country over which he had so recently fought. His eye for detail was acute; there is an illusion that every rock, stream and bush is included. Extensive annotations along the upper edge of each drawing supply the names of salient topographical features and the precise position of French batteries and fieldworks. The finished effect is far removed from the often fanciful battle scenes produced for the home market at this time, and illustrates vividly some of the difficulties of terrain with which Wellington and his men had to contend.

Batty's sketches depict a countryside of great natural beauty, but one which must have presented monumental difficulties for the com-

Lieutenant-General Sir John Moore (1761-1809)
Oil on canvas by Thomas Lawrence c1805.
National Army Museum   6607-22

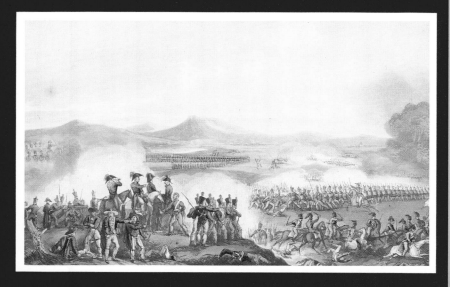

Battle of Talavera, July 28th 1809
Coloured aquatint by Thomas Sutherland after William Heath, from the series 'The Martial Achievements of Great Britain and her Allies', published by J Jenkins, London, 1815.
National Army Museum
7102-33-532-15

**'Mt. La Rhune South of France
from a Spanish Camp Octr. 9th
1813'**
Pencil, pen and ink, from the
sketch-book of Ensign Robert
Batty.
National Army Museum   9007-50-9

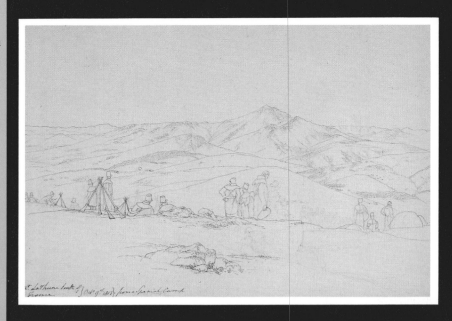

**'View of the Heights of
Buriatou, Attacked by the
Spaniards on the 7th Octr.
1813'**
Pencil, pen and ink, from the
sketch-book of Ensign Robert
Batty.
National Army Museum 9007-50-28

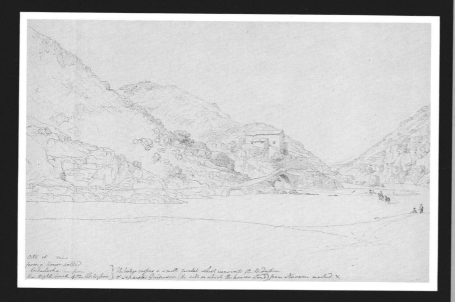

'Octr 15. View from a House
Called Endarlacha from the
Right Bank of the Bidassoa'
Pencil, pen and ink, from the
sketch-book of Ensign Robert
Batty.
National Army Museum 9007-50-15

'View of Endarlacha on the
Bidassoa from the Left Bank
Octr. 18.
Pencil, pen and ink, from the
sketch-book of Ensign Robert
Batty.
National Army Museum 9007-50-19

'Fort de Socoa Nov. 24 1813'
Pencil, pen and ink, from the
sketch-book of Ensign Robert
Batty.
National Army Museum 9007-50-44

**'Bayonne From St. Etienne
April 13 1814'**
Pencil, pen and ink, from the
sketch-book of Ensign Robert
Batty.
National Army Museum 9007-50-58

**'S.E. View Bayonne From the
End of One of the Batteries
Forming Part of the En-
trenched Camp...'**
Pencil, pen and ink, from the
sketch-book of Ensign Robert
Batty.
National Army Museum 9007-50-61

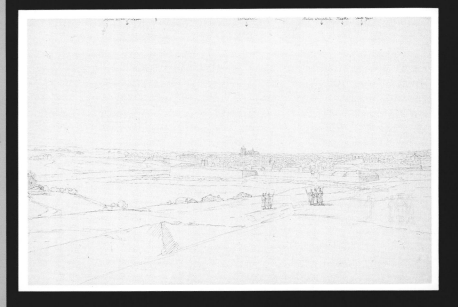

mand and movement of troops. The sides of the Bidassoa valley are steep and frequently broken by outcrops of rock. The higher slopes are almost bare, the lower levels covered with shrubs and small trees - ideal cover for French skirmishers. The hillsides are intersected by small rivulets, creating narrow but deep obstacles to movement. The few existing roads are mule tracks, and off-road movement would have been virtually impossible for cavalry or artillery.

The sketches include a scene of Spanish muleteers struggling with their beasts across the difficult landscape. Wellington's forces were dependent upon thousands of these animals to keep them supplied.[8] Other views show columns of troops toiling through the rocky terrain. A scene of a Spanish camp acts as a reminder that one of Wellington's most difficult problems was the uncertain military capabilities of his Allies. All in all, Batty's sketches reinforce the impression that the crossing of the Bidassoa was a major tactical feat, one which could only have been carried out by an army brought to the highest pitch of confidence and training by years of campaigning.

8. Michael Glover, *Wellington's Army in the Peninsula 1808-14*, Newton Abbot (1977) p109.

The Battles of the Nivelle

Soult's new position ran for some 20 miles south-east of the harbour of St Jean de Luz. The port was protected by permanent defences and the French line was further reinforced with entrenchments, redoubts and inundation.[9] Once again Soult had insufficient troops to mount an effective defence and on 10 November, whilst Lieutenant-General Sir John Hope demonstrated with the First Division in front of St Jean de Luz, Lieutenant-General Sir William Beresford smashed through the centre of the French position. Soult was forced to fall back towards Bayonne, abandoning St Jean de Luz to the British.

9. For a detailed description of Soult's position see Maj-Gen F C Beatson, *Wellington: The Bidassoa and the Nivelle*, London (1931) pp106-14.

On 18 November, Batty's Battalion went into cantonments at the port, where Wellington established his headquarters. Once again Batty employed his available time to sketch his surroundings. With his remarkable eye for detail, he recorded the harbour defences, the fortified tower of Socoa, the buildings of the town, both grand and humble, and perhaps most significantly the local boats, known as *chasse-marées*, which Wellington was assembling there in secret.

Like the sketches of the Bidassoa, these drawings are annotated to highlight natural and man-made features, for example the head-quarters of Major-General Sir Edward Pakenham. Regrettably, Batty produced no detailed studies of the diverse military and civilian population which must have thronged the port, although there are occasional glimpses, as for example in a sketch of the harbour which includes figures bathing.

For Batty, the static features of the landscape always appear to have exercised more fascination than its inhabitants, although the latter did not escape his notice altogether. He remarks that the local population did not possess '... those ears of uncommon size' recorded by Buffon (a French naturalist whose hypotheses were frequently devoid of any basis in observable fact). Batty also noted that many of the women were '... tall, and with handsome features', but if any of these were ever captured by his pencil, the sketches have not survived.[10]

A series of actions, fought between 9 and 13 December in appalling weather conditions, drove the French back on Bayonne itself, but not before Wellington's army had suffered a number of minor reverses. The deteriorating weather then forced both sides into winter quarters, where they remained until February 1814. Batty has left no sketches from this period, when keeping warm and dry was probably his major preoccupation.

Bayonne

Soult's position at Bayonne was a formidable obstacle, as Batty's later sketches make clear, but by now Wellington's numerical advantage was seriously restricting the Marshal's options. Soult concentrated his army to the east of the city, but Wellington attacked to the west, throwing a bridge of boats across the mouth of the River Adour below Bayonne. The constituents of this bridge were those same *chasse-marées* which Batty had so carefully sketched in the harbour of St Jean de Luz. As at the crossing of the Bidassoa, Wellington took a calculated risk at the Adour. No reconnaissance of

10. Batty, *op cit*, p19

the far bank could be carried out before the bridging operation was attempted, but once again the French had trusted solely to the natural strength of the river position and the attacking troops met with little opposition. By 27 February the investment of Bayonne was complete.

Leaving Hope's force, which included the Guards, to prosecute the siege, Wellington pursued Soult's field army to the east, defeating him at Orthez and Toulouse. Batty therefore missed these battles, but he was a witness to the last significant action of the Peninsular War. On 14 April, the day after he had visited the suburb of St Etienne to sketch, the Bayonne garrison made a pre-dawn sortie with over 6,000 men, overrunning most of St Etienne and catching the besiegers totally unawares. They inflicted over 800 casualties and captured the unfortunate Hope. The city finally surrendered on 27 April, on a direct order from Soult, three weeks after Napoleon's abdication.

With the war at an end, Batty, at leisure once more, was able to sketch Bayonne's defences, and the resulting drawings serve to confirm that a direct assault on the city would have been a costly operation. It had been fortified by Vauban, and Batty records a vista of massive walls, outworks and artillery emplacements, the drawings once again carefully annotated. Even sketching was not without its perils. On one occasion, the artist had his work confiscated by a French officer who reported his artistic activities to the Governor, clearly suspecting some devious design;

'The governor, however, with great politeness, restored the book, and offered to send one of his own aide-de-camps to accompany the author, whenever he wished to exercise his pencil within the limits of the intrenched camp; a permission of which he frequently after availed himself, and was, besides, conducted over the whole of the intrenched camp.[11]

11. *Ibid*, pp176-77.

This kindly offer also ensured that Batty was kept away from those areas which the French did not wish him to see, a fact which seems to have escaped him. In July 1814, the Guards embarked at Bordeaux for England and his opportunities for sketching came to an end.

Waterloo and after

The following year Batty accompanied his Battalion to the Netherlands. At Waterloo, the 2nd and 3rd Battalions of the 1st Foot Guards formed part of Major-General Peregrine Maitland's brigade, posted on the right of the Allied position behind the Chateau of Hougoumont.[12] The Brigade was exposed to repeated cavalry and artillery attack and at the close of the day was instrumental in the destruction of the French Imperial Guard. The 3rd Battalion sustained over 300 casualties during the battle, one of whom was Ensign Batty, wounded in the hip by a shell whilst the Battalion was formed in square.[13] He was absent from his unit during the march to Paris as a result of his wound.[14]

Batty was subsequently attached to the staff of Count Mikhail Vorontzov, the commander of the Russian army of occupation in France from 1815 to 1818, a position which afforded the artist time to explore the countryside over which he had so recently fought. In 1815 and 1820 he published two accounts of the Waterloo campaign, one of them illustrated with plates of the battlefield drawn by himself.[15]

Although still holding a commission in the Guards, Robert Batty travelled widely in the years which followed, and published several volumes of topographical views of European countries. These included *Campaign of the Left Wing of the Allied Army, in the Western Pyrenees and South of France, in the Years 1813-14*, published in 1823, which included reproductions of several drawings from his Peninsular War sketch-book. He became a Fellow of the Royal Society and continued to exhibit the occasional work at the Royal Academy.

In 1826, Batty served as aide-de-camp to Sir William Clinton, who commanded an expeditionary force sent to Portugal in that year. Two years later he went on to half-pay and in 1839 retired from the Army with the rank of Lieutenant-Colonel.[16] He died in London on 20 November 1848 after a long illness, having sketched and painted to within a few weeks of his death.[17]

12. Lt-Gen Sir F W Hamilton, *The Origin and History of the First or Grenadier Guards*, London (1874) Vol III p29.

13. *The Art Journal*, London (January 1849) p20.

14. Hamilton, *op cit*, Vol III p55.

15. Robert Batty, *A Sketch of the Late Campaign in the Netherlands*, London (1815); *An Historical Sketch of the Campaign of 1815*, London (1820).

16. *Army List*, 1829 and 1840.

17. *The Art Journal*, London (January 1849) p20.

PETER B BOYDEN

On 5 May 1795 an Act of Parliament was passed which allowed seamen, non-commisioned officers and private soldiers '...to send and receive single Letters by the Post, on their own private Concerns at a low Rate of Postage' of one penny per letter. The fee was to be paid by the soldier when he posted or received a letter. This concessionary rate was not introduced for any philanthropic reason, but rather to prevent the loss of revenue from re-addressed letters which, when they ultimately caught up with the soldier to whom they had been written, could not be delivered, because of his inability to pay the £2-£3 postage owing.[1] In order to qualify for the concessionary rate, the letter had to be signed on the cover by the commanding officer of the writer's unit or ship - a fairly successful attempt to prevent fraudulent abuse of the privilege by officers and civilians.[2] It was not until 1854, during the Crimean War, that officers enjoyed a reduced rate of postage.[3]

The collection and distribution of letters within regiments was the work of non-commissioned officers. The *Regulations for the Rifle Brigade* (1801) directed that the bugle major was to be the carrier of all letters, for which he was to be paid a sum per letter as determined by a board of officers.[4] Similarly, the trumpet major of the 3rd Dragoon Guards was '...to have the advantage of the letters', although NCOs in charge of parties were instructed in 1803 to '...enquire at the Post office through every town they march, whether any letters are addressed there for them'.[5] In the 76th Regiment, the drummers collected the regimental mail,[6] but the 7th Light Dragoons in 1808 appointed a letter carrier at each quarter, who ranked above the corporals. They were to deliver and collect mail to members of the regiment, for which they received one penny for each officer's letter, and a halfpenny for those belonging to the private men.[7]

The Peninsular Campaigns, 1809-14

The first ever British Field Post Office was established in Holland

1. 35 Geo III cap 53 cl 7 and 8, repealed in 1837 by 4 Wm and 1 Vic cap 32; W G Stitt Dibden, *Postage Rates of HM Forces 1795-1899*, Postal History Society Special Series, No 16 (1963) pp6-7 refers to the 1795 Act, but actually cites from and illustrates the cover of an Irish Act, 36 Geo III cap 11, which included clauses 7 and 8 of the British Act in its clauses 19-24. The Irish Act became time-expired on 25 May 1797. The present article is the revised version of an essay 'Tommy Atkins' Letters: The Postal Service of Wellington's Army in the Peninsula and France 1809-1818' first published in *Army Museum 83*, pp 19-24.
2. Dibden, *op cit*, pp31-33; see also, General Orders of 28 Feb and 14 Jun 1814, *General Regulations and Orders 1st June 1815*, London (1815) pp400, 402 where it is erroneously stated that soldiers' letters were carried free of postage. Twenty-seven letters, fraudulently posted as soldiers' letters in Great Britain and the Channel Islands during the six months to 15 Sep 1813 were detected by the Post Office when they were opened because they could not be delivered: Post Office Archives, POST 30/15, E610L/1817, folder 16.
3. P B Boyden, *Tommy Atkins' Letters: The History of the British Army Postal Service from 1795*, National Army Museum, London (1990) p8, *contra* Dibden *op cit*, pp7-8, who states that a sixpenny rate for officers was introduced in 1799.
4. *Regulations for the Rifle Brigade, late 95th (Rifle) Regiment, formed at Blatchinton Barracks August 25th, 1800*, London (1819) p85.
5. *General Standing Orders, for Third or Prince of Wales's Dragoon Guards*, Edinburgh (1803) pp53, 57.
6. *Standing Orders for the Seventy-Sixth Hindoostan Regiment of Foot, Commanded by General Sir Thomas Musgrave, Bart*, London (1807) p66.
7. *Standing Orders for the Seventh Light Dragoons*, Ipswich (1808) p37.

8. Dibden, *op cit*, pp46-51.

9. *Ibid*, p9. See also POST 35/15 E610 L/1817, file 11, Secretary to the Post Office to the Post Master General, 31 Oct 1808.

10. General Orders, 5 and 6 May 1809, *General Orders Spain and Portugal*, Vol 1, London (1811) pp15-16, 18.

11. For the background, see S G P Ward, *Wellington's Headquarters*, Oxford (1957) pp122-126. For the appointment of Cpl William Colquhoun as Assistant Postmaster at HQ, see *GOS&P*, VolIII (1812), p33. The Corps of Mounted Guides consisted of Portuguese, and Italian deserters from Junot's army, and acted chiefly as couriers along regular routes.

12. *GOS&P*, Vol II (1811) pp199-200.

13. Wellington to Stuart, 17 Aug 1811, Col John Gurwood, *The Dispatches of Field Marshal The Duke of Wellington*, Vol VIII, new edition, London (1838) p203.

14. *GOS&P*, Vol III (1812) p164.

during the Duke of York's expedition to the Helder in 1799. During the 80 days that the postmaster, Henry Darlot, was with York's army he made a handsome profit for the Post Office of £643 : 6s : 6d.[8] The next occasion when a full-scale British expeditionary force was deployed in Europe was in the Peninsula, and on 31 October 1808 the penny concessionary postage-rate was extended to troops serving in Spain and Portugal.[9] Next to nothing is known of the organisation of the postal services during the first phase of military operations, August 1808-January 1809, but on 24 April 1809, two days after he landed in Portugal, Sir Arthur Wellesley appointed Sergeant Richard Webb of the 3rd Foot Guards '...to act as Post-master with the army in the field', with an allowance of two shillings a day.[10] The Sergeant Postmaster, later joined by a Corporal Assistant, was based at Army Headquarters in Lisbon. They, together with the Portuguese Post Office, letter-parties of soldiers, orderly dragoons and the Corps of Mounted Guides, constituted the arrangements for the transmission of communications and intelligence within the army.[11]

There are indications that this ramshackle organisation, which operated within the Quartermaster General's Department, was not particularly efficient. The Sergeant Postmaster was answerable to the officer commanding the troops in Lisbon, who was ordered in November 1810 to protect the unfortunate NCO from the 'violence or impatience' of officers demanding private letters from home, which were to be sorted after the official mail had been dealt with.[12] On 14 August 1811 Wellington '...made an arrangement for the better conducting of our military posts'[13] by appointing the commander of the Corps of Mounted Guides, Major George Scovell, to superintend the whole of the military communications. In addition to the Guides, the Postmaster Sergeants at Headquarters (the assistant having been upgraded), *Senhor* Olivera (Director of the Portuguese Posts), and the messengers were all placed under his command.[14] On its formation in March 1813 the Staff Corps of Cavalry (which combined the courier duties of the Guides with the functions of a military police force) also came under the orders of the Superintendent of Military Communications, with Scovell as its first Major-Commandant.[15] He was succeeded in both positions on 25 April 1813 by Lieutenant-Colonel Richard Sturgeon. After Sturgeon's death in March 1814, Lieutenant-Colonel Colquhoun Grant took over for the final four weeks of the war.[16]

A British Post Office had been established in Lisbon in 1790 to handle merchants' letters, and during the early stages of Wellington's campaign all the mail between England and the Peninsular army passed through the Post Office Packet Agent in the Portuguese capital.[17] In May 1812 the agent was Thomas Reynolds, who was instructed '...to ensure the regularity of the delivery of soldiers' letters in England'.[18] All commanding officers were in future to compile lists of the letters to be sent home with the mail. Regiments which communicated with home through Headquarters were to send their letters and lists to Scovell, whilst those that did not were to send them direct to Reynolds, and a copy of the list to Scovell. Soldiers paid 15 *reis* (equivalent to one penny) postage per letter. The money was remitted to Reynolds by the Deputy Paymaster General on instructions from Scovell, the sums paid over being based on the regimental lists. Later that same month, the regulations were amended to allow soldiers in Lisbon or the depot at Belem to take their letters direct to Reynolds and pay him the 15 *reis* postage, it being stated that the '...Post-Office Sergeant at Lisbon, or at Head-Quarters cannot receive soldiers' letters, and money to pay the postage for them'.[19]

The execution of these straightforward instructions apparently proved too much for the commanding officers of a number of regiments and on 1 December a General Order was issued drawing attention to the '...slovenly manner in which these orders have been carried into execution'. Reynolds had three reasons to complain: letters were often sent without lists or lists without letters, lists were not signed by commanding officers, and letters were sent loose instead of packeted up with the lists. A return of the numbers of soldiers' letters received by Reynolds during the week 24-31 October 1812 revealed that out of 972 letters sent by 22 units, only 340 were accompanied by lists. Those

15. On the formation of the Corps, see the notes on 'The Staff Corps of Cavalry', *Journal of the Society for Army Historical Research*, Vol V (1926) pp211-213. For Scovell see *Dictionary of National Biography*, 'Scovell, Sir George'.
16. Ward, *op cit*, pp185-191; J Haswell, *The First Respectable Spy*, London (1969) p208. For details of the staff of Sturgeon's office in Oct 1813 see Ward, *op cit*, p196, Both Ward, p191, and Haswell, *loc cit*, state that Sturgeon came under Wellington's displeasure (and got himself killed as a result of it) because of the disorganisation of the Post Office after the Battle of Orthez.
17. Dibden, *op cit*, p14. For orders respecting the closing of the mail for the weekly packet from Lisbon see *GOS&P*, Vol 1 pp209-10, and *ibid*, Vol II p5.
18. *GOS&P*, Vol IV (1813) pp79-80.

19. *Ibid*, pp88-89.

20. *Ibid*, pp224-27.

21. Jac Weller, *Wellington in the Peninsula, 1808-1814*, London (1962) pp274, 303. Pasajes was normally spelled 'Passages' by the British.

22. POST30/15 E610L/1817, file 24, Sevright to Freeling, 21 Nov 1813.

23. *Ibid*, Same to same, 7 Dec 1813.

24. *Ibid*, Same to same, 13, 16 Dec 1813, 2 Jan 1814.

from six units 'came loose and without lists, all mixed up', whilst those from another half-dozen were also jumbled together, and had arrived two days ahead of their lists. Some of the loose letters, added Reynolds, were 'ground to dust by the carriage'.[20]

As his forces advanced across Spain and approached the French border, Wellington needed to shorten his lengthening supply-lines from Lisbon. In July 1813, the northern port of Santander replaced Lisbon as the principal base for communications with Britain, while the harbour at Pasajes, east of San Sebastian, was used by many vessels bringing stores and supplies for the army.[21] Also there by November 1813 was a packet agent named Charles Sevright who had the job of attempting to provide an efficient postal service for the army. By this time the Army Post Office in Lisbon had been closed and bags for England were made up at divisional level and forwarded to the agent. Unfortunately, they frequently contained mis-sorted letters and this problem, exacerbated by the negligence of the Spanish Post Office, led Sevright to press for the reopening of an Army Post Office, and the establishment of a Spanish Post Office at Pasajes.[22] While the latter request was acceded to, he could not persuade Sturgeon to re-open the Army Post Office.[23] Instead Sturgeon pressed Sevright to sort the army's mail himself, but he refused because he did not have any suitable premises. In December Sevright felt it desirable to move the Packet Station to San Sebastian, and after resistance from Wellington had been overcome the move was accomplished in January 1814.[24]

The closure of the Army Post Office by Sturgeon made the Packet Agent's already difficult job even harder. On 22 November 1813, Sevright was driven to express to Francis Freeling, Secretary to the Post Office, the view that it would be more convenient if the military post was carried on naval vessels. Army postal traffic overloaded the packet system and since many of the letters were free of postage or sent at reduced rates, the additional work was 'counter -balanced by no return'. Since warships were sailing weekly to and from Plymouth he felt that it would be no extra burden to the Royal Navy, and a major saving for the packet boats, if the army post was transferred to men-of-war. The idea met with a cool reception at the Post Office and was not proceeded with.[25] Some relief was at hand however, for in his larger premises at San Sebastian, and later in Bordeaux, where the Packet Station had moved by July 1814, Sevright was supported by a civilian principal sorter (paid 12 shillings a week) and three NCOs or soldiers who were allowed six shillings per mail between them. This system operated from 13 January to 16 June 1814, and was eased by the establishment of a Military Post Office in Bordeaux. In his report to Freeling on the operation of his packet station, Sevright explained that an incoming mail for the army usually consisted of 20 bags, which were first sorted to extract letters for Wellington, Beresford and other senior commanders, then mail for chiefs of departments, and then by divisions and brigades.[26] When Lisbon ceased to be the packet station for the British army in the Peninsula, the agent there was owed £192:4s:10d in unpaid postage on soldiers' letters that had been dispatched to England. On 9 July 1814 Freeling had been advised that it would be almost impossible to collect the money and that the Post Office should abandon its claim. Sevright urged the Postmaster General that the Paymaster General should be made to produce the cash, but on 12 August 1814 the Treasury agreed to write off the outstanding balance on the Lisbon Packet Agent's account.[27]

Flanders and France, 1815-18

When Wellington assumed command of the Allied Armies on 5 April 1815, he had to create a command infrastructure for his force from nothing. The British army that fought in the Peninsula had been dispersed during the summer of 1814, and although experienced officers and men were available, the smooth-running headquarters which had evolved during the earlier campaigns had to be re-established. Captain James Frazer of the 90th Regiment was at first in charge of the communications of the army, but on 10 June 1815 Lieutenant-Colonel Sir George Scovell was recalled to take over the position he had last held in 1813.[28] Under him were two clerks in the

25. *Ibid*, file 27, Sevright to Freeling 22 Nov 1813, with a minute to the Post Master General from Freeling, 31 Dec 1813. For Wellington's views on the move and the use of the packet vessels and men-of-war to convey letters, see his letter to Bathurst dated 11 Aug 1813 in *Dispatches*, Vol X, pp631-633. *JSAHR*, Vol XXXVI (1951) p45 has a note on the vessels used.

26. POST30/15 E610/1817, file 23, Sevright to Freeling, 19 Jul 1814.

27. *Ibid*, file 24, same to same 23 Jul 1814; file 28, Torrens to Freeling 9 Jul 1814; Freeling to the Post Master General, 26 Jul, to the Treasury, 30 Jul, and the Treasury to Freeling, 12 Aug 1814.

28. PRO.WO37/4, Papers of Gen Sir George Scovell, Out-Letter Book 1816-18; Scovell to the Deputy Commissary General, 28 Sep 1818.

29. *General Orders, France and Flanders*, Vol VII, Paris (1815) p193.

30. PRO.WO37/4, Scovell to Bisset, 22 Nov 1816; Scovell to Col Hervey, 17 Oct 1816. Hinchcliffe died on 16 Sep 1816.
31. National Army Museum, 7709-6-1, Papers of Sir Richard Hussey Vivian; Book of General Cavalry Orders, p7, 6 May 1815, pp119-21, 2 Aug 1815; pp119-21, Apr 1816.
32. PRO.WO37/4, Scovell to Maj Bentick, 3 Mar 1817.

33. *GOF&F* Vol VII, p52, 11 Apr 1815; pp164-164, 18 Jul 1815; *ibid* Vol VIII, p117, 3 May 1816, National Army Museum, 7709-6-1, pp119-121, 3 Apr 1816. See also B Austen, 'Dover Post Office Packet Services 1633-1837', *Transport History*, Vol V, (1972), pp29-53, in particular p41.
34. PRO.WO37/4, Scovell to Bissett, 20 Oct 1816; Scovell to Sevright, 17 May 1817, 7 Jun 1817, Scovell to Grindley, 29 Sep 1818.

35. *Ibid*, Scovell to Lt-Col Darling, 8 Jan 1817; Scovell to Lt Maclean, 27 Mar 1817; Scovell to Freeling, 20 Feb, 11 Mar 1817; Scovell to the Brigade Major, 3 Cav Bde 27 Mar, 26 Apr 1817; Scovell to OC 2nd Dragoons, 19 Jul 1818.

Post Office at Headquarters, paid two shillings and one shilling and sixpence per day respectively. The civilian Director of Posts at Mons was paid 200 francs a month from 20 June 1815 'for his trouble in arranging the correspondence with Head Quarters'.[29] All mail addressed to and sent from the army had to pass through the Post Office at Headquarters, which was initially situated at Brussels, later moving to Paris, and by May 1816 to Cambrai. There are references to a Post Office Sergeant at Headquarters, and to a Post Office in Paris in the charge of Cornet S C Hinchcliffe of the Staff Corps of Cavalry.[30] Mail, both private and official, was made up by brigades and sent through the French Post Office to Headquarters.[31] Official correspondence, and packets of private letters for England went free of charge, but other items had to be paid for.[32] Two packets a week were sent to England, the days of dispatch being altered three times between April 1815 and May 1816.[33] They passed through the packet agent at Ostend, who from October 1816 (if not before) was Sevright. The method of paying him the postage on the soldiers' letters was similar to that operated in the Peninsula, with few signs of problems on the scale witnessed during that campaign.[34] Scovell did however have to contend with complaints from regiments that their newspapers had been stolen in the post, mis-sorted letters addressed to the 'Isle de France' (Mauritius), a bottle of spirits shattered in transit, and a claim by the officer commanding the 2nd Dragoons that his regiment was 'constantly overcharged by the Military Post Office'.[35]

From the sketchy evidence available it would appear that the postal service provided for soldiers between 1809 and 1818 was adequate, although given the undermanning from which it suffered and the bureaucratic nature of its organisation, it required someone of Scovell's ability to keep it running smoothly. More importantly, it provided a means for families at home to keep in touch, however fitfully, with sons and husbands serving overseas.

Rory Muir

In the spring of 1814 the Allies captured Paris; Napoleon abdicated and went into exile on the island of Elba; the Bourbons were restored, and the long series of wars that had convulsed Europe for over 20 years seemed to be over at last. Wellington's army did not reach Paris, but by the time peace came it had secured a firm hold on southern France and captured Bordeaux and Toulouse. This was the culmination of a series of glorious campaigns in which Wellington had led his army from the Lines of Torres Vedras, through Spain and over the Pyrenees in three short years. Wellington's reputation stood higher than any British soldier since Marlborough; the Prince Regent had created him a Field Marshal for his victory at Vitoria (21 June 1813); the Portuguese and Spanish armies had been entrusted to his command and his Government had progressively made him a baron, a viscount, an earl and a marquess. Now, with the coming of peace, he was given the last and highest promotion in the peerage and made Duke of Wellington.

But Wellington was far more than a soldier, no matter how glorious. He was the brother of one of the leading politicians of the day - although by 1814 the Marquess Wellesley's star was in decline. He had advised the Grenville and Portland Governments on strategic questions; planned an expedition to South America and taken part in the seizure of the Danish fleet in 1807. He had held the important and difficult political position of Chief Secretary of Ireland for two years, impressing both the Lord Lieutenant and the British cabinet with his ability. In the Peninsula he had constantly handled important diplomatic as well as strategic issues so that he more than anyone else had shaped Britain's relations with Portugal (from 1809) and Spain (from 1812). He had gained the trust of the British Government so that by 1814 there was no one else outside the cabinet in whom the ministers felt such confidence.[1]

1. Liverpool to Castlereagh, 1 Dec 1814, Arthur 2nd Duke of Wellington, ed. *Supplementary Despatches, Correspondence and Memoranda of Field Marshal Arthur, Duke of Wellington KG*, London (1858-72) Vol IX pp461-62.

The Paris Embassy

Almost as soon as the guns had stopped firing Lord Castlereagh, the Foreign Secretary, offered Wellington the position of British Ambassador to Paris. It was natural that Castlereagh and his colleagues would wish to harness Wellington's talents, yet it was a strange idea to make a victorious general the emissary of peace to a defeated and resentful enemy. But Castlereagh believed that Wellington's 'personal weight, decision and judgement' would help to harvest 'the auspicious results of this most glorious war'.[2] Wellington accepted the offer without hesitation. He was used to serving his country and had no taste for a life of idleness. He could have crossed the Atlantic and commanded the British armies in America, but no triumph there could equal what he had already achieved, and besides, he doubted whether force alone would settle that troublesome war.

Wellington did not take up his new appointment for four months. Castlereagh sent him on a diplomatic mission to Madrid where he tried, without success, to persuade King Ferdinand VII to accept a constitution and to moderate the persecution of the liberals. Wellington then bade farewell to his army at Bordeaux, and returned to England for the first time in five years. He was fêted and praised. Balls and dinners were held in his honour, he was formally thanked by Parliament and gave thanks at St Paul's. Parliament expressed its appreciation of his services by voting him a grant of £400,000 to add to the £100,000 he had been given in 1812. In between all the festivities Wellington found time to see his family and to have talks with the King's Ministers.

In August he set out for Paris. On the way he carefully inspected the border of what is now Belgium, but was then the territory of Britain's ally, the newly created United Netherlands, and prepared a memorandum on its defence against possible French attack.

Wellington arrived in Paris on 22 August 1814. His duties as Ambassador were many and varied, ranging from the mundane and trivial to serious matters of state. Thus his correspondence shows him arranging with the French government for the deportation of an

2. Castlereagh to Wellington, 27 Apr 1814, *ibid* Vol IX pp42-43.

English vagabond; complaining of the quarantine needlessly imposed on British visitors at Le Havre; and making representations on behalf of the English Benedictines, some of whose papers and works of art had been seized during the Revolution. All these minor matters and many more which might now be dealt with by junior officials, received Wellington's personal attention - but ambassadors in those days were fortunate if they had even a handful of staff.

More substantial was a clutch of issues left over from the peace settlement. A dispute over the ownership of prizes claimed by the British as having been captured at Bordeaux annoyed Wellington, for he felt he had been particularly generous in the affair. The French government was also slow to pay compensation to British citizens who had been imprisoned or had their property seized by Napoleon, despite the fact that the British Government had conceded the far greater claims which it had for the maintenance of French prisoners of war in Britain. There were also irritating disputes over the fate of the warships which Napoleon had been building in Antwerp, in which the French government showed itself to be far from conciliatory. This unfriendly attitude was even more evident in the way that France permitted American privateers to take refuge in her ports. But the most difficult issue in bilateral relations at this time was undoubtedly the slave trade.

Thanks to the long campaign of William Wilberforce and his many supporters, Britain had abolished the slave trade in 1807, and Castlereagh had included a provision in the Peace of Paris requiring France to abolish its own trade within five years. This produced almost equal outrage on both sides of the Channel - though for different reasons. Although Louis XVIII and Talleyrand both privately supported abolition, there was little public support for it in France, and those with an interest in the trade had no difficulty persuading the public that the whole business was a devious British attempt to prevent the revival of France as a colonial and maritime power. In Britain the public reaction was stronger and much better organized. Wilberforce was deeply disappointed and his supporters organized a massive campaign of petitions and public protests which proved beyond doubt the strength of feeling on the issue. Not for the last time Castlereagh and his colleagues had badly misjudged the public mood and had to scramble to recover the ground they had lost. Wellington was instructed to press the French to agree to abolish the trade immediately or, if this was impossible, within three years at the most. Wilberforce's friend Zachary Macaulay went over to Paris to try to educate French opinion. The British Government offered through Wellington to cede a valuable colony or provide cash compensation in return for immediate abolition, but in vain. Opinion on both sides had hardened and the French found it impossible to concede. Wellington personally abhorred the traffic in slaves and he worked hard to see it abolished, but he recognized that the public furore in England only hindered his chance of success. In the end it was left to Napoleon to abolish it in 1815, a step which the Bourbons had neither the ability nor the wish to repeal when they were once again restored.

Less contentious and much less public than the question of the slave trade was Wellington's role in co-ordinating British and French policy at the Congress of Vienna. Both powers were in a similar position with broadly similar interests. Britain's own particular concerns in the Low Countries and elsewhere had already been secured by a combination of adroit diplomacy and the fortunes of war, while the settlement involving France had been spelt out in the Peace of Paris (May 1814). The discussions at Vienna related to other issues in the settlement of Europe in which the most difficult were the fate of Saxony and the Grand Duchy of Warsaw (Napleon's satellite state in Poland). The Russians wanted control over the Duchy of Warsaw, and the Prussians wanted to absorb Saxony, but the Austrians feared that these accessions would make their rivals too powerful and so disturb the balance of power.

If Britain and France could act together they might be able to hold the ring between these competing claims. But co-operation did not prove easy despite a visit Castlereagh made to Paris on his way to

Vienna. He and Talleyrand had some serious disagreements over tactics early in the negotiations, and Castlereagh used Wellington to put pressure on Talleyrand through the French government. In the end the Russians defeated Castlereagh and got their way over Poland, but the creation of a formal alliance of Britain, France and Austria and the threat of war, forced the reluctant Prussians to compromise over Saxony.

The French government was delighted not only with saving Saxony, but with the implicit recognition in the negotiations of their place among the great powers. The British Government on the other hand was simply relieved to escape from the Continental entanglements into which Castlereagh had led them without loss of face, and without war.

Wellington in Paris obviously could not play a large role in the negotiations at Vienna, yet he told Lord Liverpool: 'I flatter myself I am daily becoming of more use to Lord Castlereagh here, and am acquiring more real influence over the government'[3]. Castlereagh confirmed and went beyond this modest assessment;

> 'I cannot sufficiently express to you my thanks for your most useful and seasonable co-operation. You have succeeded in rendering the French influence here much more accommodating; and [Talleyrand] has been to me personally most obliging and conciliatory, and has ceased to thwart me as he did, possibly unintentionally, at first[4].

All the evidence suggests that Wellington performed his official tasks competently, and that he clearly understood the diplomatic and strategic issues at stake. But at another level - as the public embodiment of his country - his embassy was less successful. Among close friends Wellington could be charming, even playful, but his social graces were over-stretched by the demands of Paris. His marriage was not a happy one and in his five years in the Peninsula he had not been devoid of feminine company, although he was discreet. In Paris, he threw discretion to the winds, despite the fact that his wife joined him in October. No one (except perhaps the Duchess) would have minded his

3. Wellington to Liverpool, 7 Nov 1814, *ibid* Vol IX pp422-33.

4. Castlereagh to Wellington, 21 Nov 1814, *ibid* Vol IX pp446-47.

infidelity if only he had obeyed the rules of society, but even Lady Bessborough, (no narrow-minded paragon of virtue), condemned his behaviour;

> 'The D[uke] of W[ellington] is so civil to me, and I admire him so much as a hero, that it inclines me to be partial to him, but I am afraid he is behaving very ill to that poor little woman; he is found great fault with for it, *not* on account of making her miserable or for the immorality of the fact, but the want of *procédé* and [the] publicity of his attentions to Grassini[5].

Nor was Grassini, the famous opera singer, his only liaison; it has even been suggested that he had a most undiplomatic affair with Mlle. George, a Parisian actress and a former mistress of Napoleon, who was currently causing a scandal by appearing on stage wearing a bouquet of violets - the symbol of Bonapartist hopes[6].

Yet the real problem lay not in Wellington's behaviour but in the symbolism of his appointment. As Napoleon remarked from Elba, the choice of Wellington was tactless, for no one - let alone the French - liked to be constantly reminded of their defeat. Lord Holland condemned Wellington's bad taste in accepting the embassy, yet Castlereagh must bear much of the blame for offering it to him[7]. A man of wit, charm and polish might possibly have succeeded in softening French hostility to Britain, if not making her popular, at least in the salons. But Wellington - though far from a simple soldier - lacked the ease of manner to succeed in this most nebulous of tasks.

Paris in 1814 was not a contented city. Thousands of officers and soldiers discharged from Napoleon's armies and finding the adjustment to civilian life extremely difficult, drifted to the capital where they talked over happier days, dreamt of the Emperor's return from exile, and nursed their grievances against the restored Bourbons and the Allies. Rumours and half-baked conspiracies abounded. Shots were fired at Wellington and the *Duc* d'Angoulême, and the British Government became so alarmed that Liverpool strongly urged Wellington to come home. Wellington himself felt that an uprising or coup

5. Lady Bessborough to Granville Leveson Gower, 13 Nov 1814, in Castalia, Countess Granville, ed., *Lord Granville Leveson Gower (First Earl Granville) Private Correspondence, 1781 to 1821*, London (1916) Vol II p507.

6. For Wellington's alleged liaison with Mlle George, see Elizabeth Longford, *Wellington: the Years of the Sword*, London (1969) p375; on the bunch of violets, Edith Saunders, *Napoleon and Mlle. George*, London (1958) p163.

7. Napoleon's remark is quoted by Richard Aldington in *Wellington*, London (1946) p202; Lord Holland's comment is in his *Further Memoirs of the Whig Party 1807-1821*, London (1905) p196.

was more than likely, but was reluctant to leave precipitately lest his departure alarm the King's friends. He therefore stayed until January 1815 when Paris appeared calmer.

Wellington's Paris embassy had thus been a mixed success - he had done his official business well, but his presence had probably done more harm than good. On the whole, an unobtrusive career diplomat like Sir Charles Stuart might have been a better choice. For Wellington the experience was however very important. In the Peninsula he had been exposed to the problems in Britain's diplomatic relations with Spain and Portugal, but in Paris he was faced with relations with an equal power, not a dependent ally, and so learnt the usages of peacetime diplomacy while becoming familiar with the principal difficulties facing European statesmen at the time.

At the Congress of Vienna

From Paris he went to Vienna to replace Castlereagh who was having to hurry home to defend the Government in the House of Commons. Although the social whirl of the Congress continued (albeit a little jaded by nearly five months' incessant activity) the main work had already been done. Poland and Saxony were settled, as were most of the other contentious issues, while some technical questions had been referred to specialist commisions. Yet some of the minor outstanding issues - such as the border between Austria and Bavaria - had been made much more difficult by the bitterness aroused by earlier decisions. Wellington acted carefully and cautiously, supporting Britain's friends but avoiding committing his Government where little was at stake. Castlereagh, if he had been present, might have played a more decisive role, but he had built up influence over months of negotiations which Wellington lacked. Not that Wellington was an unworthy replacement - his military victories afforded him a stature among the Continental rulers that no alternative British representative would have had - and the British Government felt more confidence in him than in any of their professional diplomats. He justified their trust by handling issues with care and skilfully avoiding entanglements and blunders. More important for the future were the contacts which he made with leading Continental statesmen, many of whom, like Count Metternich of Austria, were to dominate European diplomacy for the next 30 years.

But Wellington's presence at the Congress might have remained an obscure footnote in his long life if it had not been for the return of Napoleon from Elba. News of the Emperor's escape electrified the atmosphere. At first no one knew where he was heading. Soon word came that he had landed in southern France, but Wellington did not give him much chance of success. 'It is my opinion', he wrote to Castlereagh, 'that Buonaparte has acted upon false or no information, and that the King [Louis XVIII] will destroy him without difficulty, and in a short time'[8], while he told Lord Burghersh that Napoleon's conduct was nothing more than an *effet d'illusion*[9]. Given Wellington's extensive knowledge of the discontent in France this was not perceptive. On the other hand he did recognize that if Napoleon's progress was not nipped in the bud the affair could become serious. Even so, he was imagining the necessity for large-scale Allied intervention in a civil war in France, not the complete collapse of support for the Bourbons. But if Wellington's predictions were wide of the mark, his actions were not. There was no need to incite the Allies to unite against Napoleon - they were all anxious and determined to do so - rather, his role was to 'moderate these sentiments as much as possible, and get them on paper'[10]. He did not expect Napoleon to succeed, but he worked hard on preparations just in case. Wellington's presence in the Austrian capital, and his firm statement of British support for a new war against Napoleon if it should prove necessary, were very important. He played an active role in the military preparations and ensured that Britain - through him - would command the armies in the Low Countries, her area of greatest strategic interest on the Continent. On 28 March 1815 he left Vienna to take up this command and to begin the most famous episode in his entire career.

The Waterloo Campaign tends to obscure the significance of Wel-

8. Wellington to Castlereagh, 12 March 1815, Col John Gurwood, ed., *The Disptaches of Field Marshal the Duke of Wellington*, London (1837-44) Vol VIII pp2-3.
9. Wellington to John, Lord Burghersh, 13 March 1815, *ibid*, Vol VIII p3.

10. *Loc cit*.

lington's diplomatic activities of 1814 and 1815, making them appear a frivolous episode sandwiched between matters of greater importance. In some ways of course this is quite true: nothing in his later life, not even the great political crisis of 1828-30 when he was Prime Minister, could equal in significance the re-establishment of Britain as a great military power on the Continent for the first time since Marlborough, or the final overthrow of Napoleon. Yet the months of diplomacy in Paris and Vienna were a foretaste of what was to come - of Wellington's second career as a statesman. Wellington was never as successful as a diplomat or as a politician as he had been as a soldier. His early training, character and habits of mind made him better suited to bearing heavy responsibility on his own with the matching authority to act decisively without consulting others, than to the give and take of political compromise. Nonetheless it is too easy to overlook his contribution as one of the most senior members of Liverpool's cabinet for a decade; as the Prime Minister who introduced Catholic Emancipation, and as an elder statesman in the emerging Conservative Party. Yet even Lord Holland, that ardent Whig, acknowledged of Wellington that, 'He was a great man in the field, and a more considerable one in a Cabinet than his sorry exhibitions in the Senate led the Parliamentary public to suppose'[11].

11. Lord Holland, *op cit*, p193.

LESLEY SMURTHWAITE

1. Major-General Sir W F P Napier, *History of the War in the Peninsula*, London (1895) Vol II p401.

'Napoleon's troops fought in bright fields where every helmet caught some beams of glory, but the British Soldier conquered under the cold shade of aristocracy. No honours awaited his daring, no despatch gave his name to the applauses of his countrymen, his life of danger and hardship was uncheered by hope, his death unnoticed...[1]

Whether the soldier serving with Wellington's army in the Peninsula, or further afield in North America or the West Indies, gave any thought at the time to honours and mentions in despatches, or whether his concerns lay with more immediate and mundane rewards, is a matter for conjecture. Far from worrying about the decorations his country might bestow upon him, it is probable that the average soldier, often attempting to survive under appalling conditions, scarcely hoped to see that country again.

Economy was no doubt a contributory factor in the Government's reluctance to issue visible and tangible rewards to every one of the thousands of soldiers and sailors who performed loyally in the service of their country. For officers however, a need had long been felt to encourage and reward service in the Army through the bestowal of honours, a need which was eventually to be met, somewhat unsatisfactorily, through the Order of the Bath, and the institution of the Army Gold Medals and Crosses during the Peninsular War.

Early Awards

In late-eighteenth century Britain, although military rewards in the form of Orders and medals were, by comparison with most European countries, sparingly given, they were by no means unprecedented. During the English Civil Wars a number of medals and badges had been struck for issue both to Royalists and Parliamentarians, most notably perhaps, Charles I's 'Forlorn Hope' Medal of 1643. The Dunbar Medal, authorised by Oliver Cromwell in 1650, had the distinction of being the first campaign medal officially sanctioned by the Government for award to officers *and* men of the Army alike, although there is no evidence to confirm that it was intended for award to *all* officers and men.

Awards made by the East India Company

During the following century medals were not awarded officially on any scale, until in 1784 the East India Company saw fit to reward its native troops by issuing medals for their services in the First Maratha War (1778-82) and the Second Mysore War (1780-83). The Deccan Medal was to be the first of several campaign awards issued by the East India Company at its own expense, with the sanction of the British Government, which, it would appear, had no objection to these and other medals awarded by private institutions, provided that no cost was incurred by the Crown. However, the example set by the Company was to be a major influence in changing the Government's policy with regard to the issue of medals to its own troops.

Most awards made by the East India Company were designed and struck at the Calcutta Mint, usually in gold for officers and silver for other ranks. The medal for Seringapatam (1799) however was designed by the German engraver Conrad Heinrich Küchler, working at the Birmingham Mint, who was responsible for a number of fine commemorative medals struck during the reign of George III. Awarded to both British troops and sepoys who served in the successful operations against Seringapatam in 1799 which ended the wars against Tipu Sultan, it was produced in five different metals. The design on the obverse is of the British Lion triumphing over Tipu's tiger, and the reverse depicts the fortress of Seringapatam under attack. Officers of the East India Company received royal sanction to wear the medal in 1815, while British Army officers were denied that privilege until 1851. The medal was issued unnamed, although the National Army Museum has in its collection one in silver-gilt, privately engraved with the name of Major-General Ross Lang, who was at the time command-ing the 2nd Division, 2nd Regiment of Madras European Infantry. This example has been enclosed in a decorative gilt rim and bears on the ribbon an ornate gilt clasp inscribed SERINGAPATAM. It is suspended from a crimson ribbon with dark blue edges, and would have been worn around the neck, as was the practice for General Officers, (NAM.6310-49).

In a General Order dated 31 July 1802 the Governor-General authorised the award of a medal for troops despatched from India to Egypt in 1801 under Major-General David Baird, to support Sir Ralph Abercromby's attack against the French army of occupation. The EIC's medal was engraved and struck at the Calcutta Mint, in gold and silver, and depicts on its obverse a sepoy supporting the Union Flag, below which is a Persian inscription which translates as 'This medal has been presented in commemoration of the defeat of the French Armies in the kingdom of Egypt by the great bravery of the victorious army of England'. On its reverse, a man-of-war is shown sailing towards the coast of Egypt. The medal was intended to be worn suspended from a yellow silk cord and bears a ring suspender for this purpose. Among British troops eligible to receive the medal were the 8th Light Dragoons, the 10th, 80th, 86th and 88th Regiments of Foot and the Royal Artillery. Although authorised in 1802 it was not actually to be issued until nine years later (General Order, Commmander-in-Chief 13 May 1811).

Another medal, struck in gold and silver and awarded by the East India Company to their troops, commemorates the capture of Java from the Dutch in 1811. Although a number of British troops took part and received the Java Medal, only those in the service of the Company were allowed to wear it, (NAM.8707-43).

Foreign Awards to British Officers

British officers who served during the campaign in Egypt in 1801 received a medal distributed by the Sultan of Turkey. This medal in gold, bearing a crescent and eight-pointed star within an ornamental border and, on its reverse, the cypher of Sultan Selim III, is generally suspended by means of a small gold chain and sharp pointed hook. It was made in four sizes according to the rank of the officer who received it, and was an extension of the Order of the Crescent, founded by Sultan Selim in 1799, originally as a special reward to Admiral Nelson for his victory at Aboukir Bay in 1798. The medal awarded to Sir John Moore, who served in Egypt under Abercromby, is inlaid with diamonds, (NAM.6310-61-3). Another example in the Museum's Collection was awarded to Captain Alexander Godley of the 28th (or North Gloucestershire) Regiment of Foot, which fought with distinction under Moore's command, (NAM.7112-34).

The experience of the Peninsular War brought a greater realisation of the wide discrepancy between Britain and her Allies with regard to the method and extent of rewarding distinguished service, and to the fact that no equivalent existed in the British Army to the numerous Orders and decorations that were handed out to their Continental counterparts.

British officers who served in the armies of other nations were often rewarded with their highest honours. Major-General Thomas St Clair of the Buffs, who fought in the Portuguese Army with the 5th Regiment of *Cacadores*, received the Portuguese Officers' Cross for four and five Peninsular actions as well as a Portuguese Cross and a medal for the Battle of Nive in 1813, and was subsequently invested with the Portuguese Military Order of St Benedict of Aviz, and the Ancient and Most Noble Order of the Tower and Sword, (NAM.6907-30).

The Order of the Bath

An awareness of the difference between our own country's attitude to honours and awards and that of other nations had helped in some measure to bring about the evolution of the Order of the Bath during the eighteenth century as an award for distinguished military service. Fourth in seniority after the Orders of the Garter, the Thistle and St Patrick, the Bath had been revived by George II in 1725 initially as a political rather than a military institution, but it progressively came to represent an award for military merit. George II celebrated his victory at the Battle of Dettingen in 1743 by the appointment of four General Officers to the Order, and as time went by it became more and more restricted to men of naval and military or diplomatic distinction, a process hastened by George III after his accession in 1760.

Distinguished commanders such as General George Augustus Eliott, defender of Gibraltar during the War of American Independence, and Lord Nelson were admitted to the Order of the Bath on this basis, and it no longer devolved upon the Knights of the Order to pay their own fees, following Nelson's refusal to do so. John Moore was admitted to the Order in 1804, in recognition of his many years of outstanding service, (NAM 6310-61-1) and Sir Arthur Wellesley succeeded to a vacancy in the Order of the Bath created by the death of Nelson in 1805. At that time the restriction on numbers admitted to the Order had not yet been lifted. The original statutes set the limit at 35, but in 1812, when it became evident that the war had produced far too many deserving candidates to adhere to this restriction any longer, a new statute removed all limitations on numbers.

The Maida Medal

The first and perhaps rarest medal of the wars against France to be sanctioned by the Crown for service on land was occasioned by Major-General Sir John Stuart's triumph at Maida in 1806. A gold medal, bearing the portrait of George III, was to be given to officers of field rank and above who had been present at the battle. The General Order, signed by HRH the Duke of York, Commander-in-Chief and dated 22 February 1808 reads: '…His Majesty having approved of the Medal which has been struck upon this occasion, is pleased to command that it should be worn suspended by a Ribband of the colour of the sash [crimson], with a blue edge, from a button of the coat, on the left side'. Thirteen officers of the rank of Lieutenant Colonel and above, including Major-General Stuart, commander of the British troops in Sicily, are listed. In the event, four others of major's rank are known to have received the medal, making a total of 17 in all. This superbly executed gold medal bears on its reverse the figure of Britannia in a warlike attitude, aiming her spear, with a trinacria, the symbol of Sicily, behind her; in front of her the word MAIDA and the date (1806) in Roman numerals. Stuart received the thanks of Parliament plus £1,000 a year for life, was created a Knight of the Bath, and also Count of Maida by the King of Naples. The City of London voted him its freedom and a sword.

The Army Gold Medal and Army Gold Cross

The Maida Medal set a precedent for the award of medals to those senior officers who distinguished themselves in subsequent campaigns. On 9 September 1810 a General Order was issued from Horse Guards announcing that, 'His Majesty having been graciously pleased to command that, in commemoration of the brilliant victories obtained by Divisions of His Army over the Enemy in the battles of Roleia, Vimiera, also in the several instances where the Cavalry had an opportunity of distinguishing themselves against the Enemy in Spain, and in the Battles of Corunna, and Talavera de la Reyna, the undermentioned Officers of the Army, present on these occasions, should enjoy the privilege of bearing a Medal'.

The gold medals were struck in two sizes, though the design of both (by Thomas Wyon Jr), is identical, the larger intended for General Officers, and the smaller for field officers. Examples of these most elegant awards are rare, especially the large version, of which only 85 were issued, while 596 small gold medals were awarded in total. The medals could be awarded posthumously, as was Sir John Moore's posthumous Large Gold Medal for Corunna, (NAM.6310-61-2).

Often erroneously described as 'Peninsular Gold Medals', these medals represent actions in the war against France, not only in Portugal, Spain and France, but also in Egypt, the West and East Indies and North America. Obviously, many officers were entitled to receive more than one medal, in consequence of services performed in a number of campaigns. From the necessity of recognising several distinctions and the inconvenience of having to wear two or more medals, arose the decision to institute a further decoration, the Army Gold Cross. Under a General Order of 7 October 1813, officers who distinguished themselves in further actions after receiving a medal were entitled to wear up to two gold clasps, bearing the names of the actions, upon the ribbon. On entitlement to a fourth distinction they would receive a gold cross. Further actions would be denoted by clasps similar to those worn with the medals. The maximum number of clasps to be awarded to any one recipient was nine, denoting 13 actions in all, the Duke of Wellington himself being the only bearer of such a distinction. In all, 163 Gold Crosses were issued, with an additional 237 clasps.

The National Army Museum's Collection includes the Gold Cross of General Sir John Ormsby Vandeleur, who after a brilliant military career in India, served with equal distinction in the Peninsula and at Waterloo. His Cross is inscribed: Cuidad Rodrigo, Salamanca, Vittoria and Nive, and his Gold Medal for Cuidad Rodrigo bears clasps for Salamanca and Vittoria, (NAM 6310-47). In 1815, when the Order of the Bath was revised, and General Vandeleur was one of those officers appointed to the newly created division of Knight Commanders.

Despite the widespread award of Army Gold Crosses and Medals to senior officers in recognition of their services in the Wars against France, officers of lower rank still received no equivalent encouragement or reward, an omission which occasioned much criticism and discontent. In 1811, Lieutenant-General Sir Thomas Graham, later Lord Lynedoch, writing to the Prime Minister, Lord Liverpool, said of the Army Gold Medals , 'I own it is impossible for me to understand on what principle (generally speaking) *all* the officers of a *particular description & Rank* shd. be entitled to a reward of this kind, while *none* of an *inferior Rank* can be admitted for the most transcendent merit'.[2]

2. Anthony Brett-James, *General Graham, Lord Lynedoch*, London (1959) p222.

The Order of the Bath Extended

When the war in the Peninsula ended, it was decided that the Naval and Military Gold Medals and Crosses should cease to be issued, and their place should be taken by the revised Order of the Bath. Under its new constitution (laid down in the Royal Warrant of 2 January

1815), the Order was '...to be composed of three classes "differing in their ranks and degrees of dignity"'. The First Class of the Order (Knights Grand Cross) which admitted 72 members (including all those hitherto admitted as Knights) was to be limited to officers in the Army with the rank of Major-General and above. The Second Class (Knight Commanders) extended to colonels or above. Out of 180 places, ten were reserved for foreign officers holding British commissions. The Third Class (Companions) had no limitation in numbers, but was open to officers who already held a 'medal or other badge of honour' - thereby effectively reserving this class for field officers. An additional clause (6 January 1815) enabled 15 KCBs to be elected from officers of the East India Company and an unspecified number of CBs were allowed to 'certain' officers of the Company.

Even under its revised statutes, the Order of the Bath was soon to be seen as deficient and receive criticism, not the least from the Duke of Wellington himself, who wrote, 'I confess that I do not concur in the limitation of the Order to Field Officers. Many Captains in the Army conduct themselves in a very meritorious manner and deserve it; and I never could see the reason for excluding them either from the Order or the Medal' (referring of course to the Field Officers' Gold Medal).[3] Incredibly, it was to be over 70 years before the merits of officers of junior rank could be recognised by an award in any way equivalent to the CB, by the creation of the Distinguished Service Order in 1886.

3. Wellington to the Duke of York, 28 Jun 1815, Col John Gurwood, *The Wellington Dispatches*, London (1837-44) Vol XII p520.

The Waterloo Medal

'By God! I don't think it would have been done if I had not been there.

Until 1815, little had changed the soldier's meagre expectation of tangible or visible rewards for his loyal service to the Crown. It was largely due to Wellington's personal efforts that the Waterloo Medal, a landmark in the history and evolution of British campaign medals, came into existence. In a letter to the Duke of York, dated 28 June 1815, only ten days after the battle, he wrote: 'I would likewise beg leave to suggest to your Royal Highness the expediency of giving to the

4. *Loc cit.*

5. Wellington to Bathurst, 17 Sep 1815, *ibid* p636.

6. A A Payne, *British and Foreign Orders, War Medals and Decorations*, Sheffield (1911) p54.

non-commissioned officers and soldiers engaged in the battle of Waterloo a Medal. I am convinced it would have the best effect in the army; and, if that battle should settle our concerns, they will well deserve it'.[4] Shortly after, he was to send a further despatch from Paris, declaring that, 'I have long intended to write to you about the Medal for Waterloo. I recommend that we should all have the same Medal, hung to the same riband as that now used with the [Army Gold] Medals'.[5]

Accordingly, a memorandum dated 10 March 1816 was issued from Horse Guards stating that 'The Prince Regent has been graciously pleased, in the name and on behalf of His Majesty, to command, that in commemoration of the brilliant and decisive victory of Waterloo, a Medal shall be conferred on every officer, non-commissioned officer, and soldier of the British Army, present upon that memorable occasion'.[6]

The Waterloo Medal is significant in being the first campaign medal awarded, in identical form, to officers and men of all ranks, and additionally in being given to the next-of-kin of those who died in the battle. Designed by Thomas Wyon and struck in silver, it was also the first of many medals on which the recipient's name was impressed around the edge, using a newly invented machine constructed at the Royal Mint by Thomas Jerome and Charles Harrison. Despite its title, the medal was awarded to everyone who had been present at the Battles of Ligny and Quatre Bras on 16 June or Waterloo on 18 June 1815.

Hanoverian Awards

Among the troops in British service to receive the Waterloo Medal, the King's German Legion formed a significant part of Wellington's army. One of their number, who fought with distinction in the Peninsula and France and survived to claim his Military General Service Medal with ten clasps, was Corporal Georg Oelmann (variously spelt Ohlmann or Oehlmann) of the 1st Regiment of Hussars. His group, which includes the Guelphic Medal for Gallantry, is in the

Museum's Collection, (NAM.8907-79). This medal, instituted in 1815, was intended to reward non-commissioned officers and men of the Hanoverian Army who had distinguished themselves by acts of gallantry. It hangs from a light blue ribbon similar to that of the Guelphic Order, of which it forms part, but unlike the Order, the medal could only be bestowed upon Germans. The infrequency with which this medal was awarded may have been in part due to the annual pension of 24 *thalers* (£5) that accompanied it, added to which, each recommendation for the medal had to be attested by two officers. The medal could not be awarded posthumously.

In addition to the British Waterloo Medal, the Prince Regent authorised in December 1817 an equivalent medal for award to the Hanoverian troops who had fought in the battle. Designed in silver by William Wyon, it also bore the Prince's portrait, but was inscribed in German, and on the reverse carried the legend: 'HANNOVERSCHER TAPFERKEIT' [Hanoverian Bravery], NAM.6312-25.

In 1815 the Prince Regent founded the Royal Hanoverian Guelphic Order to commemorate the establishment of Hanover as a Kingdom, and initially at least, to reward high-ranking British and Hanoverian officers of the Army who had distinguished themselves in the Waterloo Campaign. Like the newly reformed Order of the Bath, the Guelphic Order was divided into three classes. Membership of the First Class (Knights Grand Cross) was open to Lieutenant-Generals and above. Its particularly handsome insignia includes a Badge executed in gold and enamels in the form of an eight-pointed cross surmounted by the Guelphic Crown with the Brunswick lion passant gardant between the arms, and in the centre, on a red enamelled ground the White Horse of Hanover courant, surrounded by, on a blue enamelled circle the Motto of the Order: 'NEC ASPERA TERRENT' [Difficulties do not terrify], the circle being enclosed in a green enamelled laurel wreath.

Regimental Awards

Awards bestowed upon General Officers and field officers were almost certainly intended to be regarded by the soldiers who had served with them as honours in whose reflected glory they could share. At the same time, the officers who received them must have felt to some extent bound to express their gratitude for the loyal service of the common soldiers, particularly in the light of the Government's failure to do so. These sentiments undoubtedly contributed to the decisions of many regimental authorities and individual officers to commission and distribute, at their own expense, medals for campaign service, for gallantry, meritorious service or skill-at-arms.

Regimental medals, bestowed in their greatest numbers during the years immediately after Waterloo, undoubtedly influenced the Government's eventual decision to award the campaign medals that would proliferate during the later-nineteenth century. Yet their variety and individuality often makes them objects of greater immediacy and appeal than the official awards that would in time supersede them.

The creation of the Waterloo Medal heightened the Army's awareness of a need to recognise the worth of those who had fought with equal, if not greater, fortitude in earlier battles, and a considerable number of medals and decorations were produced by regiments to reward their men (and often officers) for their service in Europe, and overseas. A typical example is the Order of Merit of the 88th Connaught Rangers, authorised for issue to survivors of the Peninsular War. It was granted by Lieutenant-General Sir J A Wallace and the officers of the regiment, and sanctioned by the Commander-in-Chief in 1818. It was divided into three classes, dependent upon the number of actions in which the recipient had been involved. The First Class took the form of a silver cross in recognition of 12 actions, the Second Class was a silver medal, given to those involved in seven to 11 actions, while the Third Class medal was issued for one to seven actions. The names of the actions were inscribed upon the reverse of the cross or medal. The 94th Scotch Brigade issued a similar Order of Merit, in two classes, consisting of medals in silver and bronze, bearing a clasp inscribed with the word 'Peninsula'. Sergeant George Bain, who was awarded the 1st Class for his service in ten actions, lived to claim, many years after, the Military General Service Medal with the same number of clasps, (NAM.5102-17-8).

Medals awarded to individuals by their regiments for specific acts of gallantry or merit are comparatively rare and of correspondingly greater interest than those distributed in larger numbers for campaign service. The appeal of these early awards is enhanced by their usually being hand-engraved, with designs ranging from extreme simplicity to elaborate detail. Often, they depict the event commemorated and frequently bear an inscription which includes the name of the recipient, the officer who presented it and the circumstances of its award.

Regimental medals were no less generously awarded to the Militia and Volunteers, raised during the Wars with France to defend the country against possible invasion. It may have been felt that these part-time soldiers were in even greater need than their regular counterparts serving overseas of incentives in the form of visible rewards such as medals for merit, as they were not having to fight in order to clothe and feed themselves, but out of a sense of patriotism and loyalty to their country. Certainly the medals that were issued to the Volunteer units, occasionally by societies or private institutions, though more often by their colonels or commanding officers, have no equivalent in the armies of other European countries.

Some medals were struck to commemorate momentous events, or acts of bravery in the face of the enemy, equal to those experienced by the regulars fighting overseas. They include awards to men of the Irish Militia who helped to repel the French expedition against Ireland. The silver Bantry Garrison Medal was awarded by the Friendly Association of Ireland to the officers and men of the Galway Militia who confronted the ill-fated French expedition to Bantry Bay in 1796. Another medal, the Limerick Militia Medal for Coloony 1798, represents the defeat of General Humbert's expeditionary force by a combined army of Irish Militia and regulars.

Most of the Volunteer medals however, were given as individual awards for merit or skill-at-arms, in particular prizes won in shooting competitions or at target practice. As these medals were generally commissioned and paid for by the officers, it is not surprising that their design and quality varies, depending largely upon the affluence of the regiment or the finances of an individual officer. The Bank of England Volunteers for example could afford to distribute fine-quality gold medals to men who qualified for prizes in shooting contests. The Museum Collection includes an example awarded to Private Joseph Lewin of the Bank's light company, who took third place in a regimental shooting match in1805, (NAM.8707-37).

Some medals incorporate sentiments of a patriotic or inspiring nature, such as the impressive and weighty gold medal awarded to the Loyal Briton Volunteers, whose poetic inscription reads; 'For our country and King may our efforts ne'er cease Till from Victories palm springs the olive of peace'. More prosaically, on the reverse it records; 'Presented by Col Davison to the Best Shot of the Battalion 20 April 1807', (NAM.7506-73-10).

Most Volunteer medals, however, were engraved in silver, usually round or oval in shape, typically bearing inscriptions such as; 'For exemplary Conduct', 'Reward of Merit' or 'Testimony of Merit'. Most include some form of of suspension, and there is no doubt that these medals were intended to be worn in uniform. Sadly, few of the ribbons or other attachments that would have been used by the wearers of regimental medals at this period have survived.

Some of the finest examples were awarded to men whose terms of enlistment with the regiment or corps had expired. A number of these were issued in 1802 and 1814 when Volunteer units were disbanded. Although most individual Volunteer medals are found to be engraved, those of the latter category were often struck or cast, occasionally from coins bearing the head of the sovereign, or commemorative medals, particularly that of Küchler commemorating the Peace of Amiens in 1802, which was also converted into a medal for skill-at-arms, (NAM.8408-61). Other examples include Matthew Boulton's medal commemorating the Birmingham Loyal Association and Birmingham Light Horse Volunteers (NAM.8606-86) and the silver medal of the Royal Bristol Volunteers, struck in 1814, (NAM.6212-91).

The Military General Service Medal

It may seem unaccountable that the Duke of Wellington who so applauded the conduct of his troops in the Peninsula, and was himself instrumental in establishing the award of the Waterloo Medal, should have resisted the institution of an equivalent honour to those who had served in campaigns in Spain and Portugal. Yet in 1845, in a House of Lords debate occasioned by a petition presented by the Duke of Richmond on behalf of Peninsular veterans, Wellington defended his position with the argument that 'the battle of Waterloo was an occurrence of an extraordinary nature'. He stressed that the Army in the Peninsula had been sufficiently rewarded through the thanks of Parliament, not to mention the medals and Orders conferred upon its officers. 'New modes were discovered and adopted of distinguishing and rewarding the officers; medals were struck in commemoration of actions of gallantry performed in the Peninsula upon not less than 19 occasions, and these medals were distributed to the officers of that army .... and distributed, I understand, to not less than 1,300 officers. Will any man contend that that is not a considerable number in any army to receive such marks of distinction?'[7]

He was supported by the Marquess of Londonderry, who maintained that it was 'totally unworthy of British officers' to seek 'compensation and reward' not to mention 'unconstitutional', and 'he was certain that afterwards, when sitting by their own firesides, these very officers would think a medal so obtained totally without value'. The Duke of Richmond riposted that, 'All that these undecorated officers asked was, some memorial to show that they were the individuals to whom for these 16 actions the House had given its thanks.... It was very well' he argued 'for those who were covered with decorations to say, "Don't give medals to captains and subaltern officers, and non-commissioned officers and privates". He [the Duke of Richmond] should like to know whether, without these officers and men, they would have got their honours themselves'. He added even that 'with regard to the Waterloo honours, he knew of one corps which received them that did not know of the action till some days after it was fought'.

7. An extract from the debate is given in G Tancred, *Historical Record of Medals and Honorary Distinctions*, London (1891).

Ultimately the petition achieved its objective and long overdue recognition was given to the Peninsular veterans. Nearly 33 years and three British monarchs after the last battle it would commemorate, a medal was authorised under a General Order, dated 1 June 1847, which stated: 'Her Majesty [Queen Victoria] having been graciously pleased to command that a medal should be struck to record the services of her fleets and armies during the wars commencing in 1793 and ending in 1814, and that one should be conferred upon every officer, non-commissioned officer and soldier of the army who was present in any battle or siege...'. The Egyptian campaign of 1801 was not recognised by a clasp to the Military General Service Medal until three years later, under a General Order, dated 12 February 1850.

In all, 29 clasps were issued with the medal,[8] which, although called the Military General Service Medal 1793-1814, commemorated no campaigns earlier than 1801. The most clasps to be awarded to any individual was 15 (two recipients, Corporal James Talbot, 45th Foot and Private Daniel Loochstadt, who is listed both on the roll of the 60th Foot and of the King's German Legion), while 11 soldiers are believed to have received 14 clasps.[9] Medals could be issued to the next-of-kin of those who applied but died before the medal could be issued. It is astounding that, despite the limited life-expectancy of the period, and the fact that many survivors, owing to poor communications, may not have known of the award, over 25,000 applications were received.

The medal is designed to be worn suspended by means of a plain swivelling suspender upon a crimson ribbon with blue edges, similar to that of the Waterloo Medal only narrower. The clasps worn on the ribbon, like those of the Army Gold Medal, range through campaigns in Spain and Portugal, the South of France, the East and West Indies, North America and Egypt. Some of the more interesting examples of this medal combine actions as far apart as Martinique (30 January-24 February 1809) and Talavera (27-28 July 1809), and among the rarest are those for the cavalry actions at Sahagun (21 December 1808) and Benevente (29 December 1808), and the North American battles denoted by the clasps: Fort Detroit (16 August 1812), Chateauguay (26 October 1813) and

8. Egypt (1801); Maida (1806); Roleia (1808); Vimiera (1808); Sahagun (1808); Benevente (1808); Sahagun and Benevente (1808); Corunna (1809); Martinique (1809); Talavera (1809); Guadaloupe (1810); Busaco (1810); Barrosa (1811); Fuentes D'Onor (1811); Albuhera (1811); Java (1811); Ciudad Rodrigo (1812); Badajoz (1812); Salamanca (1812); Fort Detroit (1812); Vittoria (1813); Pyrenees (1813); St Sebastian (1813); Chateauguay (1813); Nivelle (1813); Chrystler's Farm (1813); Nive (1813); Orthes (1813); Toulouse (1814).
9. The Medal Roll however lists only nine: John Hughes, Royal Artillery; George Legg, Royal Artillery (only 13 clasps recorded on the roll); Sgt John Hardy, 7th Foot; Drum-Major John Green, 45th Foot; Edward Kean, 45th Foot; Sgt James Nixon, 45th Foot; Major James Campbell, 50th Foot; Patrick Haggerty, 52nd Foot; James Morris, 52nd Foot; Lieutenant Sir J H Schoedde, 60th Foot; Sgt Joseph Hindle, 95th Foot. A L T Mullen ed., *The Military General Service Medal Roll 1793-1814*, London (1990).

Chrystler's Farm (11 November 1813).

A number of medals bearing one or more of these last three clasps was awarded to Indian warriors who with the Canadian Militia made a significant contribution to the British cause in the American War of 1812. Sadly, their efforts in many areas went unrecorded, as no clasps were authorised for actions at such places as Fort York (Toronto), Beaver Dams and Queenston Heights, where Indians fought bravely on the British side. Medals bearing the clasp Chrystler's Farm have however been found with unofficial clasps for 'Stoney Creek', 'Fort George' and 'Queenston' added to the ribbon. Many of the Indians probably did not apply for the medal at all, as it is unlikely that in all cases news of its award ever reached them. The example bearing the clasp: Chrystler's Farm and inscribed with the name John Pegeon Omeme, Warrior 1813, is all the rarer and more interesting for this reason. Omeme is believed to be one of 30 Mohawk Indians recruited to fight under Lieutenant Colonel Joseph Morrison, commanding the 2nd Battalion, 89th Foot, in a successful bid on 11 November 1813 to repel the advance of the Americans on Montreal, (NAM.7006-27).

Two other rare examples relating to the American War of 1812 are the Medal bearing the clasp: Fort Detroit, awarded to Private George Bond, serving in the 3rd York Regiment, Upper Canada Militia, (NAM.8203-1) and another with the clasp: Chateauguay, to Sergeant Joseph Baillargeon, 5th Battalion, Select Embodied Militia of Lower Canada, (NAM.7704-49).

The Army of India Medal

Following the precedent created by the Military General Service Medal, the Government, was to recognise in 1851 the need for the award of a Medal to all those survivors of the numerous campaigns in India between 1799 and 1826. The Army of India Medal is relatively rare, in view of the span of years that elapsed between the first action it com- memorates - Allighur (4 September 1803), and the actual issue of the medal. The ratio of survivors to those who would have qualified must have been exceedingly low, especially for the early campaigns, and hence those awarded for the Maratha War of 1803-4, particularly to Europeans, are among the most interesting. Wellington himself received the medal with clasps for Assaye (23 September), Argaum (29 November) and Gawilghur (15 December 1803), a combination of which only 13 were awarded. Twenty-one clasps were issued with the medal, ten for campaigns during the Maratha War of 1803-04. The medal awarded to Private King of the 76th Foot carries four clasps: Allighur (4 September 1803), Battle of Delhi (11 September 1803), Laswarree (1st November 1803) and Battle of Deig (13 November 1804). Only nine men of the regiment received these four clasps, and the latter clasp is especially rare, being awarded to only 49 soldiers, (NAM.7711-235).

Unlike the Military General Service Medal, and most other campaign medals that were to follow, this medal is unusual in that the clasps worn on the ribbon read downwards, or chronologically with the earliest campaign represented by the clasp positioned highest. The medal is suspended by means of an ornate swivelling bar suspender, upon a pale blue ribbon.

Commemorative Medals

A survey of awards and medals during the period of the Napoleonic Wars cannot exclude those medals which were produced purely for commemorative purposes. Although they were rarely intended to be awarded or worn, the themes, subjects and events that they record, and the technology and artistry that helped to create them, make them important not just as an enduring pictorial record of historical events and persons, but also as having a lasting influence stylistically on the production of medals intended for official award throughout the nineteenth century and later.

A landmark in the history of medal production in Britain was the establishment, towards the end of the eighteenth century, of Matthew Boulton's Soho Manufactury at Birmingham. The technical advances in medal manufacturing in Birmingham attracted the work of highly talented and celebrated artists in the field, many from the Continent, such as Conrad Heinrich Küchler, and the Wyons, a distinguished family of medal engravers originally from Germany, who not only produced many significant commemorative medals recording military, political and social events, but were between them responsible for the designs of most of the campaign medals awarded throughout the century.

Perhaps the most famous group of medals commemorating Britain's victories against France in the period 1794 to 1815 was the series of 40 medals struck in 1820 under the direction of the publisher James Mudie, by Edward Thomason, apprentice and partner to Matthew Boulton. Mudie's series of 'National Medals' provides an impressive record of British military and naval achievements, and includes scenes of the various battles and events of the war together with several fine portraits of Wellington and his generals. The Duke of Wellington was himself the subject of an unprecedented number of commemorative and souvenir medals that were issued bearing his portrait, from the time of his Peninsular victories onwards, recording every public event of his life, whether military, political or social up to and including his death.

A prominent and influential medallist working at this time was Benedetto Pistrucci, an Italian who arrived in Britain in 1815, and was to rival William Wyon not only technically and artistically, but also politically in the field of medal production, eventually becoming Chief Medallist at the Royal Mint when Wyon was appointed Chief Engraver in 1828. Pistrucci was commissioned in 1819, for the handsome fee of £2,400, to design a large medal which would commemorate the victory at Waterloo, and be presented in gold to each of the four Allied sovereigns, and to the two Commanders-in-Chief, Wellington and Blücher. Unfortunately, disagreements over Pistrucci's terms of employment, combined with the technical difficulties of hardening the dies for a medal of its dimensions (135 mm. in diameter), meant that by 1849 the medal had still not achieved completion, and all but one, (the Duke of Wellington), of the intended recipients had died. The original idea had to be abandoned, and the medal was eventually produced only in bronze electrotype form, (NAM.6310-94) or in gutta-percha.[10]

10. Gum produced from the Malayan percha tree, first used in medal production, c1845.

The Wearing of Medals

It was during the Napoleonic Wars that decorations first began to appear on British Army uniforms in any quantity, and it was therefore at this time that the problem of regularising their method of wear was first given serious consideration. Decorations were worn, as contemporary portraits can testify, with considerable panache by many of their recipients, though admittedly often with more regard to effect than to rules of precedence or practicality. Rules were included with the statutes of the Army Gold Medals and Crosses, to the general effect that they should be worn upon ribbons around the neck by General Officers, and for all other officers the ribbon should be attached 'to the button-hole of their uniform' i.e. worn through a button-hole in the lapel of the coatee and attached by a loop on to a button behind it. This method of wear was largely dictated by the style of uniforms worn at the time, and although it was originally intended that the Waterloo Medal should be worn in this way, after 1815 the removal of open lapels from the uniform necessitated the introduction of a buckle, which formed, in the case of the Companion Badge of the Order of the Bath, an integral part of the decoration.[11]

The Duke of Wellington himself commented upon the impracticality of medals worn around the neck in a letter to Earl Bathurst, dated 16 March 1813; 'I am not certain that it would not be best that all general officers, as well as others, should wear the medal or cross at the button-hole... It is very awkward to ride in round the neck'.[12] In general, at this period, and for some time after, as contemporary portraits show, medals, decorations and even Orders of chivalry, were worn very much at the personal whim and design of their wearer. The Duke of Wellington himself was no exception in this respect.

The Influence of Wellington

Any discussion of the system of honours and awards and its evolution in Britain during and after the the Napoleonic Wars must inevitably involve the views of the Duke of Wellington, whose influence pervaded all aspects of military and political life from that time until his death.

11. For a further discussion of this topic, see S C Wood, 'Soldiers, Decorations and the Dictates of Fashion', *National Army Museum Annual Report 1978-1979* pp21-29.

12. Gurwood, *op cit* Vol X, p199.

He was, as we know, a firm believer that amongst officers of the Army and indeed in other spheres, honours and awards should be freely and fairly given regardless of rank where they were due. Writing of the Gold Medals and Crosses for the Peninsula he declared; 'In regard of the medals, I have always been of the opinion, that government should have extended the principle more than they did; and in executing their orders, I believe it will be found that, whenever a medal could be given to an individual under the orders of government, I have inserted his name in the return'.[13] In later years, regarding the Order of the Garter, Lord Stanhope recorded; 'The Duke thinks it of great importance to the Order that it should now and then be given (as his own and Lord Wellesley's) for actual service. If it be merely assigned as a sort of appendage to high birth and rank, it will ere long come to be despised by these persons themselves'.[14]

He accepted with modest appreciation the numerous Orders and medals that were bestowed upon him by his own and other countries. When asked to resign the Order of the Bath, on his admission to the Garter in 1813, he wrote to the Prime Minister, Lord Liverpool 'God knows I have plenty of Orders, and I consider myself to have been most handsomely treated by the Prince Regent and his Government, and shall not consider myself the less so, if you should not think it proper that I should retain the Order of the Bath'.[15] Although this request was denied him, he was of course to be created GCB in 1815.[16]

He may have remained intractable to the end on the question of awarding a medal to the thousands of soldiers who had fought beside him through the campaigns that led up to his final victory over Napoleon. Yet, just as it was to Wellington that the nation owed this victory, it was to him the army owed the creation of the Waterloo Medal, the first campaign award to all officers and men alike, making no distinction in rank, that would serve as a model upon which to base all future campaign medals.

13. Letter to Sir William Carr Beresford, 6 Nov 1813, ibid, Vol XI p256.

14. Philip Henry, 5th Earl Stanhope, *Notes of Conversations with the Duke of Wellington 1831-1851*, Oxford (1938) p281.

15. Wellington to Liverpool, 21 Mar 1813; Sir Nicholas Harris, *History of the Orders of Knighthood of the British Empire*, London (1842), Vol III, *History of the Most Honourable Order of the Bath*, p132.
16. Together with the other previously created Knights of the Bath. After 1815 the Bath ceased to be resigned on appointment to any other British Order.

DAVID G CHANDLER

'After battle sleep is best,

After noise, tranquillity.

1. In his poem, 'The Old'.

So wrote Roden Berkeley Noel (1834-1894), the minor Victorian poet.[1] Such a famous battle as Waterloo was from the first fated to receive much attention and give rise to considerable Europe-wide controversy: neither 'rest' nor 'tranquillity' was to be vouchsafed either the subject or the surviving participants.

One young man who was to become completely fascinated with the subject of Waterloo was Ensign William Siborne, who in the autumn of 1815 had found himself serving in Paris as part of the Allied Army of Occupation in the 1st Battalion of the 9th Foot (later the Royal Norfolk Regiment and today the 1st Royal Anglian Regiment).[2] This

2. *Army List*, 1815, p180.

formation, in which his father was already serving as a captain, had arrived in Belgium from Canada (where it had been taking part in the 'War of 1812' against the United States) just too late to participate in the Battle of Waterloo. While serving as part of the Allied Occupation forces in Paris, young Siborne probably saw several French battle-field 'Models of Actions' then on display in the French capital. From this conjunction of events was to arise in later years the inspiration for the research, design and construction of the two models of Waterloo which bear Siborne's name.

The Siborne Family, Father and Son

William Siborn (the family finally added the 'e' in 1834) was born at Greenwich on 18 October 1797. His family was of Scottish extraction. His father, Benjamin Siborn (c1772-1819), had married Charlotte MacCulloch, and William was their only child. His father acquired an ensigncy in the West Kent Militia in 1798, and exchanged into the 9th (East Norfolk) Regiment in August the next year, with which he served until his death in 1819.

In the intervening period he saw a great deal of active service with the 2nd Battalion under General Sir John Moore in 1808-09, under

Lord Chatham in the fever-plagued Walcheren episode of 1809; and then under Wellington's command in the Peninsula from 1810, Benjamin Siborn was gravely stricken at the battle of Nivelle (10 November 1813), receiving wounds that ultimately led to his death. In 1814 the 9th accompanied General Sir Edward Pakenham to North America, and took part in the defence of Canada returning to Europe in 1815 too late for the Battle of Waterloo. At this stage he transferred to the 1st Battalion - doubtless due to the peacetime reductions - and shared in occupation duties in France. Then the battalion was ordered to the unhealthy West Indian station, and there Siborne senior died on St Vincent on 14 July 1819, 'from the after-effects of his wounds'.[3]

His only son, meantime, had also taken up the military profession. Aged 14, William Siborn joined the Royal Military College (then still at Great Marlow) as Gentleman-Cadet, and shortly after moved to Sandhurst. He left Sandhurst in December 1814, aged 17, and was appointed to an ensigncy (backdated to 9 September 1813), in his father's battalion. He served at Canterbury, Chatham and Sheerness, but in August 1815 he transferred, like his father, to the 1st Battalion, and was posted to France, marching from Ostend to Paris, to encamp at St Denis. He was promoted lieutenant on 8 November 1815, and served until 3 April 1817, when he was placed on half-pay, the 9th having been reduced.[4]

It is clear that his interest was already strongly drawn to carto-graphical matters, for during the five years he spent on half-pay he published the first of two books on the subject: *Instructions for Civil and Military Surveyors in Topographical Plan-Drawing* (1822), followed five years later by *A Practical Treatise on Topographical Surveying and Drawing*, the revealing sub-title of which was ... *to which are added Instructions on Topographical Modelling etc.*, 'together with a very important improvement in the delineation of ground by which heights and declivities are clearly and satisfactorily expressed'.

'Nothing can tend more to facilitate the acquirement of a proper knowledge of physical geography', he wrote in June

3. National Army Museum, 7510-93, M Henderson, *A Short Memoir of the Siborne Family*.

4. *Army List*, 1817.

185

1827, 'than the study of models of different portions of the earth's surface...The importance of Topographical Modelling in a military point of view is sufficiently obvious: the government in possessing a model of the country which has become the seat of its military operations, can more fully enter into, and more justly appreciate the dispositions...The comparison of models of celebrated fields of battle with authentic descriptions of the military movements...forms an important branch of military study. The practice of constructing models from topographical drawings cannot fail to prove of very great utility to students at military seminaries and to officers in general, since it teaches them fully to comprehend the meaning of a topographical map or plan...

Earnings from Siborne's first book, which ran to a modest ten pages of prelims and 329 pages of text and illustrative plates, did not lead to a radical improvement in the young man's finances, certainly not of one now contemplating matrimony. Accordingly, on 11 November 1824 William Siborn was gazetted as lieutenant into the 47th (Lancashire) Regiment of Foot (later the Loyal Regiment (North Lancashire), and today the Queen's Lancashire Regiment), with 'Army Rank' dating back to 8 November 1815.[5] That same year saw his marriage to a Scottish lady, Helen Aitken, the daughter of a Fifeshire banker who was also colonel of the local Militia. In due course the union produced three children - one son, Herbert Taylor Siborne (1826-1902) - destined to become a Major-General and to edit *The Waterloo Letters* (1892) from a selection of his late father's papers and correspondence - (see below), and two daughters, (one of them destined to be the forbear of General Frederick 'Boy' Browning of Second World War Airborne Forces fame).

Although his new regiment was soon ordered to the Far East, Lieutenant Siborne and his bride were not destined to accompany it to India and Burma, for in March 1826 he was appointed as Assistant Military Secretary to the staff of Lieutenant-General Sir George Murray, Commander-in-Chief in Ireland, and later served in the

5. *Army List*, 1825, p204.

same capacity Sir John Byng, Sir Richard Hussey-Vivian and Sir Edward Blaker - until 31 January 1843, when he was at last promoted captain, albeit on half-pay (unattached list) and posted to the Royal Military Asylum in London.

During the long period in Dublin Siborne moved in literary circles and was a member of the dining club founded by novelist Charles Lever (1806-72). We catch a glimpse of Siborne in William Kirkpatrick's *Life of Charles Lever*: - 'Of Captain Siborne it will suffice to say that he was a perfect gentleman and a most able officer. A man of fine intellect and judgement, truly scientific, most unpretending in his manner and very well informed. Pity that the British Army was so constituted as to condemn a man like Siborne to an utterly subordinate and inadequate sphere of duty'.[6]

Nevertheless, this would not prevent him from becoming the most celebrated military modellist of his age and the author of the well known two-volume *History of the War in France and Belgium in 1815* (1844), which between them earned him an entry in the *Dictionary of National Biography*.[7]

6. W Kirkpatrick, *Life of Charles Lever*, cited in Henderson, *op cit* pp3-4.

7. *Dictionary of National Biography*, 'Siborne or Siborn, William (1797-1849)'.

The Genesis and Construction of the 1838 Waterloo Models

General Murray's Assistant Military Secretary eventually came to the notice of General Sir Rowland Hill (1772-1842), Commander-in-Chief in England, and in 1830 'Daddy' Hill invited the clearly gifted officer to construct a model of the Battle of Waterloo. The time was ripe. Already the Dutch government had erected the 125-foot high mound ('*la Butte*'), topped by its Belgian Lion, completely changing the lie of the ground along the critical sector of the Mont St Jean ridge where Napoleon's Imperial Guard was defeated. In 1830 proposals to build houses constituted a new threat (and as late as the 1960s the proposal to build a motorway across the main battlefield was only narrowly averted), so it was necessary to hasten. It was clearly intimated that the work would be paid for from public funds, and so William Siborne applied for long leave, and set off for Waterloo, where he lodged for eight months on the battlefield at the farm of La

Haie Sainte. There he made an accurate survey of the ground, and set about modelling the topographical features accurately. It had already struck Siborne that if he was to achieve accuracy with his proposed model in terms of military detail it would be necessary to gather the recollections of as many surviving officers as possible who had participated in the action on 18 June 1815. With Hill's permission, therefore, he had sent out a circular letter, which asked precisely where their units had been sited at 'about 7pm', what enemy formations were to their front, and the state of the crops in their vicinity, and invited further comments on the parts they had played at Waterloo and during the preceding days.[8]

8. A version is reproduced in H T Siborne, *The Waterloo Letters* London, (1891) reprinted 1983, ppix-xi. See also NAM.7612-19 p8, Questionnaire sent to Sir H Merry, 8th Hussars, and his replies.

He seems to have elicited some 700 replies, only 200 of which were later selected by his son for inclusion in *The Waterloo Letters* at the end of the century. The remainder, gathered in six volumes, have lain, virtually unnoticed until quite recently, among the Additional Manuscripts at the British Library.[9] This diligence amounts to an early attempt by a British soldier to conduct operational research on the basis of participants' memories, gathered though these were years after the battle. Siborne hoped that by comparing sources he could arrive at '...a most faithful and authentic record of the battle despite the passage of time'.

9. BL. Add. MSS. 34,703-08.

The project, initially funded through Sir Rowland Hill's office, and pursued mostly during Siborne's spare time, proceeded well enough until 1833, When the new Whig Government of Earl Grey caused this high-level patronage to be abruptly rescinded. The authorities now clearly began to regard the persistent Captain Siborne and his confounded model as something of a liability. As a result, his petition for further funding met with a curt refusal on the grounds '...that His Majesty's Treasury, had found no precedent to continue these payments'. Siborne was now too deeply involved to draw back, however, and '...though ill able to afford it'[10], he decided to undertake the completion of the task at his own expense. He lived to regret it, for from this time forwards he was plagued by financial problems. As expenses and overdue bills mounted, he was soon making pleas for

10. D C Hamilton-Williams, 'Siborne - the Unpublished Letters', *The Bulletin, The Military Historical Society*, Aug 1987, p20.

donations from his correspondents - with results to be discussed later. In the British Library a circular letter survives in which Siborne requests the loan of five pounds, but had on reconsideration crossed this figure out and substituted ten, to be repaid from the proceeds earned from public display of the model.[11]

One way or another the work went ahead. The model was built in Ireland, although exactly where or by whom has not yet been discovered. At last, in 1838 - eight years after conception - it was completed, and in all its 39 crated sections it was moved to England for display.

Financial problems were far from being solved. In 1830 Siborne had been promised £1,500, but received only £280. Later requests for further installments were, as we have seen, rebuffed. In desperation by 1833, Siborne had to raise a loan of £1,500 on his own recognizances. His attempts to obtain funding from his correspondents did not bring in much - yet the total costs of the model and its large glass case, added to his original expenses in Belgium and now the physical movement of the model across the Irish Sea, came to a daunting £3,000. Displayed to the public from 4 October 1838 at the Egyptian Hall in Piccadilly (long ago demolished), it was visited by an estimated 100,000 people at one shilling a head. This sum, however, barely reimbursed the hire of the hall and local expenses.[12]

In financial terms, therefore, the model proved ruinous. Siborne never recouped the construction costs and in 1841 the model was back in Ireland for storage, probably in Belfast. In a letter of that year a disillusioned Siborne declared his intention to attempt its sale, proposing to '...[ship] it very shortly from this country in which it was constructed and in which every single article appertaining to it was solely and exclusively executed'.[13] Two years after Siborne's death in 1849, a subscription was raised by the regiments of the British Army depicted on the model, and it was bought. Once again it crossed the Irish Sea - this time to be set up in the Great Banqueting Hall in Whitehall as an important item of the (subsequently Royal) United Service Museum. And there it stayed until 1962 when the RUSI was

11. Henderson, *op cit* p4.

12. BL. Add. MSS. 34,703; and Hamilton-Williams, *op cit*, p20.

13. Cited on the English Heritage information panels at Dover Castle.

required to vacate its prestigious museum premises (needed for a Government entertainment centre).

No suitable site could be found for the model, and for several years its 39 crates were stored in nissen huts in the grounds of the Royal Military Academy, Sandhurst. From there it was moved to better storage in nearby Aldershot. In 1971 the National Army Museum was opened in Chelsea, and in late 1975 Field Marshal Sir Gerald Templer - its great patron and fund-raiser - asked the Commandant of Sandhurst, (the then) Major-General Robert Ford, to send a team (which included the author of this essay) to inspect the model.

Four crates were selected at random and on opening, their contents were found to be '...in surprisingly good overall condition'.[14] Although dirty, in need of repainting and slightly damaged at the joins, the sample sections were found to be damp-free and showing no signs of advanced decay. The investigators recommended that the ideal location for the model would be the National Army Museum, once space would allow. The crates were moved meanwhile to the huge Ordnance Support Unit complex at Liphook. Now, after careful restoration, firstly by members of the British Model Soldier Society and latterly by Bees Modelmakers of Sunbury on Thames, the large model has at last been installed at Chelsea, its peregrinations hopefully over for good.

For its date the model is a highly impressive piece of work. Built on a scale of nine feet to the mile, it covers 420 square-feet in completed form. Its glass case (destroyed, alas, when the model was removed from RUSI) measured 27 feet four inches long by 19 feet eight inches wide. Siborne was particularly insistent about the provision of such a case, despite the large extra expense involved. He had written in 1827 that '...models should be provided with cases to protect them from dust, and should never be exposed to the sun'. It seems that Siborne started work on a larger scale, for the daughter of Major-General Herbert Taylor Siborne (1826-1902) remembered her father '...saying work on the model had been started on a scale which proved too large, and had to be abandoned for a smaller'. One of the larger

14. 'Report to the Commandant', 27 Nov 1975, (Author's archives).

190

figures - that of Napoleon mounted - was still in the family in April 1935.[15]

15. NAM.7510-932 p6; information from P Vignon-Cointat, the husband of Annette Siborne.

The model represents the precise situation (according to Siborne) at 7.15pm on 18 June 1815, the moment when the French Middle Guard breasted the last rise to reach the summit of Mont St Jean ridge to find themselves confronted by the British Brigade of Guards and formations of the Light Infantry. It is estimated (for no-one it seems has counted every formation's strength) that it contains over 70,000 individual model soldiers. It is not, therefore, a one-for-one representation, for at that time some 200,000 men (British, Prussians and French) were present on the field.

The models were cast in a tin-lead alloy, and despite their minute size were extremely accurately designed and executed. Siborne also took the greatest trouble to portray the buildings of Hougoumont Chateau, La Haie Sainte and La Belle Alliance, exactly as they had been on 18 June 1815, and was much concerned to show the trampled crops in their correct locations.

The Accuracy of the Model -
Siborne the Historian under Investigation

The overall result is a masterpiece of the panoramic battlefield modeller's art - although it has also become the subject of some debate as to its true accuracy. In a recent article, D C Hamilton-Williams has pointed out that Siborne was highly selective in the evidence he chose to portray. It appears that many of the unpublished letters challenge points of detail shown on the model, and later expressed as historical facts in Siborne's two-volume *History of the War in France and Flanders in 1815, containing minute details of the battles of Quatre Bras, Ligny, Wavre and Waterloo*,[16] which has been much cited by military historians ever since. It would seem that many myths became incorporated in the book and upon the model. This tendency was noted at the time of first publication by Sir James Kennedy, present at the battle on the QMG's staff attached to the 3rd Division, and he was not the sole critic. Thus in 1844-45, Major Edward MacCready

16. First published in 1844 and later in a single-volume edition, London (1900).

17. Sir C Chesney, *The Waterloo Lectures*, London (1868) p20.

entered into a long and vituperative correspondence in the United Services *Journal* to show that six surviving officers wholly disagreed with the roles ascribed to their regiment, and further, had never been canvassed by Siborne at the outset of his enterprise. Charges of undue national bias were also soon being made. Colonel C Chesney noted in *The Waterloo Lectures* (1868) that the *History* '…has the essential faults of a national history written soon after a great war. Much that is in it would not have been inserted had the work not been largely dependent on the British Army'.[17]

Alas, as with the volume, so with the model. No less an authority than the Duke of Wellington commented, after seeing a plan of the model, that;

> 'No Drawing or representation as a Model can represent more than one moment of an Action, But this Model tends to represent the whole action: and every Corps and Individual of all the Nations is represented in the Position chosen by Himself.
>
> The Consequence is that the Critical Viewer of the Model must believe that the whole of each Army, without any Reserve of any Kind, was engaged at the Moment supposed to be represented.
>
> This is not true of any one moment or event or operation of this Battle; and I was unwilling to give any Sanction to the truth of such a representation in this Model, which must have resulted from my visiting it, without protesting against such erroneous representation.
>
> This I could not bring myself to do on [any] account; and I thought it best to avail myself of my absence from London, and of Indisposition, never to visit it at all.[18]

18. Gerald, 7th Duke of Wellington, ed., *Wellington and his Friends*, London (1968) No 24 (endorsed by Lady Wilton, 23 April, 1840), pp133-34.

It would appear, therefore, that Siborne was not wholly objective in the handling of the evidence he collected. Indeed, it has also been suggested that the larger the subscription an officer paid, the more credibility his evidence was given; even to the extent of his tiny figure being given an undeservedly prominent and even heroic pose on the model. Those that did not subscribe to the appeal could be ignored.

Letter to the Army in North Holland, 1799
Letter sent from Jedburgh 22 Oct 1799, to the Army in Holland, with the rare 'POST PAID/ARMY BAG' handstamp used on prepaid letters.
National Army Museum   8812-34

Letter from the Army in the Low Countries, 1814
Letter sent at the one penny concessionary rate by Sergeant John Gray, 33rd (or the 1st Yorkshire West Riding) Regiment of Foot from Antwerp, May 1814, to his brother in Leicester.
National Army Museum 9006-232-3

'Arthur, Duke of Wellington in the Cloak That he Wore at Waterloo...'
Oil on canvas by Peter Edward Stroehling c1820.
National Army Museum 6501-1

'Signing the Treaty of Peace at Vienna'
Coloured aquatint by Joseph Stadler after William Heath, from the series 'Wellington's Victories', published by Thomas Tegg, London, 1 April 1818.
Wellington signs the Treaty; across from him sits Czar Alexander of Russia with King Frederick of Prussia standing to the Czar's right. Behind the table stands Marshal Blucher.
National Army Museum 7102-33-550-30

East India Company's Medals
(left to right)
East India Company's Egypt Medal
in silver 1801.
National Army Museum 6209-35-5

Java Medal in silver.
National Army Museum 8707-43

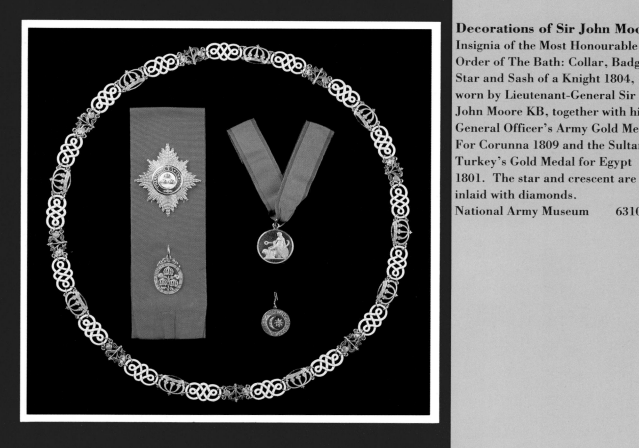

Decorations of Sir John Moore
Insignia of the Most Honourable
Order of The Bath: Collar, Badge,
Star and Sash of a Knight 1804,
worn by Lieutenant-General Sir
John Moore KB, together with his
General Officer's Army Gold Medal
For Corunna 1809 and the Sultan of
Turkey's Gold Medal for Egypt
1801. The star and crescent are
inlaid with diamonds.
National Army Museum   6310-61

Decorations of Sir John Vandeleur

Army Gold Cross for Ciudad Rodrigo, Salamanca, Vittoria and the Nive, and General Officer's Army Gold Medal for Ciudad Rodrigo, with clasps: Salamanca and Vittoria, awarded to General Sir John Ormsby Vandeleur. National Army Museum 6310-47

Orders and Medals of Major-General Thomas Staunton St Clair

St Clair served with the 5th *Cacadores*, Portuguese Army: (left to right) Army Gold Medal for Nive, type awarded to field officers; Military General Service Medal 1793-1814 with clasps: Busaco, Fuentes d'Onor, Nivelle; Order of St Benedict of Aviz, Portugal, Badge and Star of a Knight Commander c1814; Order of the Tower and Sword, Portugal, Badge of a Knight c1831; Officer's Cross for Peninsular campaigns, Portugal, awarded for five actions; Officer's Cross for Peninsular campaigns, Portugal, awarded for four actions; Portuguese Cross for the Nive 1814. National Army Museum 6907-30

Medals of Corporal Georg Oelmann, KGL
Medals awarded to Corporal Georg Oelmann, 1st Regiment of Hussars, King's German Legion: Guelphic Medal for Gallantry 1815; Military General Service Medal 1793-1814: Waterloo Medal 1815.
National Army Museum   8907-79

Regimental and Volunteer Medals
(left to right)
88th (Connaught Rangers) Regiment Order of Merit, 1st Class, 1818. Silver. Awarded to Private Patrick Burke.
National Army Museum 5602-672-1

18th (Royal Irish) Regiment of Foot medal for meritorious conduct 1801. Gold. Awarded to Private H Galley. The reverse is engraved: A/ REWARD/FOR EXEMPLARY/ CONDUCT IN/ACTION/H. GAL-LEY.
National Army Museum   6305-159
(right to left)
Bank of England Volunteer Infantry, Regimental shooting medal 1805. Gold. Awarded to Private Joseph Lewin of the light company.
National Army Museum   8703-37

Loyal London Volunteers, Regimental shooting medal 1804. Silver-gilt. The rim is engraved: 'The Gift of Captn., Hilton 2 Regt.. L.L.V. to Sergeant Weedon being the 2nd.. best Shot 6th Augt.. 1804'.
National Army Museum   8408-61

Commemorative Medals

(left to right)
The Duke of Wellington 1822.
Bronze medal by W Binfield, struck
to commemorate the Congress of the
Allies in Verona, at which Welling-
ton was present.
National Army Museum   9005-10

Napoleon Bonaparte 1815. Bronze
medal by T Webb. Reverse shown.
The obverse by G Mills bears a
portrait bust of the Duke of Wellington.
National Army Museum   9005-9

Field Marshal von Blücher 1815.
Silver. By T Halliday. Reverse
shown. The obverse bears a portrait of the Duke of Wellington.
National Army Museum   84111-203

The Duke of Wellington 1841.
Silver laudatory medal by
Benedetto Pistrucci.
National Army Museum   8712-8

Major-General Sir James Kempt (1764-1854), c1824

Oil on canvas, artist unknown,
c1824.
Sir James, in attempting to show the
full extent of his decorations, wears
his Grand Cross badge of the Royal
Hanoverian Guelphic Order (incorrectly) at the neck alongside the
lesser-grade badges of the Orders of
Maria Theresa of Austria and
William of the Netherlands.
National Army Museum   5911-278

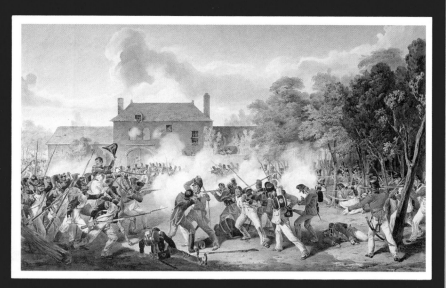

Defence of the Chateau of Hougoumont by the Flank Company, Coldstream Guards
Watercolour by Denis Dighton, 1815.
In 1811 Dighton obtained an ensigncy in the 90th Foot as a favour from the Prince Regent, but he resigned in March 1812. He made drawings at Waterloo in 1815. That year he was appointed Military Painter to the Prince.
National Army Museum   7505-7-1

Attack on the British Squares by French Cavalry
Watercolour by Denis Dighton, 1815.
National Army Museum   7505-7-2

'The Farm of La Haye Sainte'
Coloured aquatint by and after
James Rouse, published by H
Colburn, London, 1816.
National Army Museum
7102-33-546-17

'View of the Cottage of Valette'
Coloured aquatint by and after
James Rouse, published by H
Colburn, London, 1816.
Rouse's Waterloo prints were
produced in conjunction with
William Mudford's *An Historical
Account of the Campaign in the
Netherlands*, London (1817). It is
highly likely that these views of the
battlefield were drawn on the spot.
National Army Museum
7102-33-546-15

Furthermore, Siborne did not, its seems, attempt to procure French or Prussian evidence - and ignored letters from German officers in Wellington's army. For example, amongst the unpublished letters, the commander of the Orange-Nassau Regiment's divisional report has the comment written on the back, 'By an unknown KGL [[King's German Legion - hardly an Orange-Nassauer] officer'. This does not increase faith in William Siborne's credibility as an historian, nor his son's. It would seem that neither could read German, nor was prepared to have such letters translated.[19]

19. Hamilton-Williams, op *cit* p27.

To be fair, perhaps we should point out in his defence that William Siborne was very much a typical 'John Bullish' Victorian gentleman of his time, probably of the type later lampooned by W S Gilbert;

'For he himself has said it,/And it's greatly to his credit,

That he is an Englishman!/That he is an Englishman![20]

20. Gilbert and Sullivan, *HMS Pinafore*, Act Two.

He was a patriot, and probably subscribed to the view represented by the famous press statement of about this time - 'Storm in Channel. Continent isolated'. He was not, however, wholly insensitive to criticism. The hand-bill announcing a new showing of the model to the public in 1845 - to mark the thirtieth anniversary of the Battle - stresses that many changes of points of detail, especially concerning the Prussian involvement around Plancenoit, had recently been incorporated.[21]

21. Report in *The Illustrated London News*, 14 June 1845.

Siborne's Second (1844) Model

Furthermore, there is the evidence of a second model which must be examined. Captain Siborne was clearly undaunted by the financial failure of his first model, and set about designing and building a second series of five models, portraying earlier critical moments in the Battle. These were to be built on a larger scale than the 1838 version, namely one of 15 feet to one inch for the countryside, and six feet to one inch for the buildings and the miniature soldiers. Siborne hoped that all six models would be displayed in a single place.[22] In fact, only one was completed - that showing the rout at 2pm by the British Union

22. 'Guide to Captain Siborne's New Waterloo Model', in *Military Tracts*, Vol XVIII (MOD Library, Central and Army). I am indebted to the cartographer, Mr Stephen Maison, for bringing this work to my attention.

Brigade (including the 2nd North British Dragoons (or Scots Greys), and the Household Brigade of Lord Uxbridge's heavy cavalry) of General d'Erlon's 1 Corps attack against the farm of La Haie Sainte and Picton's 5th Division. This second model measures (case included) 18ft 7ins by 7ft 9ins, and comprises ten sectional parts. The infantry soldiers are approximately an inch high, made of a lead-tin alloy. Each soldier's arms are movable, and his back-pack, held in place by minute iron pins, is detachable. Each cavalryman has a separable head, arms and breastplate (the latter made of lead foil or brass). The cannon are made of lead alloy, but their limbers contain wooden parts. The buildings are constructed from wood and card.[23]

First displayed to the public in London's Egyptian Hall in late 1844, the model was again shown alongside the 1838 version from Christmas Eve 1845. The models again attracted a large crowd of admiring visitors, who were required to buy two one-shilling tickets for the privilege. Siborne had paid £600 for the 7,000 soldiers of his 1844 model, and was still eager to recoup his original losses and new costs - vainly, as it was to prove.

The second model was later displayed by a Mr Evans (possibly a lessee) in Germany on two occasions, one being in 1848, 'the Year of Revolutions'. It may also have been exhibited elsewhere on the Continent, but by 1851 it had safely returned to Ireland, where it was stored at an iron-works in Dublin until it was displayed at a store during the Irish International Exhibition in 1907. Thereafter, it spent some years in the loft of a house at Cabinteely, Co. Dublin, where it was re-discovered by Mrs Barrington Malone. She had the model set up before loaning it to a Mr Bonaparte Wyse. She later offered it to the Royal United Services Museum, but as the larger model was already there, it was eventually presented to the Staff College at Camberley, following a period of repair at the Tower of London workshops, supervised by Mr Charles ffoulkes, Master of the Armouries, HM Tower of London, in 1935.

It is painful to report that the Staff College did not care for the gift, and it was even threatened with destruction when the room where it

23. *Soldier Magazine*, Vol 39, No 18 (5-18 Sept 1983).

stood in a neglected state was required for other purposes. Fortunately, it was rescued by Charles ffoulkes in the nick of time, transported to the Armouries once again for repair, and subsequently displayed at the Tower for a time. When ffoulkes took some sample figures to Wm. Britain's Ltd, the renowned model soldier makers, they refused to divulge any trade secrets as to how they could have been constructed, but admitted that Siborne's figures '...were better than anything they could produce'.[24] As *The Daily Telegraph* reported on 15 June 1935, 'A wonderful model of the battlefield of Waterloo is being placed on public exhibition in the Tower of London today'.[25] There it remained, for more years again in store, before being transferred to Dover Castle in 1965 on long loan. It was found that some deterioration was taking place, a substantial number of the figures and cannon suffering from corrosion, and the cause of this was eventually traced by the laboratory of the Ancient Monuments Commission to a corrosive vapour emanating from the material and/or the adhesive used for the 'grass' surfaces of the 1844 model.[26] After a major overhaul and repair undertaken on the instuctions of English Heritage between 1983 and 1985, it was re-opened to the public at a ceremony held at Dover Castle on 25 May 1985, and performed by Mr George Siborne of Vancouver, Canada - the great-grandson of Captain William Siborne.[27] Installed in the Castle's Great Chamber, it has been given a new case and an eight-minute computerised sound-and-light programme describing the scene, and is supported by a display area giving more information on the model, its creator, and the military events of 1815.[28]

The End of William Siborne's Life

As mentioned above, Siborne had intended to build four more displays illustrative of key moments in the battle, and several of these were started, including one showing the French cavalry onslaught against the Allied squares. But either the spirit weakened or, more likely, the financial implications unnerved him, and on 14 June 1845, we find him trying to sell - with what success is unknown - the part-

24. NAM.7510-93: Letter from Charles ffoulkes, 29 April, 1935.

25. *Loc cit*.

26. *Soldier Magazine*, *loc cit*, attributed the problem (incorrectly) to hardboard used during the 1835 repairs.

27. See the Siborne Family Tree in NAM.7510-93 p5.

28. Designed by English Heritage, with texts and sound recordings provided by the author.

29. As reported in *The Illustrated London News*, 14 June 1845.

30. National Library of Scotland, Mss.2843/110, Siborne's letter to Gen Brown, soliciting support.

31. NAM.7510-93, p4.

finished models.[29]

It would be pleasant to be able to record that William Siborne eventually recouped the money he laid out on these models. Unfortunately, that did not prove the case in his lifetime. In November 1843 his long stint as Assistant Military Secretary at Dublin at last came to an end. He was now appointed - in the rank of captain on half pay - Adjutant and Secretary of the Royal Military Asylum, Chelsea (later the Duke of York's School - today at Dover).[30] And there he died on 13 June 1849, '...a disappointed man, depressed by the neglect or inability of the authorities to give him well-earned promotion, or to refund him the large sum (nearly £3,000) he had spent on the Waterloo Model'.[31] Clearly, the second model involved considerable additional expense that was never recouped from his share of the entrance fee at public displays. As the larger model was only bought by regimental subscription - presumably to spare it from destruction - in 1851, two years after after his death, William Siborne never saw any return on his investment.

However, his models - after many and varied travels and tribulations - have survived safely for posterity to admire, and form the true and lasting monument to a remarkable man. They may not be strictly accurate - how could they be? - any more the Siborne's *History* is to be regarded as sound in every scholarly sense, but the pains he put into researching his work from first-hand sources and on the ground at Waterloo (most of it in his own leisure time), deserve a full measure of respect and gratitude.

So William Siborne may lie quietly at Brompton Cemetery, London, where his gravestone records that he was the maker of '...the Waterloo Models'. With the re-opening to public display of his larger '7.15pm' model of the Battle of Waterloo in the National Army Museum - only a few hundred yards from where he spent the last years of his life - the story that began in 1830, or possibly in 1816 in Paris, has come full circle.

The British Army's legacy from the Revolutionary and Napoleonic Wars was not what the conventional wisdom of European military history suggests it ought to have been. The French Revolution, with its extension in the powers of the state, allowed the full application of conscription for the first time in modern warfare. Mass armies enabled sustained and continuous combat. They also demanded fresh systems of organisation: in Prussia the foundations of the modern staff system were laid, and in France the development of the corps allowed the enlarged army to function as an articulated chain of independent yet interlocking parts. Tactically, the infantry of the revolutionary armies gave primacy to the attack column rather than to the line, to mobility, rather than to firepower. Napoleon, himself a gunner, increasingly treated artillery as the third arm rather than as a secondary support. These generalisations, however over-stated, encapsulate some of the key changes in warfare conventionally attributed to the period 1793-1815. Yet none of them is applicable to Britain. With the possible exception of Austria, Britain was France's most consistent opponent; 1802 was the only year between 1793 and 1815 when Britain was not at war with France. But Britain did not adopt conscription. The development in its military administration was limited. Although corps began to figure towards the end of the war, the highest normal field formation was the division, and even this enjoyed no permanence after 1815. Tactically, Wellington, with his emphasis on the two-rank line and infantry firepower, and his derogation of artillery, remained closer to the precepts of Frederick the Great than those of Napoleon. The British Army in 1815 looked curiously old-fashioned.

And yet it was successful. The victory at Waterloo, the final defeat of Napoleon himself, gave the British as much claim to international respect and emulation as the French. Indeed, much of what happened after 1815 endorsed the British way of doing things. Truly universal conscription, with its implication that the corollary of military obliga-

HEW STRACHAN

tions was civic rights, was too revolutionary for the monarchs of the restored Europe. The vindication at Waterloo of eighteenth-century principles, albeit amended, justified a rejection or minimisation of much that was innovatory in the French armies of 1793-1815. In accusing the British Army of atrophy over the next 40 years (in itself a false accusation), it is as well to remember that what the British Army did, and how it absorbed the legacy of the Revolutionary and Napoleonic Wars, was in many respects similar to the behaviour of the armies of other great powers. The idea that armies should be small, professional in ethos, and recruited for long service, was not singular but widely held. The motivations underpinning such an approach differed: in the British case colonial service divorced the Army from its parent society willy-nilly, in the case of most European countries the dominant need was to have a reliable prop to maintain domestic order. But the consequences for military organisation were congruent rather than diverging.

The Sword and the Pen

Although not recruited by conscription, the British Army nonetheless expanded to meet the demands of the Napoleonic Wars. Twenty to thirty thousand men each year were enlisted into the regular forces between 1805 and 1813, and in the latter year the effective strength of the Army (including the Militia) stood at 330,663.[1] By 1835 peacetime contractions had cut both these figures by two-thirds. Thus an enduring consequence of the wars was a massive increase in the number of officers put on to half-pay as the Army was reduced. In 1831 there were still 9,404 officers drawing various forms of half and retired-pay as against 6,768 on full pay.[2] Technically the half-pay list constituted not a means to retirement but a form of reserve service. Officers on half-pay were available to return to active duty, and - if they expressed a willingness to do so - remained eligible for promotion. Therefore, the financial incentives to employ these officers were considerable, so reducing the burden of the half-pay list and getting some return on the investment thereby made.

1. Sir John Fortescue, *The County Lieutenancies and the Army 1803-1814*, London (1909) pp292-93.

2. Hew Strachan, *Wellington's Legacy: the Reform of the British Army 1830-54*, Manchester (1984) p114.

Nor was physical decrepitude or military inefficiency an obvious block to such a course. Wellington's army in the Peninsula was a young man's army. Its commander himself reached his fortieth birthday in 1809; among his subordinate generals, only the redoubtable Thomas Graham had passed middle age. Of those 149 officers who served in the Adjutant General's and Quartermaster General's departments and whose dates of birth are known, most were born in the 1780s, only four before 1775 and one as recently as 1794.[3] Therefore, the veterans of the Napoleonic Wars continued to dominate the current of promotion in the army for several decades after the peace of 1815. Wellington himself was Commander-in-Chief of the Army in 1827-28 and 1842-52, sandwiching the incumbency of another Peninsular veteran, Lord Hill, and being succeeded by a third, Lord Hardinge (Commander-in-Chief until 1856). Almost all the major field commanders until (and including) the Indian Mutiny had won their spurs in Spain and Portugal - Lord Combermere (Stapleton Cotton) at Bhurtpore, Sir Benjamin D'Urban, Sir Harry Smith and Sir George Cathcart in South Africa, Lord Seaton (John Colborne) in Canada, Sir Charles Napier in Scinde, Lord Gough in China and the Punjab, Lord Raglan (Fitzroy Somerset) in the Crimea, Lord Clyde (Colin Campbell) in the Indian Mutiny. Many undoubtedly stayed in service too long. Wellington himself proved a major block to change and reform. But most of them had only enjoyed middle or junior rank at the beginning of the century. Thus their education under Wellington was tempered by their subsequent experience of colonial campaigns. Not a single war, although many included their share of humiliation and incompetence, was concluded by ultimate defeat: even the disaster at Kabul in the winter of 1841-42 was followed by subsequent success. Individually, these officers shed much lustre on the British Army.

Victory on the battlefields of Empire was the most striking achievement of the veterans of the Napoleonic Wars. But not all half-pay officers could find the active employment which they craved. For some the vacancies were too few, for others their wounds too debilitating. Anxiously they scanned the *Army List*, calculating their chances

3. S G P Ward, *Wellington's Headquarters: a Study of the Administrative Problems in the Peninsula 1809-1814*, Oxford (1957) pp170-93.

of promotion or appointment. In 1840 H G Hart produced the first edition of his annual army list, which supplemented the official version with details of past services and so provided the basis for a fuller comparison of merit. Those not recognised referred to Hart to buttress their grievances. For many these were already deeply, and justifiably, etched. The victory at Waterloo had been marked in 1816-17 by the grant of a year's additional service towards a pension and by the distribution of a medal to all those who had been present in the action. Not until 1847 was a medal authorised for issue to those who had served in the preceding campaigns of 1793 to 1814. Wellington himself was a major opponent of the proposal that the Peninsular veterans should be recognised as those of Waterloo had been. The principal outlet for these professional frustrations was the military press, in particular the *United Service Journal* (or *Magazine* as it became), the *Naval and Military Gazette* and the *United Service Gazette*.

For what is remarkable about many of those soldiers who could not find continued service after 1815, or could do so only spasmodically, was that they did not cease to see themselves as soldiers. Unable any longer to wield the sword, they worked as vigorously with the pen, writing prolifically on military subjects. Some of what they wrote remained mired in the problems of promotion in a peacetime Army and in the claims to medals or pecuniary rewards. But much was both more positive and more constructive. Today we tend to think of 'war books', the combination of memoir, fiction, and history, in the context of the First World War. But the Peninsular War too produced a spate of personal accounts, the publication of which seems still not to be exhausted. In 1912 Sir Charles Oman, in a list which he admitted was not complete, was able to catalogue 108 such works.[4] Between 1837 and 1845 Colonel John Gurwood published Wellington's despatches in 12 volumes. But pre-eminent in this bibliography was General Sir William Napier's *History of the War in the Peninsula*, the first volume of which appeared in 1838 and the sixth and last in 1840. Napier, who served almost continously throughout the war he described, retired

4. Sir Charles Oman, *Wellington's Army*, London (1912) pp375-383. See also the bibliography in Anthony Brett-James, *Life in Wellington's Army*, London (1972).

on half-pay in 1819. A bullet lodged near his spine, which made painful the prolonged periods of sitting required to write, probably precluded further active service even had he wanted it. His only subsequent appointment was as Lieutenant-Governor of Guernsey in 1841-47. Half-pay, therefore, provided the financial cushion which enabled *The War in the Peninsula* to be written. It is a book which infuriates now as it did then: nonetheless Napier's prejudices, both political and military, which run throughout the *History*, have gained immortality by the quality of the prose in which they are clothed. Napier coloured all subsequent nineteenth-century interpretations of the Peninsular War. He minimised the contributions of the Spanish Army and the guerrillas, and exaggerated the fighting powers of the English (as he insisted on calling it) infantry. In doing so, however, he did more than anybody else to found the study of military history in Britain.[5] No previous war had merited such an output of literary effort; few subsequent wars would escape it.

Napier's study of military history was not conceived in terms of pure scholarship. His purpose was also didactic. Because the technology of warfare remained relatively unchanged from the beginning of the eighteenth century to the middle of the nineteenth, this observation does not mean that Napier was using the 'lessons' of the past to illuminate the possibilities of the future. The war he was considering represented much more of a continuum than twentieth-century notions of inevitable and rapid technological change lead modern observers to expect. *The War in the Peninsula* does not in itself spell out its author's theories on the conduct of war in the way in which Liddell Hart would do a hundred years later: for Napier, the reader's understanding and assimilation of the events which he was describing were themselves a lesson. However, *The War in the Peninsula* was used in a more overtly didactic sense, by Napier as well as by others, in the columns of the military press and in publications devoted specifically to military theory. Frequently, Napier's researches provided illumination or illustration in debates on tactics. Thus the Peninsular veterans - Sir John Kincaid or Colonel Jonathan

5. On Napier, see Jay Luvaas, *The Education of an Army*, London (1965) pp7-38; also Hew Strachan, 'The British army and "modern" war: the experience of the Peninsula and the Crimea', in John Lynn, ed., *The Tools of War*, Urbana (1990).

Leach - fused reminiscence and history with the advocacy of reform. Most celebrated was Colonel John Mitchell, whose writing of history was far more pragmatic and didactic than Napier's and who took issue with the latter in the pages of the military press. Particularly heated was their exchange on the bayonet, castigated by Mitchell as a 'rickety zig-zag', and which he claimed had achieved far less in combat than the bombastic and flowery descriptions of despatch-writers (and of Napier) suggested.[6] Mitchell was also (in contrast to Napier) a defender and advocate of the achievements of the cavalry. What all this debate highlighted was that for the British Army the Napoleonic Wars constituted a sustained succession of experiences, the value and burden of which would take time to comprehend and assimilate.

The Legacy of Wellington and the Legacy of Moore

The British Army of the first half of the nineteenth century is described as Wellington's Army. Although complaints against his conservatism and calls for reform multiplied in the last decade of his life, only his death in 1852 removed the major obstacle to change. For the Duke, not even the imperfections revealed by the Army's experiences in the Peninsula should necessarily be rectified, hallowed as they were by the fact that they had worked in practice.

In some senses, however, the Army after 1815 was not Wellington's, but Sir John Moore's. Naturally enough the legacy which the Army carried forward from 1815 was that of the latter stages of the Napoleonic Wars, a period which also contained its major victories. Little attention was given to the West Indies, to the Low Countries, to Maida or Walcheren. The crack troops of the Peninsular War were those of the Light Division, the 43rd and 52nd Light Infantry, and the Rifle Brigade. It was in these regiments that William Napier, Kincaid and Leach, as well as Harry Smith, Charles Napier and Colborne, had served. Their tasks were those of outposts, of skirmishing, of marksmanship. They were not the troops of the thin red line, and their responsibilities and direct contact with the enemy were continuous, not confined to battle itself. The overwhelming majority of

6. Hew Strachan, *From Waterloo to Balaclava: Tactics, Technology and the British Army*, Cambridge (1985) pp27-29.

post-war publications on tactics concern themselves with the work of rifle corps and of light infantry, or with the not unrelated tasks of field fortification. And as the disillusionment with Wellington deepened, so the memory of the putative founder of the Light Division, Moore, burned brighter. Shorncliffe camp, where in 1802-03 under Moore's command the training of the light infantry had been developed, cast a long shadow forward on to the post-Waterloo Army. The principles appropriate to light infantry were, Moore argued, universally applicable to all infantry. His pupils and juniors reflected the same line of thought in the 1830s and 40s.[7]

The training of the Light Division was not, however, purely tactical. The skirmisher, operating in relative isolation from his fellows, required greater qualities of initiative and individuality than did the infantry of the line. Moore's system was therefore an approach to discipline, a philosophy in the handling of men. The role of officers, particularly company officers who were in closer contact with their men, was to encourage rather than to repress, to make emulation rather than punishment the basis of a regiment's internal working. Wellington's views on his soldiers and how to manage them were - notoriously - very different. Formally speaking, much of the Duke's approach remained in the post-1815 Army, enshrined in the debates on corporal punishment and in Wellington's resistance to proposals for the amelioration of the soldier's conditions of service. In reality, a great deal changed, and it did so from the bottom up. The precepts of Shorncliffe and of the Light Division found their applications within the individual regiment. Commanding officers, frequently heading battalions which were serving in isolated colonial postings for up to 15 years at a time, presided over self-contained societies increasingly marked by a spirit of paternalism. This does not mean that the ethos of the armies of Revolutionary France found its eventual application in the British Army: equality and democracy remained alien and threatening words. What Moore represented was the Enlightenment, not the Revolution. The basic order remained the same, but it did so while acknowledging more fully the rights of the

7. The most recent account, which plays down Moore's actual contribution, is by David Gates; *The British Light Infantry Arm c1790-1815: its Creation, Training and Operational Role*, London (1987).

individual, and by recognising that under such conditions he would do his job more effectively.

The most important positive legacy of the Napoleonic Wars for the British Army was therefore its contribution to the development of a sense of professionalism. The victories of the Peninsula and Waterloo, the final defeat of the greatest commander yet known, and their recording by Napier and others, gave the Army a sense of worth and self-esteem which was vital to its development as an institution. Although the antics of cavalry subalterns stationed at home suggested a different picture, most officers of the British Army saw themselves as committed to a career. This professionalism was already nascent in the eighteenth century;[8] the expansion of the army during the Napoleonic Wars, the relative decline of purchase and the emphasis on seniority in promotion, gave it vigour;[9] post-war contraction, the concerns of the half-pay officers, and their continuing identification with the Army and its needs (rather than their re-absorption into civilian society), were evidence of its deep-rootedness; and the dominant post-war military experience, battalion service overseas, consolidated the process.

The importance of the legacy of the Napoleonic Wars was obliterated by the first winter of the Crimean War. The initial setbacks of that campaign, exaggerated by the Press and in Parliament, were attributed to the complacency of an Army that had rested unchanged since 1815. But such an interpretation confused long-term developments with short-term expediency. Between 1815 and 1854 two processes shaped the development of the Army: the first was its commitment to colonial garrisoning, and the second was technological innovation, encapsulated in the development in small-arms beginning in the late 1840s. The former was peculiar to Britain, the latter common to all armies. In addition, much necessary institutional reform - including the consolidation of the Army's administration, the revision of the military penal code, and the introduction of educational qualifications for officer promotion - provided the stuff of ongoing debate, its advocates again and again coming to grief in the face of

8. J A Houlding, *Fit for Service: the Training of the British Army 1715-1795*, Oxford (1981) pp99-115.

9. Michael Glover, 'The Purchase of Commissions' *Journal of the Society for Army Historical Research*, Vol 58 (1980) pp223-35.

Wellingtonian opposition. In some areas of reform, progress was made despite the Duke's tenure at the Horse Guards, but it required his succession by Hardinge for real change to get under way. Thus the Crimean War broke upon an Army in a state of flux, and looking more towards imperial and home defence than to expeditions overseas. The changes that followed the Crimean War had their origins less at Sebastopol than in the longer-running currents already observable before 1854. But after 1854, the British Army's experience of the Revolutionary and Napoleonic Wars could never again have the same immediacy and vitality. The positive effects of that legacy were rendered suspect by the negative, and both firmly associated with an outmoded order.

Alan J Guy

A brief and subjective bibliography such as this one, which is only intended to supplement the references already provided by the twenty contributors to this book and to draw attention to some of the more recent secondary sources of information about campaigns and events not otherwise dealt with (the Defence of the Realm, or British operations in the Mediterranean or in North America for example), can hardly pretend to come to grips with the vast and ever-expanding literature devoted to the Revolutionary and Napoleonic era. Accordingly, readers are first of all referred to the standard bibliographical guides, starting with Robin Higham's *A Guide to the Sources of British Military History*, London (1972) and Gerald Jordan ed., *British Military History: A Supplement to Robin Higham's Guide to the Sources*, New York and London (1988). Professor Donald D Horward ed., *Napoleonic Military History: A Bibliography*, New York and London (1986) provides a comprehensive guide to the teeming literary scene, while A P C Bruce, *An Annotated Bibliography of the British Army 1660-1914* concentrates on the British dimension. Readers wishing to place Britain's military effort in the wider diplomatic, economic, social and imperial vista should consult the articles and annotated bibliographies in H T Dickinson ed., *Britain and the French Revolution*, London (1989), which includes essays by several of the contributors to the present publication, and C A Bayly, *Imperial Meridian: The British Empire and the World, 1780-1830*, London (1989).

In terms of pure narrative, the starting point for any study of the British Army's tribulations and eventual triumphs during this momentous era must still surely be Sir John Fortescue's *History of the British Army*, Volumes III-X, London (1911-20), although Sir John's swingeing dismissal of such hapless administrators as Sir George Yonge (Secretary at War, July 1782-April 1783, December 1783-July 1794) *must* now be corrected by reading J L Pimlott's doctoral thesis, 'The Administration of the British Army, 1783-1794', University of Leicester (1975). Dr Pimlott's work, which certainly deserves to be published, should also be used to supplement Richard Glover's now somewhat dated *Peninsular Preparation: The Reform of the British Army 1795-1802*, Cambridge (1963), reprinted Elstree (1988). The background in terms of tactics and training is filled in by J A Houlding, *Fit for Service: The Training of the British Army 1715-1795*, Oxford (1982) and Piers Mackesy, 'What the British Army Learned' in Ronald Hoffman, Peter J Albert eds., *Arms and Independence: The Military Character of the American Revolution*, Charlotteville (1984) pp191-215. See also the important study by David Gates, *The British Light Infantry Arm c1790-1815: its Creation, Training and Operational Role*, London (1987) and the chapter 'Firepower of Wellington's Infantry' in the revised edition of Paddy Griffiths' *Forward into Battle: Fighting Tactics from Waterloo to the Near Future*, Swindon (1990).

Life in the ranks in the period up to the outbreak of war in 1793 has been explored by Dr Glenn A Steppler in an (as yet) unpublished doctoral thesis, 'The Common Soldier in the Reign of George III, 1760-

1793', University of Oxford (1984). J R Western has tackled the recruiting problems of the 1790s in another unpublished doctoral dissertation, 'The Recruitment of the Land Forces of Great Britain, 1793-1799', University of Edinburgh (1953).

In addition to the justly celebrated memoir literature of the period, insights into the world of the late-Georgian officer can best by gleaned from Michael Glover's *Wellington's Army in the Peninsula 1808-1814*, Newton Abbot (1977) and such classic texts as Sir Charles Oman's *Wellington's Army, 1809-1814*, London (1913) reprinted London (1986), Godfrey Davies, *Wellington and his Army*, Oxford (1954) and D Bell, *Wellington and his Officers*, London (1938). See also two important articles by Michael Glover, 'Purchase, Patronage and Promotion in the British Army at the time of the Peninsular War', *Army Quarterly*, Vol. CIII (1972-73) pp211-15, 355-62.

Stimulating introductions to the problems of field-command in the British Army are provided by S G P Ward, *Wellington's Headquarters: A Study of the Administrative Problems in the Peninsula 1809-1814*, Oxford (1957) and the contributors to Paddy Griffiths' symposium, *Wellington Commander: The Iron Duke's Generalship*, Chichester (1984). There is also a section on the Duke of Wellington 'the anti-hero' in John Keegan's *The Mask of Command*, London (1988). The experience of combat in the period is best approached via the masterly Waterloo section in John Keegan's *The Face of Battle*, London (1976) and, latterly, Christopher Duffy's *The Military Experience in the Age of Reason*, London (1987). Some consequences of battle, administrative and otherwise, are examined by Richard L Blanco in *Wellington's Surgeon General: Sir James McGrigor*, Durham (NC), (1974).

Fortescue excepted, there is a startling dearth of scholarly accounts of British strategy and campaigns over the whole period, nowhere more obviously so than for the opening moves in the Low Countries during 1793-95, where Lieutenant-Colonel Alfred H Burne's *The Noble Duke of York: the Military Life of Frederick, Duke of York and Albany*, London (1949) does at least provide a corrective to the unenthusiastic view of affairs presented by Sir John. A recent article by R N W Thomas, 'Wellington in the Low Countries, 1794-1795' in *The International History Review*, Vol XI, No 1 (1989) pp14-30 indicates a heartening renewal of interest in these early battles, while there is a useful chapter devoted to the Battle of Tourcoing in Michael Glover, *Warfare in the Age of Bonaparte*, London (1980).

Fortunately, the situation improves a great deal once we turn to the Army's Caribbean campaigns, where Michael Duffy's *Soldiers, Sugar and Seapower: The British Expeditions to the West Indies and the War against Revolutionary France*, Oxford (1987) offers the first full-scale examination of the politics, economics, administration and execution of a series of military expeditions hitherto condemned as ruinous side-shows. David Geggus, *Slavery, War and Revolution: The British Occupation of Saint Domingue 1793-1798*, Oxford (1981) and R N Buckley, *Slaves in Red Coats: The British West India Regiments, 1793-1815*, New Haven (Conn) (1979) are important accounts of institutions and events, while V S Naipaul, *The Loss of Eldorado*, London (1969), offers an impressionistic glimpse of the Caribbean's tortured heart of darkness (and chronicles an unsavoury incident in the career of Sir Thomas Picton).

During many of the years under review, Britain was overshadowed by the fear of invasion. Clive Emsley, in his *British Society and the French Wars 1793-1815*, *London (1979)* offers a stimulating background study of issues ranging far beyond the basic problem of the defence of the realm, and which are further explored in his article 'The Military and Popular Disorder in England, 1790-1801', *Journal of the Society for Army Historical Research*, Vol LXI (1983) pp10-21, 96-112. See also two seminal articles by Linda Colley in *Past and Present*; 'The Apotheosis of George III, Loyalty, Royalty and the British Nation, 1760-1820', *P&P*, No 102 (1984) pp95-129 and 'Whose Nation? Class and National Consciousness in Britain 1750-1830', *P&P*, No 113 (1986) pp97-117; also Robert R Dozier's *For King, Constitution and Country: The English Loyalists and the French Revolution*, Lexington (Ken) (1983). The religious character of the period and its bearing upon the conduct of the war, touched on in my essay in this volume on Lieutenant-Governor Melvill of Pendennis Castle, are examined by E R Norman, *Church and Society in England 1770-1970*, Oxford (1976), William Stafford, 'Religion and the Doctrine of Nationalism at the Time of the French Revolution and Napoleonic Wars' in Stuart Mews, ed., *Religion and National Identity*, Oxford (1982) pp381-95 and by Ian R Christie, *Stress and Stability in Late-Eighteenth Century Britain: Reflections on the British Avoidance of Revolution*, Oxford (1984).

Turning to the Auxiliary Forces embodied for home defence; the Militia is studied by J R Western, *The English Militia in the Eighteenth Century: The Story of a Political Issue, 1660-1802*, London (1965) and Sir

John Fortescue, *The County Lieutenancies and the Army 1803-1814*, London (1909). Pamela Horn, 'The Mutiny of the Oxfordshire Militia in 1795', *Cart and Cockhorse*, Vol 7, No 8 (1979) pp232-41 and David Neave, 'Anti-Militia Riots in Lincolnshire, 1757 and 1796', *Lincolnshire History and Archaeology*, No 11 (1976) pp21-27, focus on local incidents which have a far wider significance, while Duncan Anderson, 'The English Militia in the Mid-Nineteenth Century: a Study of its Military, Social and Political Significance', unpublished doctoral thesis, University of Oxford (1982) extends the discussion of 'the Constitutional Force' beyond the time-frame of the Napoleonic Wars.

There is, as yet, no modern general study of the Volunteer Movement in print, and the best account remains Cecil Sebag-Montefiore, *A History of the Volunteer Forces*, London (1908). There is also much valuable material in H F B Wheeler, A M Broadley, *Napoleon and the Invasion of England*, London (1908), Fortescue, *County Lieutenancies*, and Dozier, *For King, Constitution and Country*. The views propounded by J R Western in 'The Volunteer Movement as an Anti-Revolutionary Force, 1793-1802', *English Historical Review*, Vol LXXI (1956) pp603-14 should be re-examined in the light of a recent and sophisticated analysis by J E Cookson, 'The English Volunteer Movement of the French Wars 1793-1815: Some Contexts', *The Historical Journal*, Vol 32 (1989) pp867-92. Drawing as it does on the insights of Linda Colley and other recent important work on Georgian civic affairs, this article is far and away the most lucid exploration of the topic for years. Some County Record Offices have produced books and collections of documents covering their county's role during the French Wars: among the best are M Y Ashcroft, *To Escape the Monster's Clutches: Notes and Documents illustrating the Preparations in North Yorkshire to repel the Invasion threatened by the French from 1793*, North Yorkshire CRO Publications No 15, Northallerton (1977) and R G E Wood, *Essex and the French Wars*, Essex CRO Publications No 790, Chelmsford (1977). For a general assessment of the role of the Volunteers in the event of invasion, see Richard Glover, *Britain at Bay: Defence against Bonaparte 1803-14*, London (1973).

Professor Glover's book includes important material on the fortification of Britain's coastline against invasion, a topic only dealt with in passing in the present book. Important studies of this subject are by S G P Ward, 'Defence Works in Britain, 1803-1805', *JSAHR*, Vol 27 (1940) pp18-27, Sheila Sutcliffe, *Martello Towers*, Newton Abbot (1972) and P A L Vine, *The Royal Military Canal*, Newton Abbot (1972). Up-to-date surveys are provided by A D Saunders, *Fortress Britain, Artillery Fortification in the British Isles and Ireland*, Liphook (1989) and Paul Kerrigan, *The Defences of Ireland*, Liphook and Sandy Cove (Co. Dublin) (1990). Kerrigan is also the author of an important series of articles, 'The Defences of Ireland, 1793-1815', which appeared in *An Cosantoir* (The Irish Defence Journal), at intervals from 1974 to 1988, also a study of the massive *tete du pont* under construction at the strategic position of Shannonbridge from 1803, 'The Shannonbridge Fortifications', *The Irish Sword*, Vol XI (1974) pp234-45.

Weapon-procurement aspects of the British Army's campaigns have only been relatively lightly covered to date. Howard Blackmore's *British Military Firearms 1650-1850*, London (1961) is a classic account, to be supplemented by D W Bailey, *British Military Longarms, 1715-1865*, London (1986) and Graham Priest, *The Brown Bess Bayonet*, Norwich (1986). Two authoritative works currently in preparation will greatly extend our understanding of firearms design, manufacture and procurement; D W Bailey, *British Military Smallarms: Board of Ordnance Production, 1690-1815* and D F Harding, *Firearms of the East India Company: Smallarms of the British Indian Armies, 1600-1856*. A glimpse of how individual firearms and bayonets were accounted for at regimental level is provided by Graham Priest, 'Private Marks of Distinction - Individual Numbering of Weapons in a Company of Foot, 1815', *Military Illustrated, Past and Present*, No 29 (October 1990) pp33-38.

For swords, the standard account is by Brian Robson, *The Swords of the British Army: The Regulation Patterns, 1786-1914*, London (1975). Additional facts can be gleaned from entries in W E May, P G W Annis, *Swords for Sea Service*, London (1970) and Hew Strachan, *British Military Uniforms 1768-1796*, London (1975). Supplementary information is to be found in Richard Glover's Peninsular Preparation, R H Thoumine's *Scientific Soldier: A Life of General Le Marchant, 1766-1812*, London (1968), Thomas Gill Junior's 'Recollections of his Father, the late Mr Thomas Gill', printed in the *Journal of the Arms and Armour Society*, Vol III (1960) pp171-93 and G R Worrall's article 'The 1796 Light Cavalry Sword', Part One, *Antique Arms and Militaria (1984)* pp14-16.

For affairs in the Indian sub-continent during the

period of the Revolutionary and Napoleonic Wars, Sir Penderel Moon, *The British Conquest and Dominion of India*, London (1989) provides a magisterial, albeit traditional, survey. This book should be read in conjunction with C A Bayly's *Imperial Meridian* and C H Philips, *The East India Company 1784-1834*, Manchester (1960). The rule of the Wellesleys is scrutinised by P E Roberts, *India under Wellesley*, London (1929), Iris Butler, *The Eldest Brother*, London (1973), Edward Ingram, *Two Views of British India: The Private Correspondence of Mr Dundas and Lord Wellesley, 1798-1801*, Bath (1970), also in the first volume of Elizabeth Longford's biography of Wellington, *Wellington: The Years of the Sword*, London (1969), and by A S Bennell, 'Arthur Wellesley as Political Agent, 1803', *Journal of the Royal Asiatic Society* (1987) pp272-88. A recent and typically astringent account of the Wellesleys' forward policy in the sub-continent is by Edward Ingram, 'Wellington in India' in Norman Gash, ed., *Wellington: Studies in the Military and Political Career of the First Duke of Wellington*, Manchester (1990). Jac Weller, *Wellington in India*, London (1972) offers a lucid account of warfare in India which is now subject to revision, not least by Randolf G S Cooper, 'Wellington and the Marathas in 1803', *The International History Review*, Vol XI No 1, 1989 pp31-38. See also John Pemble, 'Resources and Techniques in the Second Maratha War', *The Historical Journal*, Vol XIX (1976) pp375-404, and M B Deopujari, *Shivaji and the Maratha Art of War*, Nagpur (1973).

Irish affairs, culminating the tragedy of 'Ninety-Eight' and the Union, are dealt with by R B McDowell, *Ireland in the Age of Imperialism and Revolution,*

1760-1801, Oxford (1979). Professor McDowell is also a contributor to T W Moody, W E Vaughan eds., *A New History of Ireland*, Vol IV, *Eighteenth Century Ireland 1691-1800*, Oxford (1986). The standard modern account of the Rebellion itself is Thomas Pakenham's *The Year of Liberty: The Story of the Irish Rebellion of 1798*, London (1967). A copy of Dr Kenneth Ferguson's study of 'The Army in Ireland from the Restoration to the Act of Union', unpublished doctoral thesis, Trinity College, Dublin (1980) has been deposited in the National Army Museum. See also the unpublished doctoral thesis by P C Stoddart, 'Counter-Insurgency and Defence in Ireland, 1790-1805', University of Oxford (1972) and Thomas Bartlett 'Indiscipline and Disaffection in the Irish Armed Forces in the 1790s' in P Corish ed., *Rebels, Radicals and Establishments*, Belfast (1985) pp115-34. A relatively elderly volume which is still a model for thoroughness in research is Sir Henry McAnally's *The Irish Militia, 1782-1816: A Social and Military Study*, Dundalk (1949). See also in this connection an article by Thomas Bartlett, 'An End to Moral Economy: The Irish Militia Disturbances of 1793', *Past and Present* No 99 (1983) pp41-64.

The War of the Second Coalition, of which Sir Ralph Abercromby's successful invasion of Egypt was one of the culminating events, is covered in two books by Piers Mackesy which, in their successful integration of political, diplomatic, naval and military affairs, are models of their kind; *Statesmen at War: The Strategy of Overthrow 1798-1799*, London (1974) and *War without Victory: The Downfall of Pitt, 1799-1802*, Oxford (1984). Edward Ingram, *Commitment to Empire: Prophecies of the Great Game in Asia*

1797-1800, Oxford (1981) offers an alternative (and controversial) interpretation of the War. An earlier and equally authoritative study by Professor Mackesy, *The War in the Mediterranean, 1803-1810*, London (1957) extends the strategic perspective onward through the decade. More recently, a sequence of books by Desmond Gregory has focused on individual strategic locations; *The Ungovernable Rock: A History of the Anglo-Corsican Kingdom and its Role in Britain's Mediterranean Strategy during the Revolutionary War (1793-1797)*, London and Toronto (1985), *The Insecure Base: A History of the British Occupation of Sicily, 1806-1815*, London and Toronto (1988) and *The Beneficent Usurpers: A History of the British in Madeira*, London and Toronto (1988). See also an important general study by Quentin Hughes, *Britain in the Mediterranean and the Defence of her Naval Stations*, Liverpool (1981).

Many British operations are not at all well covered in the available literature, although Gordon C Bond, *The Grand Expedition: The British Invasion of Holland, 1809*, Athens (Georgia) (1979) demonstrates what might be achieved. The principal British theatre of war from 1808, the Iberian Peninsula receives, in contrast, massive coverage, much of it remorselessly Anglo-centric. The classic modern account is by Sir Charles Oman, *A History of the Peninsular War*, Oxford (1902-22). Anglo-centricism is effectively challenged by David Gates in a recent one-volume study, *The Spanish Ulcer: A History of the Peninsular War* London (1986) and in a still more searching way in two books by Charles J Esdaile; *The Spanish Army in the Peninsular War*, Manchester (1988) and *The Duke of Wellington and the Command of the Spanish*

Army, 1812-14, London (1990). See also Donald D Horward, 'Wellington and the Defence of Portugal' and Charles J Esdaile, 'Wellington and the Military Eclipse of Spain, 1808-1814', both in *The International History Review*, Vol XI, No 1, (1989) pp39-54, 55-67 and John K Severn, 'The Wellesleys and Iberian Diplomacy, 1808-12' in Gash, *Wellington*, pp34-65. Certainly not to be forgotten is D W Davies' critical reassessment of the Corunna campaign; *Sir John Moore's Peninsular Campaign, 1808-1809*, The Hague (1974) which should be contrasted with the account in one of the most enduring (and endearing) biographical studies of a British hero, Carola Oman's *Sir John Moore*, London (1953). A brisk modern study of one of Wellington's ablest subordinates in the Peninsula is by Gordon L Teffeteller; The *Surpriser: The Life of Rowland, Lord Hill*, Brunswick (NJ) (1983). As for Wellington's army itself, in addition to the important studies by Sir Charles Oman and Michael Glover mentioned above, Anthony Brett-James offers an enjoyable survey of the Peninsular War's extensive memoir literature topic by topic in *Life in Wellington's Army*, London (1972).

The other major conflict of this period, the War of 1812, has received significantly less attention on this side of the Atlantic but an excellent recent account by Donald R Hickey, *The War of 1812: A Forgotten Conflict*, Urbana and Chicago (1989), along the lines made familiar by the work of Professor Piers Mackesy, goes a long way towards making up the deficiency. Also of value is Reginald Horsman's *The War of 1812*, London (1969) and, for primarily Canadian views of the fighting, J Mackay Hitsman, *The Incredible War of 1812*, Toronto (1965) and George F G Stanley, *The*

War of 1812, Land Operations, Canadian War Museum Historical Publication No 18, Ottawa (1983). Those wishing to sample the full range of American publications on the War should consult two bibliographies compiled by John C Fredriksen; *Free Trade and Sailors' Rights: A Bibliography of the War of 1812*, New York and London (1985), *Shield of Republic, Sword of Empire: A Bibliography of United States Military Affairs, 1783-1846*, New York and London (1990).

As for the concluding campaign of the Napoleonic Wars, the account of the Battle of Waterloo in Lady Longford's *Wellington: The Years of the Sword* is a renowned feat of extended description, which should be complemented by Jac Weller's *Wellington at Waterloo*, London (1967), and the account of Waterloo in Michael Glover's *Wellington as Military Commander*, London (1968). For a modern study which presents the Battle firmly in the context of the linked engagements at Ligny, Quatre Bras and Wavre, see David G Chandler's *Waterloo, the Hundred Days*, London (1980). Alan Lagden and John Sly, The 2/73rd at Waterloo, Brightlingsea (1988) break new ground with their biographical analysis of a battalion in action. See also the anatomy of a single company of the 2/73rd by John Sly, 'An Infantry Company at Waterloo', *Military Illustrated, Past and Present*, No 23 (June 1990) pp20-27.

For the British foreign policy in the period and Wellington's transformation from fighting general to European statesman see, in general, Michael Duffy, 'British Diplomacy and the French Wars 1789-1815' in Dickinson, *Britain and the French Revolution*, C K Webster's *The Foreign Policy of Castlereagh 1812-15*, London (1931) and, once again, Lady Longford's *Wellington: The Years of the Sword*.

Britain's military legacy from the Revolutionary and Napoleonic Wars is discussed by Sir Michael Howard in an influential essay, 'Wellington and the British Army', *Studies in War and Peace*, London (1970) and by Edward M Spiers, *The Army and Society 1815-1914*, London (1980). Two linked studies by Hew Strachan, *Wellington's Legacy: The Reform of the British Army 1830*, Manchester (1984) and *From Waterloo to Balaclava: Tactics, Technology and the British Army 1815-1854*, Cambridge (1985) argue convincingly that the post-War British Army was by no means the reactionary, hide-bound institution of popular renown.

Dr De Witt Bailey is a scholar of firearms technology, in particular, Board of Ordnance manufacture of small-arms about which he is completing a major study, Brit*ish Military Smallarms, Board of Ordnance Production, 1690-1815*. In addition to many scholarly articles he is also the author of *British Military Longarms, 1715-1865*, London (1986).

Michael Ball is a Curator in the Department of Fine and Decorative Art, National Army Museum. An Associate of the Museums Association, he was a major contributor to *1688 - Glorious Revolution? The Fall and Rise of the British Army, 1660-1704*, National Army Museum, London (1988) which accompanied the Special Exhibition of the same name.

Dr Ian F W Beckett is a Senior Lecturer in War Studies at the Royal Military Academy, Sandhurst. Author of a number of important scholarly studies of the British Army, including *Riflemen Form: A Study of the Rifle Volunteer Movement, 1859-1908*, Aldershot (1982), he is currently completing a volume on the Auxiliary Forces in the forthcoming multi-volume *Manchester History of the British Army*, to be published by Manchester University Press. He is also Secretary to the Council of the Army Records Society.

A S Bennell is an Historian with the Ministry of Defence and a member of Council of the Army Records Society. A former Research Associate with the International Institute for Strategic Studies and a former Vice-President of the Royal Asiatic Society, he is the author of a number of important articles on politico-military affairs in India at the turn of the eighteenth and nineteenth centuries.

Dr Peter Boyden is Head of the Department of Archives, Photographs, Film and Sound, National Army Museum and an historian of his home county of Essex. He is the author of *Tommy Atkins' Letters: The History of the British Army Postal Service from 1795*, National Army Museum, London (1990), which accompanied the Special Exhibition of the same name.

David G Chandler is Head of the Department of War Studies, Royal Military Academy, Sandhurst, Vice-President of *La Commission Internationale d'Histoire Militaire* and author of 20 books specialising in warfare during the age of Napoleon and the period of Marlborough's Wars. Among them are the oft-reprinted *The Campaigns of Napoleon*, London (1967), *Waterloo: the Hundred Days*, London (1980) and the recent symposium *Napoleon's Marshals*, London (1987).

Randolf G S Cooper is a University of Cambridge research student based at Selwyn College. During the last four years he has held a Fellowship in Military History from the Social Sciences and Humanities Research Council of Canada. He is the author of a number of articles on Asian military strategy, tactics and technology.

Dr Michael Duffy is a Senior Lecturer in History at the University of Exeter. Author of many scholarly articles on Britain's struggle against Revolutionary and Napoleonic France, his principal publications include the collection of essays *The Mili-*

tary Revolution and the State, Exeter (1980), *The Englishman and the Foreigner*, Cambridge (1986) and *Soldiers, Sugar and Seapower: The British Expeditions to the West Indies and the War against Revolutionary France*, Oxford (1987).

Dr Clive Emsley is Reader in History at the Open University, and has been Visiting Professor at the University of Paris VIII and the University of Calgary. His publications include *British Society and the French Wars, 1793-1815*, London (1979), *Policing and its Context, 1750-1870*, London (1983) and *Crime and Society in England, 1750-1900*, London (1987). He is currently working on a history of police and policing in England from the eighteenth century to the present.

Dr Charles Esdaile was until recently Wellington Research Fellow at the University of Southampton and now teaches at the University of Liverpool. Joint-organizer of the Wellington Congress at the University of Southampton in 1987, he is the author of a number of important revisionist articles on the Peninsular War and two books; The *Spanish Army in the Peninsular War*, Manchester (1988) and *The Duke of Wellington and the Command of the Spanish Army, 1811-14*, London (1990) He was special adviser to the 1986 National Army Museum Special Exhibition, 'Patriots and Liberators: Anglo-Spanish Military Co-operation in the Peninsular War'.

George Evelyn is an external research student at King's College, University of London, and is working on a re-appraisal of the British Army of the 1790s. A contributor to scholarly journals in Britain and the United States, he has presented papers at the Wellington Congress, University of Southampton

(1987), the International Congress on the Iberian Peninsula and the Consortium on Revolutionary Europe.

Dr Kenneth Ferguson, whose 1980 doctoral thesis on the Army in Ireland from the Restoration to the Act of Union pioneered studies in an area where many vital records have either been destroyed or dispersed, is a Dublin barrister, and a Council Member of the Military History Society of Ireland. He is the author of a number of important articles in the Society's journal, *The Irish Sword*.

Dr Alan J Guy is Assistant Director (Collections) at the National Army Museum and a Member of Council of the Army Records Society. His publications include *Oeconomy and Discipline: Officership and Administration in the British Army, 1714-63*, Manchester (1985) and *Colonel Samuel Bagshawe and the Army of George II, 1731-1762*, Army Records Society, London (1990). He is working on an edition of the Crimean War Diary of Captain Louis Edward Nolan of Light Brigade notoriety.

David Harding served in the 10th Princess Mary's Own Gurkha Rifles, 1974-77 and the 2nd Battalion The Yorkshire Volunteers, 1977-78. He is regimental archivist of 10 GR and has been a contributor to the National Army Museum's annual publication *Army Museum*. He is currently working on a major study, *Firearms of the East India Company: Smallarms of the British Indian Armies, 1600-1856*.

Dr Piers Mackesy FBA is an Emeritus Fellow of Pembroke College Oxford and a Member of the Council of the National Army Museum. He is the author of an influential sequence of books on British Grand Strategy in the reign of King George III; *The*

War in the Mediterranean 1803-10, London (1957), *The War for America 1775-1783*, London (1964), *Statesmen at War: The Strategy of Overthrow, 1798-1799*, London (1974) and its companion volume *War without Victory: The Downfall of Pitt, 1799-1802*, Oxford (1984); also a revisionist study of a notorious incident in the Seven Year's War; *The Coward of Minden: The Affair of Lord George Sackville*, London (1979). He is currently working on a study of the British Campaign in Egypt, 1801.

Dr Rory Muir is Visiting Post-doctoral Research Fellow in the Department of History at the University of Southampton. He is currently working on a two-volume study of Britain and the War Against Napoleon from 1807 to 1815.

Brian Robson CB has served in the British and Indian Armies. A career Civil Servant in the Ministry of Defence, he was Deputy Under Secretary of State (Personnel and Logistics) from 1984 to 1986 and a Member of the Army Board. He is a Member of the Council of the National Army Museum, a Member of Council of the Society for Army Historical Research, and was a founding Member of Council of the Army Records Society. He is the author of the standard work on British Army swords, *The Swords of the British Army: the Regulation Patterns*, London *(1975)*, an account of the Second Afghan War, *The Road to Kabul: the Second Afghan War, 1878-1880*, London (1986) and has recently completed a history of the campaigns in the Eastern Sudan, 1884-85. He is preparing a volume for the Army Records Society on the Indian service of Lord Roberts.

Mrs Lesley Smurthwaite is a Senior Curator in the Department of Uniform, Badges & Medals at the National Army Museum, and an Associate of the Museums Association. She is the author of numerous articles on badges and medals which have appeared in the Museum's published *Annual Reports* and successor annual publication *Army Museum*.

Dr Glenn A Steppler is a Canadian military historian currently working in London. He has published a number of scholarly articles on the eighteenth and nineteenth century British Army, and is the editor of the eighteenth century entries for the English language edition of Professor André Corvisier's *Dictionnaire D'Art et D'Histoire Militaires*, to be published by Basil Blackwell, Oxford. He is also completing a volume on the history of the Volunteers for the Leicestershire Museum Service and a ground-breaking study of the Common Soldier during the reign of King George III for Cambridge University Press.

Dr Hew Strachan is a Fellow and Senior Tutor of Corpus Christi College, Cambridge. His publications include *European Armies and the Conduct of War*, London (1983) and two influential studies of the post-Waterloo Army; *Wellington's Legacy: The Reform of the British Army 1830-1854*, Manchester (1984) and *From Waterloo to Balaclava: Tactics, Technology and the British Army, 1815-1854*, Cambridge (1985). The latter book was awarded the Templar Medal of the Society for Army Historical Research. Dr Strachan is currently working on a history of the First World War.

A

Abercromby, General Sir Ralph 166-67; in the West Indies 25-26, 28; opinion on Militia 36; C-in-C-Ireland 92, 99; in Egypt 101-110; as a trainer 102-106,tactics 103-106; assault landing 107; advance to Alexandria 107-109; assessment 109-10

Acts of Parliament
April 1794 re Yeomanry 40; Act of Union of Great Britain & Ireland 1800 100; Army of Reserve 1803 37; Defence of the Realm Act 1798 41; Habeas Corpus 1796 89; Insurrection Act 1796 89; Levy en Masse 1803 41; Local Militia Acts 1808 41; Mutiny Act 8; Permanent Additional Force Act 1804 37; Training Act 1806 37, 47; Volunteer Consolidation Act 1804 41

Addington, Henry, Viscount Sidmouth 77

Aitken, Helen 186

Aldington, Richard 85

Allied Army of Occupation (France) 184

America, North 22, 164, 169, 185

American War of Independence 6, 7, 9, 13, 14, 28, 40, 41, 48, 94, 168, effect on tactics 103-104

American War of 1812 179, 184

Amiens, Peace of 1802 30, 35, 41, 45, 47, 55, 119, 126, 176

Amphibious operations 27, 101, 107

Ancient Monuments Commission 195

Anstruther, Sir John 107, 109, 137, 138

Armed Associations 41, 42

Armstrong, Capt John Warnford 96

Army, British (see separate entries for Fencibles, Militia, Volunteers, Yeomanry)
Administration of 5, 16; aid to civil power 10, 94; cavalry 19-20, 59, 60, 63, 64, 66; colonial commitment 6, 9, 23; commissariat 4; drill and training 8, 10, 17, 19, 65, 102, 106, 109; infantry 17-18; light infantry 17-18, 19, 104, 105-106, 108; medical 18, 29-30; morale 6, 7, 14, 21-22, 30-31, 96-97, 101; officers 10-13, 36, 199-201; other ranks 13-15; pay and social aspects 7, 14; post (see under P); recruiting 21, 30, 36-39, 88; regimental organization 4, 8-10, 16, 58; state of, in 1793 4-15; strength 4-7, 18, 36-39, 93, 198; support

services 16, 21; tactics 17, 19, 27-28, 103-106, 197

Units of, Artillery, Horse Artillery 7, 12, 20, 166; Engineers, Military Artificers 7, 12; Foot Guards 23, 56, 142, 147, 148, 150; Dragoon Guards: 2nd 61, 3rd 149, 5th 20, 6th 20, 94; Dragoons: 1st 64, 67, 2nd 20, 68, 154, 194, 3rd 67, 5th 96, 6th 59, 7th 21, 149, 8th 166, 9th 94, 13th 29, 15th 64; Foot: 2nd 98, 3rd 167, 4th 56, 8th 108, 9th 184, 10th 166, 14th 21, 56, 18th 108, 28th 167, 29th 98, 31st 29, 33rd 22, 25, 71, 43rd 202, 47th 186, 52nd 56, 202, 54th 91, 67th 28, 71st 56, 73rd 112-13, 76th 149, 180, 80th 166, 86th 166, 87th 30, 88th 88, 166, 174, 89th 179, 90th 106, 108-109, 153 94th Scotch Bde 174; 95th 134, 100th 98, Rifle Bde/Regt 56, 149, 202; Staff Corps of Cavalry 150, 154; Corps of Mounted Guards 150; Garrison Bns 120; Veteran Bns 121; Invalids 114, 115; West Indian 23, 26, 29, 30

Army Gold Medal/Gold Cross 169-70

Army of India Medal 179-80

Austria, Austrians 20, 197; cavalry 60-61, 63, 65

B

Babur Jung 87

Baillargeon, Sgt Joseph 179

Baillie, Lt-Col William 112-13

Baji Rao II, *Peshwa* 70-71, 73-75

Bain, Sgt George 174

Baird, Sir David 113, 166

Bal Gandadhur Tilak 80

Ballesteros, General Francisco 139

Bath, Order of 167-78, 170-71

Bathurst, Henry, 3rd Earl 139

Batty, Dr Robert 142

Batty, Lt-Col Robert; early life 142; arrival in Spain 142; sketches in Biddassoa 142-45; in St Jean de Luz 145-46; in Bayonne 146-47; wounded 148; subsequent career 148

beacons, fire126-31; home defence requirement 126-27; financing 127; erection of and manning 127-29; effectiveness of 129-31

Bentinck, Lord William Cavendish 119, 135

Beresford, General William Carr, Viscount 145, 153

Bessborough, Lady 160

Birmingham Mint 165

Blaker, Sir Edward 187

Blücher, Field Marshal Gebhard Leberecht von, Prince of Wahlstadt 181

Board of Control (India) 50, 53

Board of General Officers 9

Board of General Officers of Regiments of Cavalry 59, 62

Bonaparte, see Napoleon

Bond, Pte George 178

Boulton, Matthew 176, 180

Bragge, Capt William 67

Braybrooke, 2nd Baron 129

Britains, William Ltd 195

British and Foreign Bible Society 121

British Field Post Office 149, 151

British Library 188, 189

Browning, Gen Sir Frederick Arthur Montague 186

Bryant, Sir Arthur 82

Buckingham, Marquess of 36, 101

Buffon, George Louis Leclerc, Comte de 146

Bunbury, Sir Henry Edward, Bart. 4, 5, 7-13, 15, 102

Burghersh, John Fane, Lord, later 11th Earl of Westmorland 162

Burgess, Capt Isaac 118

Burke, Edmund 89-90, 92, 93

Burket, James 129

Byng, Gen Sir John, Earl of Strafford 187

C

Caffarelli du Fulga, *Général* Mario 139

Calcutta Mint 165, 166

Cambridge University 142

Campbell, Maj-Gen 98

Canada 178-79, 185

Carey, Peter 65

Carhampton see Luttrell

Caribbean 7, 22, 23, 102, 105, 164, 169, 185, 203; importance of, to Britain 23; war in 24-26; casualties 26, 29-30; tactics 26-29; morale 30-31; results 31

Castlereagh, Viscount 37-38, 47, 136, 156-161, 162

Cathcart, Gen Sir George 199

Cawdor, Baron 45

Ceylon 73

Chatham, Gen John Pitt, Earl 185

Clinton, Gen Sir William Henry 148

Clive, Baron 71

Close, Maj-Gen Sir Barry Bart 73-76

Clyde, Field Marshal Sir Colin Campbell, Baron 199

Combermere, Field Marshal Sir Stapleton Cotton, 1st Viscount 199

Conway, Field Marshal Sir Henry Seymour 59

Coote, Gen Sir Eyre 107

Copenhagen Expedition 37

Cornwallis, Charles, 1st Marquess 54, 95, 99, 101, 105

Cornwell, Bernard 64

Costello, Edward 39

counter-insurgency operations 29; in India 84-85, 86; in Peninsula 132-41, French appreciation of 132-34; evidence of recent research into effectiveness 135-35; British attitude towards 135-36; Wellington's mistrust of 136-40

Cowley, Henry Wellesley, Baron 69, 77

Craig, Gen Sir James Henry 129

Crimean War 204, 205

Cromwell, Oliver 164

D
Dalhousie, Earl of 103

Dalrymple, Gen Sir Hew Whitefoord 93, 129

Dalrymple, Lt-Col James 83

Darlot, Henry 150

Davidson, Col A 176

Doddridge, Dr Philip 123

Dhoondiah Waugh 73, 81-87

Dover Castle 195

Duke of York's School see Royal Military Asylum

Dundas, Gen Sir David 8, 10, 17, 18, 65, 104, 108, 109

Dundas, Henry, Viscount Melville 25, 29, 30, 49, 50, 53, 88

Dundas, Ralph 93

D'Urban, Lt-Gen Sir Benjamin 199

E
East India Company 50-53, 55, 69, 70, 75, 85, 112, 165-66, 171

Egremont, Lord 43

Egypt 18, 22, 36, 73, 83, 101-10, 166, 167, 169, 178

Egyptian Hall, Piccadilly 189, 194

Eliott, Gen George Augustus - see Heathfield

Elphinstone, Mountstuart, Baron 76

English Civil War 115, 164

English Heritage 195

Esmonde, John 97

Evans, Mr 194

Ewart, Sgt Charles 68

F
Fencibles35, 93; infantry 98; cavalry 98; Scottish 45; Irish cavalry 93

Ferdinand VII, King of Spain 156

ffoulkes, Charles 194-95

Fitchettt, William Henry 81, 83

Fitzgerald, Lord Edward 91, 96

Flanders 16-22, 36, 60, 101, 102, 105, 149, 203; preparation for War in, 1793 17-18; French supremacy on battlefield 20-21; morale of British Army in 21

Ford, Maj-Gen Robert 190

foreign troops in British pay 18, 19, 28, 54, 68, 193; King's German Legion 56, 66 note 9, 172

Fortescue, Sir John William 4, 7, 38, 81, 112

Frankfurter, Felix 80

Fraser, Maj-Gen John Henry 79

Frazer, Capt James 153

Frederick II, King of Prussia 103, 110, 197

Freeling, Francis 152-53

Furbisher, Master 49

G
George II, 167

George III 12, 96, 168

George, Prince Regent, later George IV 172, 173, 183

George, *Mlle* 160

Gibraltar 29

Gilbert, Capt Roger Pomeroy 115

Gilbert, Sir William Schwenck 193

Gill, Thomas 58, 59, 62

Gleig, Revd George Robert 82

Godley, Capt Alexander 167
Gooch, Sir Thomas 40

Gough, Sir Hugh, Viscount 199

Graham, Gen Sir Thomas, Baron Lynedoch 136, 170, 199

Grant, Lt-Col Colquhoun 151

Grassini, Josephine 160

Grattan, Henry 100

Green, William 39

Grey, Gen Sir Charles, Earl 24-26, 28, 188

guerrilla warfare, see counter-insurgency

Guernsey 114, 201

Gurwood, Col John 200

H

Haidar Ali, Sultan of Mysore 70, 81, 112

Hamilton-Williams, D C 191

Hamley, Prof Edward 81

Hanoverian Army 172-73

Hardinge, Field Marshal Sir Henry, Viscount 199, 205

Harris, Gen George, Baron 72

Harris, Rifleman John 114

Harrison, Charles 172

Hart, Henry George 200

Hay, Robert 46

Heathfield, Gen George Augustus Eliot 168

Hennem, Jonathan 49

Herries, Col Charles 41, 45

Hill, Gen Sir Rowland, Viscount 187-88, 199

Hinchcliffe, Cornet S C 154

Hitchins, Revd. Richard Hawkin 120

Hoche, *Général* Louis Lazare 89, 91, 93

Holkar, Jaswant Rao 70, 75-79

Holland, Henry Richard Vassall Fox, Bart 160, 163

Holland, see Flanders

Hope, Gen John, Earl 27-28, 145, 147

Hugues, Victor 24, 26

Humbert, *Général* Joseph 45, 99

Hunter, General 98

Hyderabad, Nizam of 70, 71, 72, 74, 83

I

India 16, 22, 68; Mutiny 199

Ireland 88-100, 115, 186, 189; recruitment in 88-94; disaffection in 89; counter-insurgent operations 95; disbandment of 5th Dragoons 96; morale 96-97; course of military action 97-99; casualties in 99

Irish International Exhibition 194

Irish Militia, see Militia

J

Jackson, Thomas 39

Jacobins 40, 42, 47, 90

Java 73, 83, 166

Jerome, Thomas 172

Johnson, Gen Sir Henry 98

Jomini, Baron Antoine Henri 102

Jones, Capt Lewis 21

K

Keatinge, Col Maurice 90

Kennedy, Gen Sir James Shaw 191

Kincaid, Capt Sir John 201-202

King, Pte 180

Kirkpatrick, William 187

Knox, Brig-Gen 94

Kolhapur, Raja of 82

Küchler, Conrad Heinrich 165, 176, 180

L

Lake, Gen Gerard, Viscount 75-79, 93, 94, 96

Lang, Maj-Gen Ross 165

Lawrence, Maj-Gen Stringer 52

Leach, Col Jonathan 201-202

Leinster, Duke of 91

Le Marchant, Maj John Gaspard 61-65, 67

Lever, Charles James 187

Lewin, Pte Joseph 176

Liddell Hart, Sir Basil Henry 132, 135, 136, 140-41, 201

Liverpool, Robert Banks Jenkinson, 2nd Earl of, 37, 138, 160, 163, 170, 183

Local Militia, see Militia

Londonderry, Robert Steward, Marquess of 177

Longford, Thomas Pakenham, Earl 45

Louis XVIII, King of France 157, 162

L'Ouverture, see Toussaint

Low Countries, see Flanders

Lowe, Maj Hudson 107

Luddite disturbances 1811 and 1812 34, 45

Luke, Dr Stephen 118

Luttrell, Henry Lawes, Earl of Carhampton 89, 92, 93, 99

Lynedoch, Baron see Graham, Gen Sir Thomas

M

Macaulay, Zachary 158

MacCready, Maj Edward Nevil 191

MacCulloch, Charlotte 184

Mackenzie, Lt-Gen Kenneth 106, 109

Maitland, Maj-Gen Sir Peregrine 148

Maitland, Lt-Gen Sir Thomas 26

Majendie, Lewis 128

Malcolm, Capt John 74-76, 79

Malone, Mrs Barrington 194

Mao Tse Tung 86

Maratha Wars 53, 73-77, 81, 165, 180

Marlborough, John Churchill, Duke of 155, 163

Masséna, *Maréchal* André, *Duc de* Rivoli, *Prince d'*Essling 133, 138

Maxwell, William Hamilton 92

Mayett, Joseph 34-35

medals164-183; campaign 165-173; Order of the Bath 167-68; regimental 173-176; commemorative 180-81; foreign 166-67, 172-73; Maida 168-69, 172-73; Mudie's National Medals 181; how worn 182

medical 4, 18, 21, 29-30

Melvill, John 112

Melvill, Capt Philip 111-25; joins 73rd Ft 112; in India 112-13; Capt of Invalids, Guernsey 114-15; removed to Falmouth 115; improvements to garrison and fortifications of Pendennis 117-19, 123-24; charitable and religious interests 119-24; death and funeral 111, 124-25

Mendizabal, Gen Gabriel 139

Metternich, Count Winneburg Clemens Wenzel Lothar 162

Military General Service Medal 177-79

Militia 17, 30, 32-40, 43, 47, 95, 96, 97, 98, 102, 103, 111, 116, 118, 124, 126, 128, 175, 184, 186; enlistment into 32-33, 35, 37; disaffection in 33-35; strength of 35, 36; transfer of Militiamen to regular Army 36-39; Canadian 179; Irish 38, 91, 93, 96-98, 175; Local 41, 47, 119, 131; Supplementary 35, 36, 37, 54

Mina, Gen Francisco Espoz y 140

Minorca 102, 105

Misericordia Society 120

Mitchell, Col John 202

Moore, Lt-Gen Sir John 28, 95, 102, 107, 108, 109, 135-36, 167, 168, 169, 185; effect on the British Army 202-203

More, Hannah 121

Morillo, Gen Pablo 139

Mornington, Richard Colley Wellesley, Earl 69-80, 82, 155

Morrison, Lt-Col Joseph 179

Mudie, James 181

Murray, Gen Sir George 186

Mysore Wars 71-73, 81, 165

N

Napier, Lt-Gen Sir Charles James 199, 202

Napier, Gen Sir William Francis Patrick 200-201, 202, 204

Napoleon, Bonaparte 22, 31, 42, 102, 123, 126, 143, 147, 155, 160, 162, 191, 197

Naval and Military Bible Society 121

Needham, Gen Francis 99

Nelson, Vice-Admiral Horatio, Viscount 47, 167, 168

Netherlands, see Flanders

Newenham, Thomas 99

Nock, Henry 49

Noel, Roden Berkeley 184

Nookta Sound Crisis 1790 7

Nova Scotia 30

O

Oakes, Lt-Gen Sir Hildebrand, Bart 107

Oelmann (Ohlmann, Oehlmann), Cpl Georg 172

Olivera, *Senhor* 150

Oman, Sir Charles William Chadwick 132, 138, 200

Omeme, Warrior John Pegeon 179

Orders, see medals

Ordnance, Board of, provision of muskets 48-57; Master General of 54

Osborne, Henry 62

P

Paget, Gen the Hon Sir Edward 108-10

Paine, Thomas 121

Pakenham, Maj-Gen Sir Edward Michael 146, 185

Paul, Sir George Onesiphorus 43

Paris, Treaty of 157, 158

Pelet-Clozeau, *Général* Jean Jacques Germain, 133

Pelham, Thomas 88

Perceval, Spencer 37

Perryn, Col (local), Maj-Gen James 27

Picton, Lt-Gen Sir Thomas 26

Pinckard, Dr George 30

Pistrucci, Benedetto 181

Pitt, William 4, 6, 7, 23-24, 37, 91

Poole, Maj Nevinson 116

Popham, Rear Admiral Sir Home 139

Porter, Maj 45

Postal Service149-54; servicemen's concessionary rates 1795 149; unit administration 149; in Holland 149-50; in the Peninsula 150-53; in Flanders & France 153-54

Prince Regent, see George IV

R

Raghuji Bhonsle of Nagpur (The Rajah of Berar) 70, 74-77

Raglan, Lord Fitzroy James Henry, Baron 199

Reeves, John 42

Reille, *Général* Honoré Charles Michel Joseph, 143
Reynolds, Thomas 151

Richmond, General Charles Lennox, Duke of 13, 48, 49-50, 53, 54

Roberts, Field Marshal Frederick Sleigh, Earl 81

Roche, Capt Philip 135

Ross-Lewin, Ensign Henry 28

Royal Academy 142, 148

Royal Military Academy, Sandhurst 190

Royal Military Academy, Woolwich 13

Royal Military Asylum 187, 196

Royal Military College, Great Marlow 185

Royal Mint 172, 181

Royal Navy 44, 88, 98, 152

Royal Society 148

Runkel, John Justus 59

S

St Clair, Maj-Gen Thomas 167

St Paul, Lt-Col Horace 42

St Vincent, Admiral John Jervis, Earl 101

Scotland, Scots 11, 14

Scovell, Maj George 150-51, 153, 154

Seaton, John Colborne, Baron 199

Selin III, Sultan of Turkey 166

Seven Years' War 32, 52, 103

Sevright, Charles 152-54

Siborn, Benjamin 184

Siborne, George 195

Siborne, Major-General Herbert Taylor 186, 188, 190; life and career 184-87;constructing models 187-95; death 196

Siborne, William 184-96

Siborne models 187-96

Sicily 168

Simcoe, Lt-Gen John Graves 105, 116-17, 123

Simmons, Maj George 134

slavery 23-24, 157

Sinde, Daulat Rao 70-71, 74-79

Smith, Maj-Gen Sir Harry George Wakelyn, Bart 202

Smith, Ensign John 116

Smithies, Trooper James 67

Soult, *Maréchal* Nicolas Jean de Dieu 143, 145, 146, 147

Staff College, Camberley 194

Stanhope, Philip Henry, Earl 183

Stuart, Gen Sir Charles, Baron Stuart de Rothesay 106

Stuart, Sir Charles 161

Stuart, Lt-Gen Sir John, Count of Maida 168

Sturgeon, Lt-Col Richard 151-52

Suchet, *Maréchal* Louis Gabriel, 132-33

Surtees, William 39

T

Talleyrand-Périgord, Charles Maurice de, *Prince de* Benavente 159

Tate, Col William 45

Taylor, Gen Sir Herbert 104

Templer, Field Marshal Sir Gerald 190

Thomason, Edward 181

Thompson, Admiral Sir Charles 98

Tipu, Sultan of Mysore 70-73, 81, 85

Tone, Theobold Wolfe 91, 100

Toussaint L'Ouverture, Pierre Dominique 26

Tower of London 64, 194, 195

Townshend, Marquess 44

Treaty of Bassein 73, 74

Treaty of Mangalore 113

U

United Irishmen 91-92, 96-97

United Service Museum (later Royal United Services Museum) 189, 194

V

Vandeleur, Gen Sir John Ormsby 170

Vauban, Sebastien le Prestre 147

Victoria, Queen 178

Vienna, Congress of, 1814-15 158-59, 161-62

Villemur, General, Conde de Penne 139

Vivian, Lt-Gen Sir Richard Hussey, 187

Volunteers 35, 37, 40-47, 111, 118, 119, 120, 126, 128, 131, 175, 176; encouragement given to 40-41; composition of 41-42; motives of 42-43; possibility of disaffection 44; efficiency of 45-47

Von Saldern, Gen Friedrich Christoph 110

Vorontzov, Gen Prince Mikhail 148

Vyse, Maj-Gen Richard William 130

W

Walcheren Expedition 1809 38, 185, 203

Wallace, Gen Sir John Alexander Dunlop Agnew 174

Ward, Stephen George Peregrine 81, 83

Weapons; artillery 60; Baker rifle 56; cavalry swords 58-68 - lack of standardization 58, 64; 1788 cavalry recommendations 59-60; testing of 58, 59-60; Le Marchant's proposals 61-62; 1796 recommendations 62-65; modifications 67; Muskets 48-57; provision, in 1793 48-50; East India Company's supply system 50-53; supply of India Pattern musket to British Army 53-57; comparisons 57
Webb, Sgt Richard 150

Webbe, Jossiah 84

Wellesley, Arthur see Wellington, Duke of

Wellesley, Richard Colley see Mornington

Wellesley, Sir Henry see Cowley

Wellington, Field Marshal Sir Arthur Wellesley, 1st Duke 15, 16, 20, 22, 25, 66, 67, 92, 101, 133, 144, 150, 152, 153, 168, 170, 180, 181, 182, 192, 197, 199; In India 69-87; Mysore wars 70-73; commands in the Deccan 75-77; political duties 80; actions against Dhoondiah Waugh 81-85; counter-insurgency operations 85-86; assessment of Indian posting 87; attitude to guerrilla warfare 136-140; crossing of the Bidassoa 144; ambassador 161-165; marital relations 159-60; at Congress of Vienna 158-59, 161-63; attitude toward medals and decorations 171-72, 177, 182-83; effect on British Army 202-203

Wesley, Arthur see Wellington

West Indies, see Caribbean

Wheeler, Pte William 39

Wilberforce, William 157

Wilkes, John 92

Windham, William 37, 47

Wyon, Thomas Jr 172, 180, 181

Wyon, William 169, 173, 180

Wyse, Bonaparte 194

Y

Yeomanry Cavalry 41, 42, 44, 45, 47, 68, 94, 99, 111; Irish Yeomanry 89, 99

Yonge, Sir George Bart 7, 12

York, Frederick Augustus, Duke of York and Albany 15, 18-22, 46, 60, 62, 88, 101, 105, 168, 171